PRAISE FOR *SPIRIT GUIDED*

"Dr. Williams' honesty in communicating with Spirit is both vulnerable and inspiring, highlighting the courage it takes to share unconventional truths.

By acknowledging the societal stigma and the risk involved, the narrative fosters empathy and encourages open-mindedness. This candor serves as an empowering example for anyone wrestling with revealing parts of themselves that may not fit societal norms.

Sharing the context of living a responsible, normative life while quietly cultivating psychic abilities provides a nuanced perspective on the coexistence of the extraordinary and the ordinary. The comparison between the stigma of being psychic and the stigma surrounding mental health issues is particularly insightful, prompting readers to question their own biases."

— **Stanley Krippner,** PhD, author of *A Chaotic Life*

"As a scientist, I value skepticism. But I also appreciate intellectual courage when lived human experience refuses to fit neatly inside materialist assumptions.

Drawing on her work as both a clinical psychologist and a practicing psychic, Dr. Williams offers a thoughtful bridge between professional rigor and firsthand experience.

Whether read as a literal account, a psychological narrative, or as a challenge to prevailing models of mind, *Spirit Guided* invites a serious reconsideration of whole realms of existence that science has only recently begun to grasp."

— **Dean Radin, PhD**, Chief Scientist, Institute of Noetic Sciences, and author of *The Science of Magic*

"In *Spirit Guided*, Dr. Catherine Anne Williams offers a luminous invitation to remember who you truly are.

Drawing from a life devoted to science, healing, spiritual inquiry, and service, Catherine gently bridges psychology and mysticism, intellect and intuition, human experience and divine presence.

Spirit Guided is a master key that opens the door to your spirit. Go get a copy for you and your best friend!"

— **Vincent Tolman**, author of *The Light After Death: My Journey to Heaven and Back*

"*Spirit Guided* feels like spending an afternoon with Catherine, who is not just a deeply profound medium, but the kind of teacher and healer that sets your heart at peace. Her words and wisdom remind us that Spirit is waiting for us, always ready to teach the lessons of our human experience and help us see beyond the veil. This is a beautiful book from a beautiful teacher that can absolutely change your life if you allow it."

— **Kristen McGuiness**, LA Times bestselling author of *51/50: The Magical Adventures of a Single Life and Live Through This*

"The extraordinary is with us all the time, yet few of us have the courage to step into its creative and healing potential. This book is exemplary in its courage to go where common norms, expectations, and taboos so often get in the way. It can serve as a beacon for readers who are struggling to assert their inner truths. This beautifully written book is an exemplar of successfully blending psychology with profound self-exploration. An encouragement for every reader!"

— **Jurgen Kremer, PhD**, Author of *Ethnoautobiography*, editor of *ReVision, A Journal of Consciousness and Transformation*

"In *Spirit Guided*, the author shares her greatest vulnerabilities—those painful, low points in life which birthed her 'coming-out story,' as she puts it. That is, taking a leap of faith to stay true to her own path, abandoning the strict materialist, skeptical scientific background from which she was raised, and opening to Oneness. Through sharing her personal testimony, Dr. Williams gifts her readers with courage and hope. Stories which touch the heart, spirituality, and scientific findings are the fabric of *Spirit Guided*. Dr. Williams has delivered an engaging, reflective, and inspiring read, reminding us of our connection to Oneness."

— **Kimberly Mascaro, PhD**, Author of *Dream Medicine*, and *Dreaming with the Earth-Mind*

"I loved the clear, conversational, and well-researched way Dr. Williams presented a myriad of helpful and insightful strategies to developing our best selves and higher consciousness. I learned a lot from this excellent book!"

— **Phyllis Mitz, MA**, Author of *Love Stars: Astrology's Secrets to Relationships, Compatibility, and Great Sex!*

SPIRIT GUIDED

SPIRIT GUIDED

Coming Home to Oneness

Catherine Anne Williams, PhD

Contents

Acknowledgments

To all who helped me to break through the limitations of my mind to believe that publishing a book was possible: Kristen McGuiness and Rise Writers for celebrating my voice; Indigo River for saying yes (!); and Anne MacDonald, Toby Israel, and Deborah Froese for their brave and wise editing.

To my colleagues at Santa Rosa Junior College, especially Jurgen Kremer, for helping me to unlearn psychology and learn anew.

To my parents, Roger, Mary, and Peter, thank you for this healthy, engaged, and gorgeous life. The lessons I share in these stories pale in comparison to your generous and selfless gifts of love. To my siblings, Mark, Diana, and Jack, only you know! To Jose, Stephen, Matthew, and Michelle, thank you for creating a family with intention. I celebrate our family's loving foundation that supports so many.

To my soul sisters, Michele, Ryn, Kristi, Lisa, Grace, Shannon, Amy, Liz, Michelle, and Galina, I am graced to "trudge this road of happy destiny" with you. To Wendy, Courtney, Laura, and Madison, thank you for supporting my inner union. To Marin and the Sisterhood of the Rose, thank you for remembering me. To my spiritual teachers and therapists, too numerous to name, I am because you walked before me. To Mount Shasta and Her loving community, thank you for calling me home. To my cheeky monkey, feather boa-wearing "god's Teri," all my loved ones in spirit, my spirit guides and master teachers, and especially to my most patient and beloved teacher Meera, humbly I thank you for your Bott's dots, guiding me to the One Who Waits.

To my beautiful, amazing offspring Ian and Ellie, you are the brightest lights in my world. I wrote this book with you in the house while you quietly honored my space. Of all my identities and endeavors, being your mama is my favorite and most fulfilling.

Dear reader, *Spirit Guided* is my gift to you. It is the sum of my understandings from my own karmic journey. It is all that I have unlearned—less than, not good enough, separation, intellectualization, scarcity—and all that I am still learning—peace, love, connection, trust, fullness. I offer this book to you with the hope that you will feel validated as a spirit on your own journey of self-discovery. What I present is my perspective; I hope that you will stand in your truth to discover yours.

There are no limits to what we can awaken to in one lifetime. Love and enlightenment are here now. We each plot our own course. Every day, my loving awareness is my most important destination.

So, as we embark, I lay Rumi's words at your feet:

> *I have fallen in love with Someone*
> *Who hides inside you.*
> *We should talk about this problem—*
> *Otherwise,*
> *I will never leave you alone.*
> —Rumi

Introduction

I landed on the pavement twenty-five feet from my bike, its front tire still lovingly cradled by the yawning pothole. I was not conscious, not dreaming, not present, and not helpful to the scene now unfolding in the middle of the narrow two-lane road. My face rested in a warm burgundy pool; far away, I heard my own groaning. As if momentarily waking up from a dream, I struggled to flip myself over. My hands, crossed under my torso and pinned by my pelvis, were unable to help break my landing and now were unable to help push me up. My best friend, Michele, off her bike and managing an emergency scene, grabbed me under my armpits to help me flip over. I felt the love in her touch. Through teeth floating in my mouth, I gargled out a prayer. "God, please help me," I said, before fading into blackness again.

I came to as a woman who was driving home from church stopped her car to ask Michele if she could pray over me.

Michele acknowledged the truth of the moment: "We need all the help we can get."

A second car pulled over, and out jumped a man who identified himself as a wilderness EMT before kneeling at my head. He asked me the year and the president's name. My mouth was still rolling with teeth and blood, so I used sign language to spell the name with my fingers. He didn't get my answer and asked me again, "Who is the president?" Painstakingly, I raised my hand higher and spelled it out again: O-B-A-M-A.

A paramedic ran out of her house and up the hill with her medical bag, followed by her husband, a retired police officer, and a third man who sprinted out of his house. All three were volunteer firefighters, responding to the 911 call that flashed on their phones. When the firetruck arrived, there was already a fully functional team attending to me.

We have everything we need.

I was placed on a wooden board and loaded into an ambulance. Someone struggled to take off my bike shoes. Meanwhile, I traveled into another reality, a swirl of colors, geometric images, and words arising alone, unattached to thought. But there was still something present, something watching, noticing. "I" was present. There was nothing else—no up or down, no gravity, no material world—just "I" traveling through a kaleidoscope. Just "I" witnessing. I didn't have a body, and there was no pain. I merely existed. None of it made sense, and none of it had to.

Even in our darkest moments, a presence endures.

I am that presence. I am pure consciousness.

I am a spirit in a body.

And in some moments, like that one on the pavement, not in a body.

There was no time to think thoughts; the slurry of colors transformed too fast to ask a question. Gravity pulled me back into my heavy body and the thud in my head that had just pressed my consciousness out.

I heard the siren taking my injuries seriously and felt every bump in the road. One man close to me talked to another man farther away, debating which hospital to go to. "Memorial," declared the man close to me. The hospital with the trauma unit.

I wished I could leave the pain in my head and go back to the swirling colors. Being in a body is hard sometimes. He inserted scissors in the leg of my favorite bicycle outfit and sliced it open to assess my injuries. I was aware that I was naked and my body was rhythmically shaking the gurney, lifting itself up and down, like a fish on the shore unable to breathe. The fish image freaked me out, and the pace of my rattling quickened.

"You are going to be OK," he said to me, and the tempo temporarily decreased. A light flashed in my eyes, and I hoped my pupils would respond, because I didn't want to be dead.

The celestial bodies set in motion that morning moved families, changing their trajectory, aligning their will with the gravitational force of love. Michele somehow rode home and returned with her husband and truck to retrieve my bike, still in pristine condition, and my sunglasses, now stripped with deep grooves where my face had slid on the road. Another friend left her family at home to drive to the hospital. My kids were having a cozy Sunday morning at their dad's house, packing up their toys to transition to my house for the week, when he declared, "Mom's in the hospital. We need to go."

In my hospital room, my daughter's head reached just above the height of my hospital bed. She gently held my hand with her small hot dog fingers and humbly asked, "Are you going to be OK?"

For the first time in her life, her grounding force, her rock, her lifeline was lost in space. With gravel still embedded in my face, I spit out part of a tooth and answered, "I don't know."

The Hallways Are a Bitch

I have often wished the Universe would communicate with me clearly, wished a billboard would appear, telling me "Turn Left," or "Turn Right," or "Just Say No." As a kid, I always looked longingly at the neon sign brazenly announcing a psychic lived in that run-down house, thinking how nice it would be to just know. But I was raised by a wolf pack of skeptical scientists, and I needed cold, hard evidence before I could believe all that.

I started my spiritual path as a young adult in recovery from addiction. Other women in recovery taught me to look for the breadcrumbs, the omens and signs that appear throughout my day, such as the guidance I get from others. Otherwise known as finding G.O.D. in "Good Orderly Direction." When in doubt, I learned how to hunt and peck my way through life by doing the next right thing. For more than thirty years, I have been writing, saying, singing, and pleading my prayers to a higher power and waiting for answers to come from the outside. Discrediting my inner knowing and desperate to understand myself better, I have paid all kinds of therapists, psychics, and healers to tell me things about myself.

This approach of moving through life like a dark hallway, fingertips grazing the walls, ended after my traumatic bike accident launched me into yet another spiritual growth period. As I learned early on in recovery, "When one door closes, another one opens, but the hallways are a bitch."

After the bike accident, I started a daily meditation practice that built a channel of communication with an all-knowing spirit guide who identified herself as Meera. (I later learned that Meera means "light" or "saintly woman" in Hebrew, and "prosperous" in Hindi and Sanskrit.) Meera is an old, old spirit who has lived every life imaginable and now dedicates herself to helping us awaken to the truth of who we are. She is not me, nor some form of my higher self. She is a different consciousness, fully awakened but not in a body. She appears as female to me, but is also every gender and no gender at all.

In my daily meditation, I quieted my internal blockages and learned to bring my consciousness to a higher vibration to communicate with her. We developed a kind of pen pal relationship, where I would sit with pen in hand and write down what I was receiving from her. Of course, like any self-respecting single woman in her forties, I brought to her my most important life questions about dating, relationships, and love. But Meera doesn't mess around. She cuts through the fluff and tells me when a concern of mine is "unimportant." Meanwhile, I continued to perform my day job as a dean at a college, and I didn't tell my family and friends that I communicated daily with spirits who don't have bodies.

It's a lot to explain.

Privately, my guides and I engaged in this writing project until, one day, their words stopped flowing. They pointed their finger at me and simply said, "You." It was my turn to write my story, of how someone who was raised by scientists, who did her level best to seek satisfaction through drugs, sex, and loud rap music, who became sober at nineteen and later became, seemingly, an upholder of society's status quo as a mother and psychologist, who also secretly took classes on clairvoyance and mediumship, who after over twenty-five years of hitting brick walls and finally hitting her face on the pavement transitioned to living a Spirit-guided life.

This book is my coming-out story. I am a psychic psychologist, but, more than that, I am a spirit at Home in the One.

Hard to Believe

> *If you stumble about believability, what are you living for? Love is hard to believe, ask any lover. Life is hard to believe, ask any scientist. God is hard to believe, ask any believer. What is your problem with hard to believe?*
>
> —Yann Martel

I get it. It is hard to believe that I communicate with Spirit. It is also hard for me to tell you this. I generally keep my mouth shut.

This public admission that I communicate with spirits that don't have bodies is more damning in my family and my white/Western/industrialized culture-of-origin than if I were to admit that I was a robber or telephone spam operator. Both of those identities still operate within their worldview. I have been developing my spiritual abilities for over thirty years, most of that time in secret from my family, friends, and colleagues. In addition to being a psychic medium, I am a responsible mother and a full-time faculty member at a college. I pay all my bills on time and live a very normative American life. In my college psychology classes, I teach about the social stigma around mental health issues, the one health issue that we don't bake a casserole for in our communities. Being psychic faces similar stigmas; it is seen as "woo-woo," flaky, made-up, or con-artistry. Meanwhile, trusting your gut is fine, talking about the vagus nerve is fashionable, and polls in the United States show we are only getting more spiritual and less religious.[1]

I welcome your doubts, skepticism, and questions. I feel the same way when I encounter other people who say they can channel Spirit. Even with thirty-plus years of spiritual practice and evidence, I daily encounter my own skepticism and invalidation about being a spirit in a body. I am still healing the lies I have absorbed. With training wheels, I have learned how to balance on my authority, certainty, and sovereignty as I ride through life. So can you.

As you read this book, I invite you to notice your skeptical thoughts and question their origin. How many come from family or cultural programming? A spiritual journey requires that we be true to ourselves above all else. Your intuition will tell you what feels true to you in this book. I respect your capacity for discernment.

This book is not about me having a special gift. I did not grow up sensing my dead grandparents. I was not special or different as a child. And yet, I receive communication from the spirit world. We are all born with this capacity in varying degrees; perhaps the only difference is that I have chosen to practice it. I have dedicated my life to developing these gifts. With this book, I hope to pass on to you a roadmap for how to do the same.

We all have spiritual abilities.

I communicate with spirits that do not have bodies, and so do you.

We are all influenced by the energy around us. How is it possible that you can walk into a room full of strangers and know instantly who you like and who you don't like? How many times, when a family member comes in the front door, have you simultaneously known they had a bad day and felt it in your body? How many of us have thought of someone, only to have them text or call moments later? In reaction, we say, "I was just thinking of you!" when we could instead reply, "I was just communicating with you as a spirit, now let's do it with our bodies."

Jill Bolte Taylor noted in her book, *My Stroke of Insight*, that while in the hospital following her stroke, she was immediately able to perceive the energy state of her visitors as they entered her room. She was so sensitive to this energy that she placed a sign outside her door that read, "Please take responsibility for the energy you bring into this space."[2] Actually, we are all this sensitive, and we don't need a stroke or brain injury to figure it out.

As spirits in a body, we are sensitive beings.

Examples of how we are sensitive to the energy around us include: tightness, constriction, or pain in parts of our bodies, especially our stomach and torso; feeling disconnected from or floating above our bodies; intense or disturbing dreams; self-criticism—as if someone else's voice is in your head; feeling pressured to do something, even if you do not want to do it; and feeling depressed or stuck. The energy around us affects our thoughts, our emotions, and how our body feels. With practice, we can use our spiritual skills to be in charge of the energy in our bodies. We can learn to own our space. Rather than letting others run us, we can be sovereign, see for ourselves, and choose for ourselves.

Medium Laura Lynn Jackson described this spirit-body relationship well when she said, "We are not bodies with souls. We are souls with bodies."[3] Many of us have heard from our families, "You are too sensitive." Really, those family members were communicating that they didn't understand when we brought forward information that we intuited. We often don't understand it ourselves. Many of us experience anxiety, and our bodies often create this anxious fight, flight, or freeze reaction because we have not yet learned how to move energy through them. Like a shaken soda can, we build up other people's energy until we blow, our bodies releasing this energy in tears, verbal outbursts, and anger, or through muscle tension and pain. Our nervous system has evolved over millennia to pick up minute details in the environment and send that information traveling through our peripheral nervous system, up into our central nervous system to be processed by our brain. Most of our processing of these environmental stimuli is unconscious.

We can also filter out the energy around us. We can learn tools and skills to remove other people's energy from our space. By practicing certain spiritual tools through prayer and meditation, we can run our own energy, come into the power of our truth, and—instead of being victimized by the energy around us—choose which energy we want to "play with" and which energy we want to keep out of our space. From this place of personal ownership, we can raise our vibration high enough to communicate with spirits that do not have bodies in a way that is safe, protected, and guided by the One.

Spiritual Hygiene

Consider this book your blueprint for the most important thing you will build in this lifetime: *you*. This book is a spiritual hygiene practice. Like a chiropractic adjustment for your spirit, this book and the practices on the companion website (see appendix) will help realign your spirit with your body. That is, your spirit will be in better, clearer communication with your body. Practicing the tools provided in the appendix link will give you the power to choose what energy you allow into your space. Instead of looking outside of yourself for answers, you will be able to turn your gaze inward and see for yourself what is true.

Being in alignment with yourself as a spirit in a body also means being in alignment with Source, the One. *Spirit Guided* helps us to see the interconnected web of which we are a part. Just like individual trees in a forest are connected and fed nutrients by a shared root system, so too are we connected, fed, and nurtured by the One.[4]

Many of us are so consumed with daily tasks and problem-solving, paying our bills, and tending to our community, that it is hard to lift our heads up out of the sand. We all experience many lives like this, learning life lesson after life lesson until, over lifetimes, we slowly start to wake up. All of us will eventually wake up to the truth of who we are: individual spirits united in Oneness.

"Sometimes quickly, sometimes slowly," as the Big Book of Alcoholics Anonymous says, the promises of spiritual growth "will always materialize if we work for them."[5] We always evolve spiritually because…

Oneness is.

Throughout this book, you will find interchangeable words for Oneness, such as Spirit, Supreme Being, Creator, and god. I use capitalization when I am referring to the One, except in the case of "god," which is a word that carries so much cultural programming that I underload it with a lowercase *g*. Therefore, when I refer to "Spirit" with a capital S, I am talking about the One; when I refer to "spirit" with a lowercase s, I am describing an individual consciousness, a soul that either is currently in a body (alive) or not (deceased). Our spirit, our soul, is who we are. It is that part of us that lives on from life to life, collecting and learning from experiences. Our soul expresses itself through our mind, personality, talents, and strengths. Our soul is the culmination of our lived experiences over lifetimes as well as our unique expression of the One.

A disclaimer for those of you with an understanding of physics: I understand that I am taking liberties with the use of the word "energy." As we will explore in later chapters, research on psychic and mediumship abilities shows that something indeed is happening, but what that something is we don't yet know. I use the word "energy" because this is what it feels like, an invisible dynamic current that moves and changes things.

For those of you with religious affiliations, please know that all roads Home are welcomed here. Meera and my soul council affirm that no one religious path is held in greater esteem than another, as long as that path does not harm others. Spirit honors our religious traditions, as they have helped many find their way. All of us enter the spiritual path with previous teachings and cultural conditioning. We all have to discern what is true for ourselves.

Spirit Guided shows us how to admit it when we are on the wrong path, how to develop our spiritual abilities to access more information and power, and how to find our way Home to Oneness. As a psychologist, I offer my understanding of how our biology and human cultures prime us for seeking through materialism, rather than experiencing our natural state of Oneness. Meera, a powerful spirit guide, explains our awakening to our spiritual nature, which blossoms over lifetimes as our souls live through cycles of birth, death, and rebirth. By design, we get lost along the way, caught up in the shiny material world and our attachments.

This book invites you along my journey—from the family that broke my heart and my early near-death experience as a child, through adolescent addiction and beginning a spiritual path in recovery, to trying to achieve in the material world as a psychologist. My story is just one humble example of the brave karmic lessons we all are working on, how we learn from relationships along the way, and how we can connect with the One.

I have organized this spiritual journey into three parts. In Part 1, we open our minds to a new destination with a road map of where we are now (self-seeking) and where we are headed (Oneness). I put on my psychologist hat, and we explore the neurobiological and cultural barriers to our spiritual awakening. In Part 2, we explore how we will get to Oneness. I wear my reverend hat as we consider how the soul takes form, the lessons a soul is here to learn, how the soul learns from relationships, and our ultimate teacher, our body. In Part 3, we arrive at our spiritual abilities and live in Oneness. We understand our spiritual abilities of clairvoyance and mediumship, as well as our relationships with spirits, guides, and ultimately the One. At the beginning and close of each chapter, you will find stories of my self-seeking attempts to meet my needs through people, places, and things until I crashed. In the rubble, I learned how to pray. The appendix provides a link to simple, practical meditations to exercise sovereignty as a spirit and determine how you wish to run and heal your energy in your body.

When I was lifted off the pavement that day, I woke up with a different brain. After crashing my way through this life, through addictions, relationships, and material success, I was ground to a halt by the bicycle accident. What woke up on the pavement that day was me. I woke up living from my center, from my spiritual core: Spirit guided. I hope that, rather than following my path, you will find your own path to your spiritual nature. I hope that you will see that your greatest struggles are the exact right secret sauce for your spiritual freedom.

Meera's Message

In my morning meditation, I regularly step into higher consciousness and then travel as a spirit to a location I refer to as Meera's Cave of Enlightenment. The base of a rock wall sits in a grassy clearing at the edge of a forest, and the cave entrance is just out of sight. There are many ways to get up to the entrance of the cave—climb, hike, or fly—but as spirits, we can also simply arrive by seeing ourselves there. Entering the cave, we see the earthen floor has been trampled smooth by generations; the light of the central fire dances golden shadows on the cave walls. A hum, a harmonic chorus, vibrates the air.

Meera steps forward, her long gray hair a waterfall of stars that cascades down to the floor. She comes close; her eyes are black holes. She takes your hand in her wrinkled hand and wipes a crumbling gray ash in a cross mark on the center of your palms, one hand at a time. She repeats the cross mark over your heart and at the center of your forehead. Meera heals your soul, vanquishing your earthly concerns, restoring you to your true power, and reminding you of your soul's trajectory. Your soul has been carrying loads for other people; here she unburdens you, like a horse released from the bellyband of the saddle, allowing your girth the freedom to expand. A golden light emanates from you, and every aspect of you is restored to gold.

Here, all of you is welcome. Gone is the invisible veil that kept you separate. A knowingness of connection radiates outward from your core. Welcome in. Welcome Home. Without moving her mouth or making a sound, Meera says:

> *It is natural to forget your spiritual nature and get lost in the material world. It is understandable to be so consumed with how sparkly the world is.*
>
> *Nearer to you than your next breath is the truth of who you are.*
>
> *Freedom from the bondage of self, true liberation of spirit, and peace of mind are already here inside of you because that freedom is you. We are already enlightened, awakened beings; that is our spiritual nature. We just have a few attachments, aversions, preferences, and perspectives clouding the lamp and obscuring its blinding bright light.*
>
> *The point of this book is to lovingly clean our own lamps so we can shine our brightest selves out into the world.*
>
> *We are in a tug of war between our dual natures: Oneness and separateness. Oneness is the actual state of all things. We can step beyond the veil of illusion and stand in the brilliance of who we are.*
>
> *This message is urgent. A shift of consciousness is happening, a second Age of Aquarius: This shift must be. The veil of illusion has been thick for so long. But it is thinning now. You will either live in your loving awareness, or you will suffer.*

This book, like a flashlight, will help guide the way. As you read or listen, simply see what resonates for you. I am guiding the information presented, and Catherine is the channel, so you will hear it through her filter of life experiences and language. We are here for you in this process. You are not alone. This book is about opening and awakening to the true joy that is already here.

It is right here in the center of your chest.

Breathe. Be.

PART 1

The Problem Is the Solution

The path is the destination, and the destination is hidden in the path, as the Creator is hidden in creation.

—Sadhguru

We are all lost at times and search for a way to feel better. Through the very act of admitting we are lost and asking for help, we find our first breadcrumb. It turns out, we are already at Home in Oneness. We just happen to have a few barriers, distractions, and fears that keep us separate—the physical limitations of our bodies and a worldview that tells us to look outside ourselves for answers. In order to reach our destination of Oneness, we must first see the things that block us from getting there. Inside each of us is both the problem and the answer. We are our own ticket to freedom.

In this first section, we consider the destination of Oneness and how our self-seeking engine will never get us there. Wearing my psychologist hat, I explore how our neurobiology evolved to seek pleasure and social acceptance. Our capacity for self-awareness is essential on the path of spiritual awakening; the first step is being honest when we are stuck. The next step is to learn from others to find our path to spiritual freedom. Although we all have neurobiological and cultural barriers to spiritual awakening, we can remove the filters and uncover our natural inborn capacity for connection through spiritual practice.

I learned the hard way that everything I struggled with about myself is the secret sauce recipe for my awakening. The suffering of addiction, divorce, near-fatal illness, and self-abandonment brought me to a place that no pill and no person could fix. The pain brought me to my knees. Alone and in the dark, I prayed.

CHAPTER 1

Crashing

Disconnection from our spiritual nature is the source of our suffering. When we are connected to our spiritual nature, we can meet all external material problems armed with inner resources. This chapter explores how this disconnection from our spiritual nature is caused by two factors: (a) the evolution of our brains to think of ourselves as separate and seek pleasure through external experience, and (b) the globalization of Western, industrialized human cultures that have obscured and denied our spirituality and taught us to look outside ourselves for the answer. When we seek to meet our biological needs for pleasure outside of ourselves, our self-seeking engine is driving the train. However, the answer to our needs is actually inside us. By filling up with the correct fuel, Oneness, we can awaken to our spiritual natures.

We can find Oneness in this life.

But some of us must crash the train first.

Hitching the Boxcar of My Life

My first spiritual experience came from smoking a cigarette. Phillip Morris could not have chosen a better model; Emma was the girl I wished I could have been. At fourteen, she had blond hair and perfectly straight white teeth. My mousy brown hair had unruly waves, and my braces had already been on for three years, with no end in sight. It was my freshman year in high school, that year when you take a random group of teenagers, put them in a vat, add so much yearning that it bubbles into acne, and see what friendships form.

Our high school was in the heart of material attainment, Marin County, California, where jokes about everyone having a hot tub stung because we did. The word privilege does not capture the wealth that surrounded me. Children's first cars were new BMWs, and high school parties were held on yachts or in the basements of mansions. My friendship with Emma only survived the first three months of freshman year. She had not yet formed her desirable popular group, and my posse had not yet formed our group of intelligent, defiant girls who did not know how beautiful they were.

At our first high school dance, I was equally terrified that someone might look at me and that no one would. I wore my white leather K-Swiss tennis shoes, athletic shorts, and a sports bra, fully ready to get down. Emma arrived wearing platform espadrille sandals and a striped mini skirt crossed with the diagonal strap of her thin silver purse. She clearly had other plans in mind.

She promptly said, "Dude, this is lame. Let's bail."

"Totally," I agreed, while feeling the bass lines thumping their way through my body.

Magnetized to her, cute boys grabbed, pushed, and taunted Emma as we walked the city blocks downtown. I laughed as if I were part of the joke. We ventured behind the local liquor store, our weekday touchstone for Big Red gum, Nerds candy, and sodas, and perched precariously on a loading dock above the cement ground. A bottle emerged and was passed around. My social capital increased just by standing in that circle. Out of Emma's purse came two packs of cigarettes, white with gold lettering: "Marlboro Lights." She wrapped her plush lips around the shaft, lit it up, and with an easy, languid inhale, sent the plume of her exhale into the cool night. I wanted to be like Emma, so much so that I was willing to mortgage who I was to be accepted in this group. I chucked aside my childhood anti-smoking stance and inhaled. I forced the brick wall of smoke into my lungs, and my healthy young body rejected it in a coughing spasm. I was instantly lightheaded, nauseous, and confused. Was this why people smoked? Emma, in her sloppiness, asked me to hold her cigarettes.

I brought my new treasures home and hid them to cover their tangy tobacco smell. I forgot about Emma and any allegiance I had to her; when she asked about her cigarettes the next week at school, I lied and said I didn't know where they were. My bedroom was two stories above ground and had two large windows that formed a corner pointing north, getting neither sun nor warmth. The next night, I slunk downstairs after dinner, slid open my large bedroom window, and stuck my head out as far into the night air as I could. The view on the left faced the western descending arm of Mount Tamalpais. In the middle, horses grazed on a hill, and on the right, Zen Buddhist monastery gardens terraced the valley below. The now black mountain and hills across the valley hemmed in the flicker of the lights from San Francisco and the greater Bay Area; for me, there was nothing but the expanse of the night sky. The wind whipped around my corner window, creating a perfect current to carry away furtive smells. Like the rookie I was, I struggled to light the cigarette in this wind and time it with my inhale. Eventually, I pulled my head inside, risking discovery for the importance of this accomplishment. And then I was doing it, all on my own, training wheels removed, proud of myself. I was smoking.

I found what I was looking for—a harder Catherine with fewer feelings, a way I could exhale deeply and let it all go. The next night, I wanted to enjoy my secret pastime again, and the night after that too. Eventually, the headaches and nausea disappeared, replaced by a calm, euphoric presence, an inner knowing that I was somebody: I was a smoker.

Meaning-Making Devices

The evolution of our neurobiology is a driving reason for our disconnection from our spiritual nature. Our brain is not one thing, but rather many small structures connected by networks that have evolved over millennia, each with different functions. These parts operate in communication with each other in a tug of war for primacy. We have a sense of ourselves as being one person because of the many superhighways carrying information across these regions and the projections of neurons (one type of brain cell) that reach across and unite the parts. By exploring key brain regions, we can become aware of which part of our brain is driving the train. Who is sticking their head out the driver's window, the lizard, the mouse, or the chimpanzee? Who is making meaning of our experiences?

Our ancestors survived and adapted to get us to this moment, affecting our thoughts, feelings, drives, and behaviors in the process. Let's start our exploration of the brain from the evolutionarily speaking oldest structures. Our spinal cords carry similar skills and abilities to those we had as invertebrates, receiving sensory stimuli from the environment and moving toward or away from each stimulus. Our brain stem and cerebellum, a lump of structures on top of our spinal cord, share capacities with other vertebrates, like fish, reptiles, amphibians, and birds. Our brain stem controls our sleep/wake cycles, motivates us to eat and reproduce, and helps us hunt by tracking prey; our cerebellum coordinates our body's movements. I have new gratitude for my brain stem, as it's the part of my brain I injured in the bike accident. I had to relearn how to walk with balance to prevent constant nausea, as if I just got off a boat.

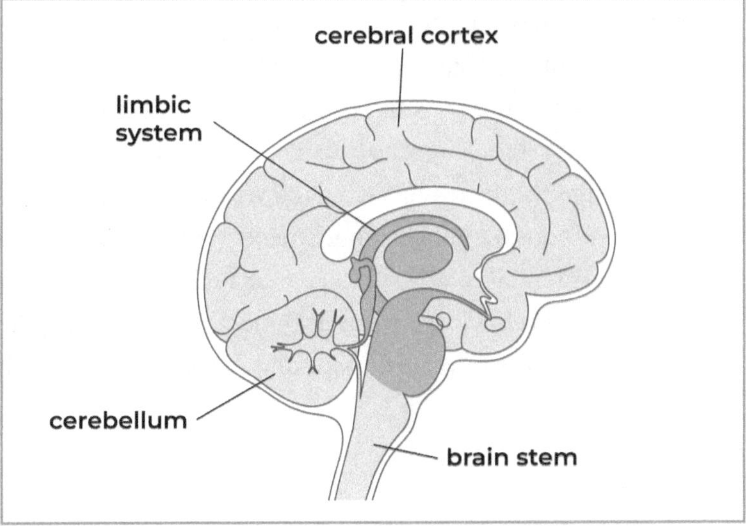

Figure 1.1: Brain Stem, Cerebellum, Limbic System, and Cerebral Cortex

Above the brain stem is the limbic system, a group of structures that further specialize our ability to respond to our environment. These specializations, shared with our mammalian
cousins, regulate emotions and behavior, form memories, and
drive motivation. On the left and right sides of our limbic system,
there are two small structures called *amygdalae* (pronounced
"ah-mig-da-lay," *amygdala* in singular, which is Latin for al-
mond). The amygdalae are powerhouses that generate fear and
anger responses. Our amygdalae respond quickly, bypassing
conscious thought so we can act with aggression when needed,
sticks at the ready and words sharp. Our fear-based amygdalae
explain why we are more likely to hear footsteps behind us than
we are to feel gratitude for the food before us. Because of our
amygdalae, we respond with interest to novelty. Also in the limbic system, the *hippocampi* (*hippocampus* in the singular, a Latin
root for sea horse) wrap around our left and right amygdalae. The
hippocampi orchestrate a memory-finding system, constructing
memories by pulling together sensory information and feelings
stored in separate locations in the brain. The proximity of the
hippocampi and the amygdalae explains why we remember
memories tinged with strong feelings so vividly. Our limbic system is also responsible for the attachments we form, our social
bonds being essential to our survival. Our limbic system drives
pleasure-seeking behavior; it helps us remember where an apple
tree is and what time of year it ripens and motivates us to check
if it is ripe, over and over.

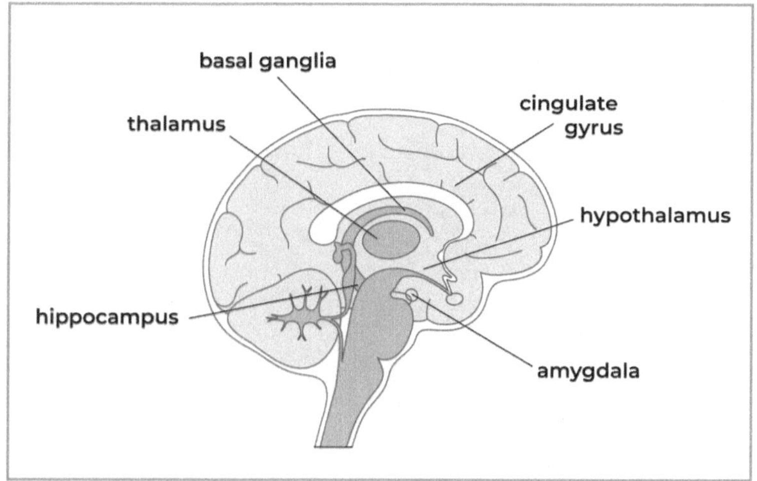

Figure 1.2: Limbic System

Around these early-to-evolve structures is our cerebral cortex, a thin, rippled, bark-like wrapping. The cerebral cortex is responsible for our higher cognitive abilities: complex processing of sensory information, planning our behavior, learning and memory, cognition, and personality. The cerebral cortex is divided into two hemispheres (left and right), each with four lobes. The occipital lobes process visual information; the temporal lobes process auditory information; the parietal lobes process touch, pressure, and body position; and the frontal lobes process olfactory and taste information as well as govern movement, personality, and mood. Our frontal lobes give us the incredible ability to pause, to think before we act, and to ask ourselves, "Hang on, is this the right time to tell this joke?" A moment I wish I had more often since my bike accident.

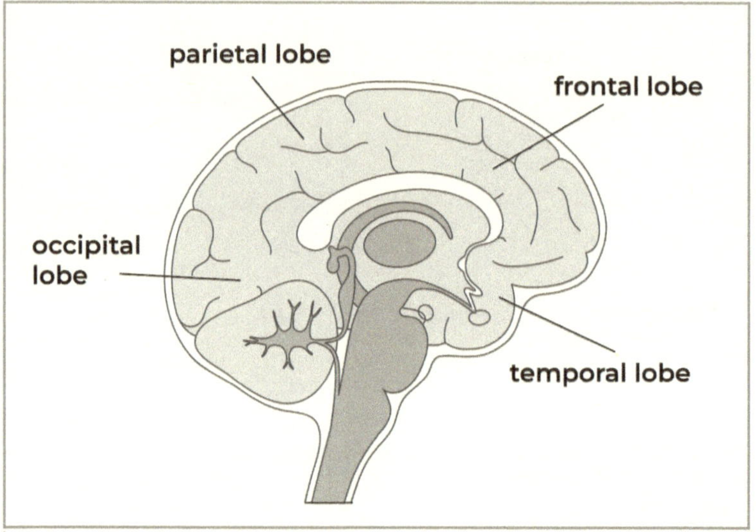

Figure 1.3: Cerebral Cortex

Our human cortexes are meaning-making devices. We can't help but turn shapes into symbols with meaning. Our cerebral cortexes naturally acquire language; we evolved to communicate. Children innately apply grammatical rules strictly at first, then later learn the exemptions. For example, many preschoolers will say someone "goed" to the store rather than "went." The language(s) that we speak then alter how we perceive the world. There might really be fifty different kinds of snow in Inuit, but my English-speaking mind wouldn't know. (It depends on the tribe; for example, the Sami have 180 words for snow/ice).[1] Rather than acting as machines that neutrally process external stimuli, our brains remember the strongest emotions best, jump to conclusions, and construct our realities as we go. It turns out, our brains have an agenda.

The House Always Wants to Win

Our understanding of neurobiology has taken a great leap in the last twenty years as we have learned about the power of brain circuitry networks to provide specialized functions. Let's explore two neurocircuitry pathways that directly relate to spiritual awakening: the default mode network and the dopamine reward pathway.

Neuroscientists aptly named the default mode network (DMN) when they found evidence of multiple areas of the brain that remain active, humming away when we are idle and at rest—in our "default mode." The discovery of the DMN revolutionized our understanding of human cognition; beyond the structure and function of separate brain regions, it gave us a map of how we think.[2] The DMN functions due to connections between: a central location in the frontal lobe called the *medial prefrontal cortex* (self-awareness, social cognition, emotional processing); multiple locations in the emotional regulation area of the limbic systems, including the *posterior cingulate cortex* (memory, self-awareness) and the *angular gyrus* (language, processing integration); and an internal area of the parietal lobe along the midline called the *precuneus* (personal memories, self-processing, consciousness). This series of connected brain regions in the DMN is responsible for our sense of ourselves, our autobiographical memories, and our understanding of others. While the DMN can be active with positive emotions such as empathy when relating our own experience to someone else's, it is also believed to be responsible for those moments when we are self-conscious, insecure, and self-critical. Being self-aware is our default mode because social acceptance is key to our survival.

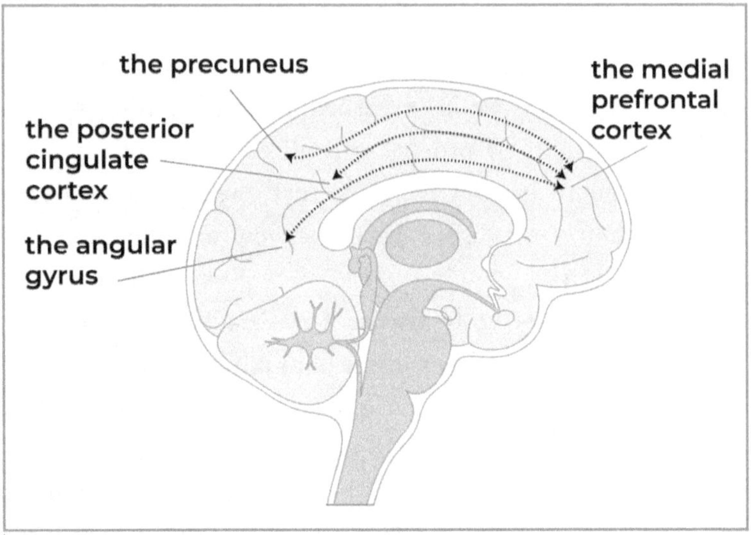

Figure 1.4: The Default Mode Network

Alongside the DMN, another powerful neurocircuitry system focuses our attention on meeting our needs: *the dopamine reward pathway*. Before we understood this brain circuitry, old-school psychological drive theory explained that humans experience tension when needs are unmet; therefore, we are motivated to act to reduce this tension. Sigmund Freud, heavily influenced by Charles Darwin, said that the most primal part of our personalities, what he called the *id*, seeks to meet our biological needs for thirst, food, comfort, and sex by any means necessary. Freud called this drive to survive and to experience pleasure the "pleasure principle." He further described a second part of the personality that develops in early childhood, the *ego*, which helps us get our needs met in socially acceptable ways, acting according to the "reality principle."[3] This explains my motivation as a toddler to pull a chair up to the cookie jar (the id's pleasure principle), while my older brother looked on, knowing we should ask first (the ego's reality principle). Freud was not too far off. In our brains, evolutionarily older structures govern needs connected to our survival, while more evolutionarily recent brain structures modify our need-driven behavior to make it more socially acceptable.

Just before our needs get met, our brains launch fireworks along the dopamine reward pathway. The dopamine reward pathway is made up of neurons that release dopamine, a chemical neurotransmitter, at their synaptic connections with other neurons. Dopamine neurons are responsible for motor control and reward-seeking behavior. The cell bodies for these dopamine-releasing neurons live in the evolutionarily oldest part of the brain, the midbrain section of the brain stem. Although we call the brain stem our "reptilian brain," in truth, we share these dopamine circuits with all vertebrates—fish, amphibians, birds, reptiles, and mammals.[4] These dopamine-making cell bodies send their circuitry connections (axonal projections) up to the evolutionarily more recent "mammalian brain." They send pathways of pleasure to our limbic system, releasing dopamine messages of pleasure with structures in the *basal ganglia* called the *striatum* and *nucleus accumbens*. These dopamine cell bodies in the midbrain also extend other pathways up to the prefrontal cortex, that part of our planning mind that figures out how we can get more.

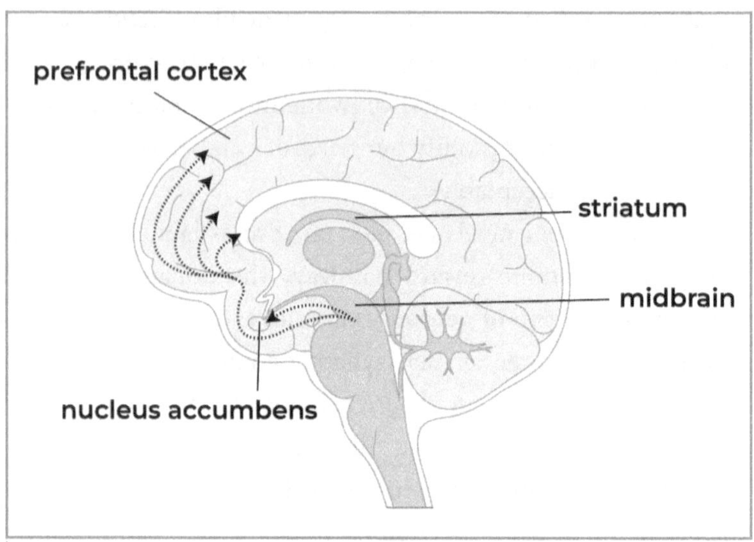

Figure 1.5: The Dopamine Reward Pathway

This dopamine system is like a string of Christmas lights in the brain that light up when we engage in pleasurable activities. The dopamine reward pathway can light up a little when we eat a wild apple, or it can light up a lot when we eat apple pie. Daniel Lieberman and Michael Long, authors of *The Molecule of More*, describe dopamine as the chemical of desire:

> From dopamine's point of view, having things is uninteresting. It's only getting things that matters. If you live under a bridge, dopamine makes you want a tent. If you live in a tent, dopamine makes you want a house. If you live in the most expensive mansion in the world, dopamine makes you want a castle on the moon. Dopamine has no standard for good and seeks no finish line. The dopamine circuits in the brain can be stimulated only by

the possibility of whatever is shiny and new, never mind how perfect things are at the moment. The dopamine motto is "more."[5]

Drugs are addictive because their chemical structure fits like a puzzle piece into this dopamine reward pathway. Like keys to a bank safety deposit box, drugs unlock our brain's stores of desire and pleasure chemicals, and we dance in the excess, forgetting we have bills to pay in the morning. We have other brain chemicals that make us feel good too: oxytocin, vasopressin, serotonin, and norepinephrine. It's a casino in there, and the house always wants to win.

The Self-Seeking Engine

Bringing it all together, when we are at rest, our minds are thinking about ourselves, and our neurobiology is programmed to maximize pleasure and avoid pain. This beautiful system, which secured the survival of our species, is the same system that can either propel our spiritual awakening or torpedo it.

I call it the self-seeking engine. All throughout the day, we are seeking something—warmth, care, comfort, validation, pleasure, relaxation. At fourteen, I chained myself to cigarettes because they gave me something in return: release from cravings, a moment to pause, identity, friends, and even a connection to nature, as I smoked outside. It is not wrong to seek; it is true to our biological nature.

We pursue the path of self-seeking to meet our needs in the only way we know how, through people, places, and things. Taking control of our lives, under the mistaken assumption that our efforts at control are the only mechanism to achieve, we pull levers and rotate knobs much like a young child does with their toy steering wheel. As a young chemist at age fourteen, I learned how the combination of cigarettes, drugs, and alcohol in my body would change the way I felt. I would transform from a depressed, quiet girl who wore only gray and thought about boys who never approached her, into a beautiful, wanted, funny, talkative, and popular young woman. Being high expanded my mindset, allowing me to think more broadly about myself and how I could be in the world. Sometimes, even when I was not high, I could be funny and, every now and then, feel pretty. Daily, I unwrapped the present that drugs gave me: calm, peace, equanimity. It would last for a few hours, then I would slide into the flat prairie of not caring before stepping back into my psyche, where I would look forward to the next time I could escape myself.

Lisa Miller, in her book, *The Awakened Brain,* applies the psychological diagnostic term "dysthymia" to this state of being. She describes it as, "The low-grade feeling that life is unfulfilling [. . .] like emptiness. Hunger. Disillusionment. Life is not what you'd hoped."[6] This feeling is pervasive in modern life, where we live paycheck to paycheck, on the headonic treadmill of accomplishment. This feeling is so familiar to us, we might just call it another day, a Tuesday. And we are smart monkeys, seeking to replace the emptiness with just a little *more* of something.

Miller used fMRI technology to demonstrate the areas of the brain that are active when we focus on getting our needs met. Connected to the frontal lobes, our planning center, are the wanting centers of the dopamine reward pathway, structures in the limbic system collectively known as the *basal ganglia.* When we are focused on a goal or idea, we rely on top-down perception, seeing the world through colored glasses that validate that goal or idea. It is not just beauty that is in the eye of the beholder; it is also money, sex, success, food, clothes, validation, power, praise, and anything that we want more of.

We perceive the world differently based on what we want. Miller states:

> This is a lonely, atomistic, and inherently empty way to be. Even having everything can feel like having nothing. This perception of emptiness just makes us want more and try harder—and so we're trapped in the cycle of motivation and reward. Overblown, it becomes craving and addiction: we need a bigger and bigger dose to feel good—but no amount of control or success will extinguish the craving.[7]

The watershed line in spiritual development is to ask ourselves, "What is it that I am seeking through this activity, person, place, or thing?" For example, I am shopping because I want to feel attractive and worthy; I am doomscrolling because I want to avoid stress; I am overeating because I am seeking comfort, and on and on. Our self-seeking patterns develop through our experiences, so while we may not relate to someone's foot fetish, we may perfectly understand salivating over Manolo Blahnik shoes. Asking ourselves what it is that we are seeking underneath this particular behavior gives us insight into who is driving the train—our lizard, seeking resources to survive, our inner mouse, seeking comfort and connection, or our inner chimpanzee, seeking social power and status. We can walk through any shopping mall, any casino, any bar, and ask ourselves, "What am I seeking here?"

Seeking to meet our internal needs only through people, places, and things causes suffering, because all material things live in time and space and therefore evaporate. For example, the cup of coffee I drank this morning cannot keep me awake tomorrow. The praise I received for doing a good job has an invisible expiration date. Seeking through chemistry and love and sex and food and praise and shopping means that we have built our train tracks in a circle and will always need more to forget that we are stuck. Chugging boxcars of coal up the hill, burning the engine ever hotter and brighter, getting the just-right mix of carbon, oxygen, and heat.

I traveled those tracks and lit that fire, over and over, until what burned up was me.

All I Need is More

I returned to school with my new identity as a smoker; this came with privileges and debts. My high school, with its vestiges of being a hippy school free from power trips between faculty and students, still had a smoking section on campus, behind the gymnasium. As the athletes would stomp by in their cleats on their way downstairs to the baseball diamond, I would light up with my new upper-class friends. This group opened doors for me, more than Emma or the likes of her ever could. I was an athlete too, that first year, on the volleyball, basketball, and soccer teams. Whatever natural talent I had, smoking took away. I developed fits of asthmatic wheezing when I sprinted and soon became one of the kids on the sidelines breathing into a paper bag.

My addictions gave me things, but eventually they took away more. Smoking got me outside, into the night air, gazing up at the stars. Every night, I slid open my big window and thrust my face up to the sky. My family had handed me a story of the universe made up of protons, neutrons, and electrons, with empty space in between. As I exhaled my trail of smoke into the broad night sky, I felt, for the first time, inexplicably connected. I befriended constellations and followed their movements night after night. Clear nights were a celebration, the river of the Milky Way spilling forth overhead. Inner questions rose up about where I came from and if there was indeed a god looking after me. The stars had these answers and held this secret. Like the mariners who found their pathways through the stars, I tried to find my own pathway through myself. My questions collided with the scientific explanation of the universe and piled up around me unanswered.

From my new, older friends, I learned how to buy marijuana, roll joints, and acquire pipes and paraphernalia. I got high alone at night, exhaling out my window, enjoying a new peace and calm. When low on buds, I would scrape my pipe and smoke the resin. I had a new identity now as a stoner; my social group opened up and narrowed at the same time. On the weekends, my best friend Phoenix and I would hang out in the city, setting up on someone's doorstep in the Haight-Ashbury district and smoking someone else's bud before cruising the record and thrift stores. We would tell our parents we were staying at a girlfriend's house, then spend the night drinking with boys, vomiting all over our clothes, and receiving lectures from their parents, who said we were too young for this. I crossed county lines and bay bridges on public transportation, reading maps and timetables in my quest to lose myself again. Unlicensed, I drove cars up and down the hills of San Francisco and to corner stores that would accept my fake ID. I drank, peed, and puked on sidewalks, behind strangers' houses, in dark alleys, in city parks, and on pristine beaches. I let guys make out with me, go up and down on me, my sexuality a doorway to connection. I walked through the neighborhoods with peeling paint and housing projects that my family avoided, my privileged white skin glowing in the foggy air. I slept on floors, making my way to bathrooms in the middle of the night with my hands pressed against dark, narrow hallways to keep from falling down.

My self-seeking eventually led me to older men, because I believed that I was not good enough for a teenage boy to like. Treated like a blowup doll, I looked into their vacant eyes for kindness, to see if they would validate a self that even I didn't like. I rode in their cars, slept in their crummy apartments, played quarters on their dirty glass tables, stood outside of bars while they worked as bouncers, and quietly crept through their families' homes at night, keeping their secret hidden. I pretended that I was hard, street smart, independent, and didn't give a fuck. I hid the truth of my sensitive nature, even from myself.

Like a train surely moving down a track, all my genetic programming for addiction was humming in sweet vibration. I had unlocked a cipher: You can ingest something and feel better. Genius. The problem? All you need is more. I pursued getting more in every way possible. I made new friends because they stood next to me waiting in line for the same ticket to oblivion. Other friends, like Phoenix, separated their train cars from mine, prioritizing their own health instead. My lies to my family about who I was, where I was going, and who I was hanging out with were a self-created script that I kept forgetting the lines to. Forgetting about the fake IDs that I stockpiled, one day I drove to the police department like a citizen to gratefully retrieve my lost wallet. Instead, I was ushered into "the box," read my rights, and arrested at age sixteen. These early external consequences were just logs on my train tracks, which my cattle guard of denial easily rationalized out of my way.

Lost in partying for two years in college, I spent time with people whose best friends were also chemical substances. My social world spiraled into a tighter circle; the daily cycle of doing what I had to do to get high was no longer enough to keep the bubble of depression from rising each morning. I began to reach out to other crystalline substances to get even higher. I attended weekly therapy to talk about my family's dysfunctional roots, only to leave the office, drive around the corner, and pull over to get high. My therapist offered me drug treatment resources, ladders up and out, but I said I was not ready. I was too shy. I was afraid. Drugs were the central relationship in my life; I could not imagine life any other way.

CHAPTER 2

Admitting Bottom Is the Price of Admission

It is possible to be free from our reliance on momentary pleasures and the gratification of desires. Through our amazing capacity for self-awareness, we can admit when we are stuck. In fact, we must admit we are lost to find ourselves.

The moment I moved through shame to admit I had crashed my train was the same moment I arrived at the solution.

I would later learn that the solution, freedom, had been within me all along.

Stuck in a Venn Diagram of Conditional Love

At the beginning of summer, I arrived home at the end of my sophomore year in college. I partied once more, combed through a stranger's house looking for drugs that I never found, slept with him one more time, and the next day boarded a plane for a life in sobriety I could not yet imagine.

The wheels of the 747 touched down on foreign land, and I slowly descended the spiral staircase, carefully entering the first day of my new clean and sober life. Hong Kong, oriented around its port, felt familiar. The smells rising from the pavement reminded me both of my hometown of San Francisco and the grime that was inside me: salt, oil, fish, exhaust. At the hotel, my father and I went for a swim in the rooftop pool looking over the bay, me ever-cool in my sparkly green bikini and him ever-dorky with his bathing trunks hiked over his belly button.

My father generally hoarded the Tiffany-blue gilded nest egg he was building, but now and then, he would create a lavish travel experience, allowing us to pretend we were a part of the gentry. My aunt and I were guests on his business trip; they were best friends and siblings, a pair of stout, matching salt and pepper shakers separated by eight years. It was not a coincidence that they shared the same sobriety anniversary. When I was nine years old, they made a pact with god to give up drinking in exchange for sparing my life while I was fighting a flesh eating bacterial infection. Now, ten years later, I was giving up drinking to spare my own life.

Swirling our arms and legs through the water next to the rock grotto waterfall, I treaded through my desire to be his good daughter and float on his praises. The first honest sentence of my life bubbled up in my chest and escaped my mouth: "I have a problem with drugs."

Like a shark smelling blood, he responded, "Drugs? What drugs are we talking about?"

I tried to reassure my father, the doctor who specialized in pharmacology and spent most of his career testing new drugs in his lab in San Francisco for safety and efficacy, now a leader in drug regulation. Drugs were deeply meaningful to him.

I searched for bravery as I bobbed in the water next to him. This was the same man who, when I was fourteen and invited him into my therapy session, took a pad of paper from his brief-case and drew two non-overlapping circles. Pointing to one, he said, "In this circle, Catherine, you go to school, you play sports, even enjoy your friends. I can be with you in this circle, be your father, and support you." He pointed to the other circle and said, "In this circle, there are your behaviors of smoking, drinking, ly-ing, stealing, and having sex." In other words, all the things I was currently doing. "Now in this circle," he continued, "if you are here, I don't know what our relationship will be." Five years later, in that rooftop pool, it was to this father, with his Venn diagram of conditional love, that I told the truth of my addiction.

"Mainly marijuana and alcohol," I confessed.

My father was familiar with hiding himself. He hid being gay under his Brooks Brothers suits, penny loafers, and marriag-es to women.

"Oh, Catherine!" He exhaled with a sigh. "We are cut from the same cloth."

He got oddly perky as he said, "You come from a long line of alcoholics. Me. Your aunt. Your grandfather. And probably many more."

My father met me in that rock grotto pool that day, waterfall thundering around us. He met me as he shared his own struggles with alcohol, how lost he had been, how he drank daily after work for relaxation and relief from anxiety. That day, I dropped my good girl facade and let my dad see me, his daughter, for the first time.

Self-Awareness Is Our Default Mode

Humans have evolved powerful cognitive abilities over time: rational deductive thought, creativity, and language. As those abilities evolved, so did our DMN's (default mode network's) ability to be self-aware as separate beings. This self-awareness is our default mode, which activates when we are not busy solving a math equation or completing a puzzle. During these moments of rest, our cognitive capacity widens and we are able to think about ourselves, make autobiographical memories, and consider our past and future. Our default mode allows us to be "meta," to think about our thinking and even to think about other people's thinking (a.k.a. social cognition).

In this mental spaciousness, we can evaluate our standing in our social group, analyze the social behavior of others, and wonder what someone else is thinking. This recently evolved brain circuitry gives us the capacity to relive memories of shame or embarrassment, such as wearing the wrong outfit or saying the wrong thing at a party. Likewise, this invisible yardstick lets us know when we are better or worse than our peers at a particular task. Our measurement of our value is a codified agreement between neurons, which excitedly whisper their chemical messages to each other between the dark gaps of the synapse: "Good enough." "Not good enough."

Social comparison theory states that we evaluate ourselves by comparing ourselves to others. Downward social comparison occurs when we look at someone who is worse off to feel better about ourselves. Upward social comparison with someone more popular or more accomplished helps us understand that we are not "there" yet. Envy or jealousy can motivate us to strive toward a new goal. Our survival as a species depends on our belongingness to the group. The discomfort of shame when we are too far outside the group norms, too "other," only eases when we find our people who are just like us, "other" in the same way.

This capacity to pause and self-reflect, to course correct on our journeys, is incredible. Some of us are more attuned to this yardstick than others. Afraid to be the "nail that sticks up" and vulnerable to being hammered down by the social group, people with social anxiety have an overactive DMN. In contrast, extroverts' DMNs are connected differently; they are more likely to think of themselves as funny and belonging to any social group.[1] They fit right in. We need both kinds of personalities in our communities—the deep-thinking introverts who go off and problem-solve in isolation, and the outgoing extroverts who are comfortable binding the group together in storytelling and laughter. We need the future-oriented farmers and the quick-acting hunters. Neurodiversity benefits the group.

Research has shown an overactive DMN, with corresponding hyper-self-awareness and social comparisons, to be more common in people with depression and anxiety who suffer from rumination.[2] The word rumination describes both the repetitive circular motion of a cow's jaw as it chews its bite of grass over and over, and the repetitive circular motion of the mind, when we chew our life decisions with regret and worry, over and over. Psychologist Susan Nolen-Hoeksema has shown that "depression reinforces rumination, and rumination reinforces depression."[3] People struggling with depression often have a bias toward negative self-processing, which corresponds to overactivity in their DMN. They are unable to quiet that inner KFUK (or WFUK) radio station that says the weather is bad all the time.

Only a few animals have a sense of themselves as separate individuals. One way that scientists measure self-awareness is the Rouge Test (also called the Mirror Self-Recognition (MSR) test). When this experimental procedure is used with non-human animals, such as other primates, elephants, and dolphins, researchers first anesthetize the animal, then place a red dot on their forehead. When the animal awakens, they are given access to a mirror. If they look for longer periods of time or attempt to investigate the red dot, then we assume that they have some sense of themselves, what they look like normally, and an awareness that something has been altered. Few animals other than humans pass the MSR test: only great apes, rhesus macaques, manta rays, dolphins, orcas, and a few birds.[4] A limitation of the MSR test is that it is based on vision; other species demonstrate self-awareness when their smell or song is altered (e.g., dogs and snakes, respectively). With babies and preschool-aged children, this self-awareness arises only after critical brain development occurs in the first two years of life. The ability to reflect on ourselves and analyze our standing within our social group allows us to be the hyper-social animals we are.[5]

Sometimes we need to know when the red dot is on our forehead. There is a critical moment when this overactive self-awareness machine can be helpful, especially when we are stuck in a loop of harmful behavior. In recovery circles, this is called a moment of clarity, when you accurately see just how stuck you are in your addictive behavior. This shattering of denial often produces guilt, shame, remorse, and hopelessness so painful that it can motivate us to take the first action toward recovery. The DMN can save our lives at these times: "Hey, you have a dot on your forehead, the sniper's rifle is aimed at you. You won't survive this one. Come on, baby, it is time to wake up."

The Ticket to Freedom Is You

We are purchasing an entrance ticket to freedom—freedom from selfish desires, attachments, longings, and our plans to get this world to suit our needs. The ticket is an entry point to come Home to the One, to rest in beingness and knowingness, in that part of us that is never afraid, alone, or confused. When we rest in Oneness, the powers we seek outside of ourselves are already available within us: grace, love, compassion, truth, power, and enlightenment. The price of admission is our ability to be honest with ourselves.

The price of admission, frankly, is you.

The first step in spiritual development, in returning Home to the One, is admitting that we have left Home in the first place. We need to see ourselves on the map, red arrow pointing "You are here," and trust that there are breadcrumbs that lead us back to where we started. First, we need to acknowledge that we feel disconnected and separate. We must admit how we have been trying to meet our needs through material means; just a little more coffee, sugar, money, hugs, validation, sex, chocolate, and I'll be fine. The gift of the self-seeking engine arrives just when we are crashing, on our knees, bankrupt, coming down, alone. We see ourselves standing on one side of the chasm, peace and harmony a distant vista where other people frolic.

For some, the language for this admission in Twelve-Step programs can feel negative. An admission of powerlessness and unmanageability can be a barrier to entry. Another option is to view ourselves as a light bulb that could be more functional, more useful, if it were plugged into the socket. There is no negative judgment with that statement. Simply, the lightbulb's potential remains untapped until that moment when it is aligned with electricity. Only then does its filament begin to glow, and a portion of that energy radiates outward as light. It can be so hard to acknowledge that we are unplugged and not shining at our brightest.

And yet, this humble admission is the cost of transformation.

Freedom comes when we see that our own unaided will-power is not enough. Freedom comes when we sink our knees into the soft sand and lay down the load we have been carrying, lashed to a stick across our shoulders. Inside these packages are the expectations of others, our parents or our community, which we have silently agreed to carry. Traveling along dusty roads, we have stopped at every town, finding the watering hole and slaking our thirst with the wrong drink—the one that ultimately dries us out. We have tried to find a warm bedfellow, only to feel more alone, cold sheets wrapped around us at night.

Admitting that this path leads to nothing is the entrance ticket. Without the first step, we remain in the delusion of self-reliance, the delusion that we can somehow solve our own problems. We can choose to stay in our delusions, but we won't wake up and taste freedom this lifetime. To step into the light, we must acknowledge that we are in the dark. This is by design; we must make the choice freely. We cannot be coerced into paying the price of admission.

When we humbly offer ourselves up, we notice how the world conspires to meet us in that moment. This, too, is by design. Grace abounds. Love transforms.

Always, we are met in our darkest moments.

Always.

My Honest Admission

Returning home from Hong Kong, I found myself on the shore of a new life, unsure of my footing. I tentatively spoke my new truth. First, I tossed pebbles nearby to my family that rippled into offers of support. My mother put her skills to work, researching treatment centers and therapists, and cleared out alcohol from our home. Then I tossed out more pebbles to my friends, ripples that spread out and hit the walls of their disbelief. The pebbles piled up, lining the pockets of our friendships, pulling them under. Still clinging to the rickety dock of my drug-dealing boyfriend, I spoke half-truths, adding to the uncertainty of us the certainty that I had to change everything about my life.

That summer, I worked at an upscale plant nursery, all 105 pounds of me slinging bags of soil and chicken manure into the pristine trunks of German automotives. At night, I drove alone to an outpatient treatment center in my extra-large station wagon, the same car that just months ago was a circus wagon caroming around Santa Cruz with friends sticking out all the windows, cruising on a cocktail of drugs to the next party. As I pulled up to the nondescript business park I had passed hundreds of times, never having any business there, the walls of my car vibrated with bass notes, and cigarette smoke streamed out my window. I encased my nervousness in my usual hard San Francisco veneer, avoiding eye contact, staring straight ahead, and acting slightly bored with everything.

Every night in treatment, we sat uncomfortably in a circle, each of us unloading our life's wreckage in the center of the room. I was surprised to be the only young person there. Where were all the other college students that I knew were out of control? The next-youngest person was a wisp of a housewife who hid her drinking from her scary, beefy Russian husband by switching to Listerine. There were four men in their fifties, one who burned the bridge of his nose clean through with cocaine, another an underwater welder capable of storing his feelings for eternity like canisters of DDT. A tan, long-haired biker dude flirted with me and told story after crazy story of his heroin and cocaine use. A straitlaced stock trader kindly treated me like I was one of them. Together, we wrote love letters to our drugs, created artwork about burying them, and said goodbye to this relationship. We listed our triggers of relapse and identified our safety plans. Everyone said how great it was that I was stopping so young; the attention made me feel different, like I didn't belong.

At nineteen, I really didn't know if I was an alcoholic. I didn't like alcohol. It took too long to work, compared to a substance that you can smoke to receive instantaneous freedom from self. I found the thirty minutes I had to wait for the alcohol to enter my bloodstream interminable at times. Alcohol made me sloppy, unpredictable, and nauseous; for me, it was a distant second favorite form of oblivion.

My counselors in treatment encouraged me to listen to the similarities as people shared their stories, rather than the differences. One man described his experience with alcoholism as a yoke around his neck. As he moved through his day, he would experience a "tug, tug" as the yoke pulled him to drink. I had known that same feeling. "Tug, tug" when I wanted to have fun, "tug, tug" when I wanted to escape my feelings, "tug, tug" when I felt stressed by life's demands, and "tug, tug" when I looked up at the clock and realized I had not yet escaped myself that day.

At nineteen, with no DUIs, no relationships torn apart, no custody of children lost, no time spent behind bars, no loss of employment, and no legal drink ever drunk, I was very familiar with the "tug, tug" of my self-seeking engine.

At nineteen, I admitted to myself: I was an addict.

The Magic Is in the Group

If the first step is admitting we have a problem, the next step is to look for a solution. For this, it is essential to have mentors, people who are a little farther along on the path and can shine a light for us. Simply by watching them, we can learn how to live without relying on the self-seeking engine. The way Home to Oneness is paved by those who have walked before us.

Boxcars Piled Up

Once a week, our family members sat with us in the treatment group circle. We enjoyed seeing them squirm with the same discomfort we had been feeling while doing so many new, vulnerable things. My mother sat upright in her professional clothes when the counselors explained to the group that addiction was a family disease. She was not just any doctor, but a full professor at a tier-one medical school and a researcher of dermatological diseases, known internationally for developing therapies to help children's skin keep the outside world out and the inside world in. She was always the good girl, the valedictorian, the flutist in a baroque quartet. As she sat in that circle, she faced the reality that half of her four teenage offspring had already succumbed to the disease of addiction and that she might have had something to do with it.

When it was our turn to pull our chairs into the middle of the circle, she softened and cried a little as she said, "I know you got lost in our family."

I tried to take care of her. "It's OK. It was a really crazy time," I said, referring to my whole childhood.

"I am so worried about you. I feel like I failed you. And I don't know what to do." She trembled. Speaking our truth is like that. When we are raw and vulnerable and messy and needy, it opens the door for others to pop the cork on their own messiness. Together, we can sit in what is.

The train crashed, and my boxcars piled up in zigzags. No research articles could answer the question; nothing could be bought nor ingested to heal this suffering. Material means cannot quench a spiritual thirst. Together, my mother and I sat on a hill and regarded the wreckage.

My mother bravely went with me to my first Twelve-Step meeting at a women's treatment center. We found the location, a nondescript house tucked into a residential neighborhood, but we were lost from the beginning. When we walked through the front door, we encountered a henhouse of women coming undone. Rules taped to the walls tried to corral their smoking and visitors. I guided my mother down a narrow hallway to a dark, anonymous back room, where the meeting started with the Serenity Prayer. Unlike my infrequent childhood experiences at church, I finally knew the prayer, while my mother was the one sitting beside me, silent. The leader of the meeting invited new people to introduce themselves. I sat opening and closing my mouth like a fish while half the women in the room said their name and identified themselves as "addicts," "alcoholics," or both. I waited until the end to introduce myself as a "visitor," a half-truth, still not quite belonging. For the rest of the meeting, I kicked myself for not fully owning why I was there.

Candles flickered at the front of the room, and the lights were dimmed in preparation for one woman to share her story. As I listened to the devastation of her journey and the power that she had discovered in these rooms, I heard only the differences between her story and mine. At the end, she selected a topic for the group's discussion, the lights flicked back on, and with them, my anxiety. Filled with self-centered fear that they would call on me to speak, I elbowed my mother and said, "Let's go." Feathers ruffled, we scuttled outside, causing a commotion as we left. I burst into tears on the sidewalk. "I don't know how to live life sober," I said. My mother was powerless at that moment. She wanted to help soothe me, to sit on me, her egg, but it wasn't her turn.

Back at my treatment group the next day, I met with my counselor, Dick, whose vascular system on his nose still betrayed his struggle with the bottle, years into his recovery. His crusty voice sounded like the private investigator from New York that he formerly was. My veneer softened. I knew that Dick knew suffering.

"I can't stop," I explained. "I've tried on my own, but I just go back to getting high every day." Blowing bubbles through tears and snot, I said, "I guess I'm just going to be a freak now. Like the only fucking college student in the whole world who doesn't party. It is so fucked up that to save my life, I also need to jump off the cliff of never having friends again."

Dick explained to me that the program used the power of the group to support recovery. "We don't do this alone," he said. "The magic is in the group."

Monkey See, Monkey Do

We learn from others how to survive. When we throw up our hands and say, "I don't know how to do this," it is an adaptive response to look around to see if anyone else knows how to navigate the conundrum. In fact, our brains are wired to learn from others. This wiring network, which lights up when we watch others, is part of the system that gives us a sense of ourselves. Our self-awareness exists within a social network. "I" exist because I am connected to you. And when I am lost, discombobulated, dysregulated, and even disfigured, I look to your body, your face, to find myself again. I can find my way back to myself through you.

We are born to learn about ourselves and the world by interacting with others. Research on twins still in utero shows that we have this capacity for social interaction even before we are born.[1] Twins are not randomly swimming around in amniotic fluid. While only halfway through baking in their mother's oven, they display other-directed behavior, which for some pairs might be an early start to sibling rivalry for more space. We are social animals.[2]

Like a lot of things about the brain, we accidentally discovered the brain regions responsible for learning from others. In a neuroscience lab in Italy, researchers Giacomo Rizzolatti and

Laila Craighero implanted electrodes in a specific region of the frontal lobe of our cousins, the macaque monkeys.[3] They were interested in studying how the brain plans motor movements. As expected, the electrodes in the frontal lobe lit up when the monkeys performed a behavior, showing that this planning region was telling the motor section, "Hey, grab that peanut."

What surprised everyone was that these same electrodes lit up when the monkey was at rest but watched another monkey grasp for the peanut. As if this planning region was saying, "Hey, if I moved my arm like he does, I could get that peanut." The researchers named this new type of brain cell *mirror neurons*. Mirror neurons became the first neurological basis for empathy and learning from others. They explain why it is so helpful to watch a yoga teacher do a pose, because in the planning region of our brains, we are doing the pose with them. Literally, monkey see, monkey do.

The discovery of mirror neurons led to innovative treatments. Neuroscientist V.S. Ramachandran studied phantom limb syndrome, the often debilitating, painful experience when the part of the body that has been amputated (e.g., hand, arm, leg) still sends sensory information, such as pain, to the brain.[4] The person missing a hand might feel that their hand is in a persistent cramp. Ramachandran developed a way to trick the brain into relaxing the missing hand. He created a mirror box, where the person missing their right hand could put their left hand in the box and then extend and flex their left fingers. Seeing the mirrored image, their brain would think they were finally able to extend and flex their right hand, massaging out the cramp. This later led to virtual reality treatments for different phantom limb experiences. For our brains, seeing is believing.

The discovery of mirror neurons launched a greater understanding of how we construct a sense of ourselves. In addition to instantly mapping others' motor movements onto our own bodies, we also feel empathy for others' sense of smell and touch.[5] If you wrinkle your nose in disgust in response to a repulsive smell, my brain will also register an empathetic response, firing in the olfactory center. Faulty mirror neuron systems can help explain why some individuals with disorders of schizophrenia and autism experience loss of self-knowledge and empathy.[6] By mapping other people's experiences in our brains, we understand who we are.

When we lie in the smoking rubble of self-destruction, we can look to others who have gently picked up the pieces of their lives. In spiritual awakening, it is essential to learn from others, relying on our social nature to survive and evolve as a species. When those of us who have been so amputated from our spirit look in the mirror, we only see what's missing, lacking, and not good enough. Like using a mirror box, we can look at others farther along on a spiritual path to see what it feels like to be so connected.

In my Western Eurocentric mindset, I use brain research to validate the fact that we learn and heal in relation to others. Other cultures figured out the power of the group thousands of years ago. In the heat of the Kalahari Desert that transverses the national boundaries of Namibia and Botswana, Indigenous wisdom keepers teach us how they heal one another in their *Ju/'hoan* community. These elders hold the knowledge of the First Psychologists: what is health, what is illness, and how to heal. In 1968, these elders allowed into their community a Harvard-trained psychologist, Richard Katz.[7] The Ju/'hoan elders shared with Katz that when there is a felt disturbance or when an individual is sick, the community gathers to dance:

Every week or so, depending on when there is a need for healing, the community gathers to create a healing dance, typically beginning at dusk and often ending at dawn the next day. As the healers dance around the women, who encircle the fire as they sing the healing songs, a spiritual energy (n/om) heats up: it becomes boiling n/om and is released throughout the dance, while most concentrated in the healers. Boiling n/om activates and enhances consciousness (laia), which makes healing possible. This n/om expands as it is released and is renewable, thereby more accessible to all at the dance. The valuable resource of healing thereby is a renewable, expanding, accessible resource for the community.[8]

This spiritual transformation of boiling n/om through dance is painful and takes skill to manage, because the dancer faces their own death. It takes practice and skill to become a healing dancer, to learn how to heat up the n/om and boil it inside one's body, starting at the base of the spine, before it rises up and out of the body and through each community member. Katz explains, "To heal, one must die and be reborn into an enhanced state of consciousness."[9] Many cultures understand that suffering can fuel spiritual growth, pain can be leveraged for a transformation of consciousness, and healing happens in community.

After a dance, the whole Ju/'hoan community is energized and healed. Katz describes this communal healing process as creating synergy. Where, in Western culture, do we stay up all night dancing and feel more energized the next day? When we share our struggles honestly with another, receive others' guidance and kindness, attend a spiritual gathering, hold hands, pray together, sing together, and even dance together, what if we are not just activating brain networks for learning, but unlocking stores of energy within us and all around us? What if, in our communal gatherings, we are releasing more healing energy than was present just a moment ago? What if we understood that just as couples can intentionally make love, generating more healing, loving power, communities can also make love, generating a coherent field of healing power?

What if the magic in the group was even bigger than we could imagine?

My Future Self

Months after swimming in that rooftop pool, I abandoned college, stopped communicating with my drug-using friends, and ended my relationship with my boyfriend. At nineteen, I attended Twelve-Step meetings nightly, diving through the wrecks of other people's lives, watching their faces as they described what it was like to open the treasure chest of recovery, searching for myself in their stories. Most of the people I went to treatment with had already relapsed. Terrified and alone, I was one of the few successes.

Letting go of self-seeking ways takes time. Back at the treatment center one night, Dick told us, "We quit things in the order they are killing us." I understood this. Although I had given up the fuel of alcohol and other drugs, I moved through my workday mornings orchestrating a new cocktail of three donuts, six cups of coffee, and hourly cigarettes. Hours before the plant nursery would open, I methodically watered the plants, sifting through my thoughts. I would escape with my favorite coworker, who was also in recovery, to the potting shed to smoke and talk shit about the customers.

"I can't believe that lady!" Marianne said. Like the Cheshire Cat, the biggest thing about petite Marianne was her blazing smile. "I can't believe she came here to return the plant after she killed it!"

"That's crazy," I joined in, capping on the customer. Marianne and I also had in common our love/hate of menthol cigarettes, hers a leftover from her crack-smoking days, mine adopted so that I could continue to smoke while coping with chronic bronchitis.

"She's like, 'There's something wrong with this plant you sold me.' I'm all, 'Yeah, it's dead.'" Cracking herself up, she said, "What a surprise, your plant needs water."

Pulling off my leather gloves, I said, "I went to my first meeting last night. It was so scary. It was at a treatment center, and everybody knew everybody."

"Good for you!" she smiled. "Trust me, meetings can be fun. You just got to find the right one."

We planned to meet up outside my second meeting. I was startled to see her cleaned up in makeup, a leather jacket, and jeans. Four hundred chairs were already set up in the large auditorium of a community center, a lectern and a microphone on the stage. The energy in the room was high, and everyone, including my soil-loving friend, was dressed for the opportunity to see and be seen. Before the meeting started, I busied myself with making tea so that I did not have to talk to people. The lights dimmed, and we opened with the Serenity Prayer. The secretary asked for newcomers, and this time, after eighteen people stood up and announced their names and identified as alcoholics, I finally did too. In front of hundreds, in the same city where I smoked my first cigarette behind a liquor store, I claimed the family lineage passed down through generations. I owned that I was different from most every other teenager I knew: "I'm Catherine. I am an addict/alcoholic."

I promptly sat down and buried my face in my hands, hiding in embarrassment. Everyone in the row in front of me turned around in their seat to shake my hand and welcome me. That night, someone humbly shared his story of destruction by the bottle and triumph through recovery. This time, I heard the similarities, tears streaming down my face. He recounted the number of cars he wrapped around trees, the marriages he destroyed, the number of times he should have died, and his total lack of faith in god. Despite all this, there was the eventual magic he felt at the end of a Twelve-Step meeting, standing in a circle holding hands with other survivors of that same shipwreck, in prayer. I recognized his desperation, and I listened intently for the secret keys to finding a power that we cannot see, hear, feel, or touch but that was somehow going to keep me sober.

At the end of the meeting, the house lights came up, and the secretary said we were going to celebrate lengths of sobriety. The energy in the room turned into a celebration of being alive, rather than shame about being addicted. People gathered at the back of the room and waited for their turn to walk down the center aisle to receive a poker chip commemorating their time in recovery. The speaker called out lengths of time starting with twenty-four hours, moving up to thirty days, sixty days, and all the way up to thirty-five years, while the crowded audience cheered, clapped, and whistled. The meeting closed with the Serenity Prayer. When four hundred well-dressed, high-energy, celebrating, self-seeking alcoholics stood in a crowded circle, jammed shoulder to shoulder, holding clean and sweaty and dirty hands, and closed their eyes in prayer to feel inside of themselves for a connection I did not yet know, I peeked around the room. Some had upturned faces with small smiles of gratitude; others squeezed the hand of the person next to them and beamed their delight. Peace flowed through the chain of connected arms and hands. Still missing parts of myself, amputated long ago, I saw a sea of humanity connected to themselves, each other, and this god I still could not see.

That night, holding the hand of my first friend in recovery, I saw my future self, a version of myself that I could become. That night, I felt the magic of hope.

CHAPTER 4

Barriers to Oneness

Jumping tracks, from fear to living a Spirit-guided life, is difficult because we have to rewire our brains to do so. We can build the needed new neural pathways through spiritual practice. Our human brains do not perceive everything; we humans are particularly inept at experiencing Oneness. Modern cultures have exacerbated this problem by further disconnecting us. Like the tight cell walls of the blood capillaries that make up the blood-brain barrier, we keep Oneness out.

And yet, Oneness exists.

We can, with practice, learn to perceive it.

First Prayer

On a hot August night during my first summer in treatment, the Santa Ana winds blew across California in the reverse direction, from east to west, covering our normally coastal climate with dry central valley air. The winds blew right through me as I waited outside the treatment center, just two months into sobriety. I felt raw and unprotected, as if the outer layer of my skin was missing. That night in the group meeting, I shared as if I were a victim in this melodrama.

"You took away my drugs. You took away my alcohol. I feel so empty, and now I don't have any way to feel better," I said.

The treatment center's director looked at me squarely and paused before he spoke. He did not talk to me about antidepressants, therapy, or anything that represented the current medical model. Instead, he declared, "The only thing that is going to make you feel better is a power greater than yourself."

Those words landed like a thunderclap in the center of my chest. I saw how far I was from any higher power. How lost I was at sea. The spirituality of the Twelve Steps was fine for everyone else, but it would not work for me, I thought. Raised by scientists, I had to see evidence to know.

I searched for this higher power but did not see how this god was influencing my life or keeping me sober. Wasn't I the one who got in my car and drove myself to meetings? Wasn't it me who lifted the weight of the ten-thousand-pound telephone when I called a sober woman to admit I felt like using again? At meetings, I listened intently when people shared about their relationship with the "god of their understanding." I learned that prayer was for asking questions and meditation was simply listening for answers. The thoughts in my head were so loud, I doubted god could have gotten a word in edgewise. I tried saying prayers out loud and thinking them silently, but my mind would hijack the stage in the middle. I worried that these interrupted prayers were somehow invalidated, as if god's attention span had an expiration date.

To compensate for my squirrel mind, I began writing my prayers to completion in bed at night. Allergic to the word "god," I wrote instead to "You," thinking that if there was an all-powerful, all-knowing god, then they would know. My first prayer read:

> Dear You,
>
> I am in between, in limbo. Neither fully dead nor fully alive.
>
> You who makes the stars, the infinite universe, will you let me down? In truth, I expect you to fail me. I am fearful of loving you. It's like putting all my eggs in one basket.
>
> Wipe away the muck from my eyes. I need to see you. I am feeling alone. I can't depend on myself for strength. I haven't got it.
>
> I NEED YOU.
>
> PLEASE.

During the day, I looked for evidence of this higher power in my life; at night, I wrote what I found with gratitude. Like a deer that hears a footstep in the woods, I became hyperaware of resources that helped me to stay sober. The women who volunteered as greeters at meetings made me feel like my arrival was wanted. A speaker, when sharing their story of recovery, would say the just-right thing to help me stay sober another day. I listened as people declared they were cared for by their higher power, their recovery specifically guarded by this presence. I looked for signs of a creative intelligence in the butterfly that landed on a flower next to me, in the plump blackberries that grew along my fence, in the birds' trails overhead, and in the blazing coastal sunsets. Crossing into new territory where my family had no roadmap, I searched on.

We Don't Know What We Don't Know

As great as we humans think we are, we have known sensory limitations. My dog doesn't just smell what's cooking for dinner better, she also smells what we cooked for dinner yesterday and the day before, measuring time in the decay of smell.[1] Some birds, mammals, and butterflies see ultraviolet light and could probably help me out by telling me when I'm getting a sunburn. Some animals feel touch before it lands on their skin, and others even sense the electromagnetic pull of the Earth's north and south poles. Still more detect earthquakes.[2] Why are we so convinced that, if the universe were in a state of Oneness, we would be the animals to perceive it?

Perhaps most life forms perceive unity. Many species behave in unison. In my house, my two yellow Labrador Retrievers lie in the same dog bed, backs sickled in the same arc, the same right ear flopped on the bed, tails curled in the same direction. Thousands of swifts fly in random directions until the moment of sunset, when they gather in a whirlpool of racing blackness, spinning faster and faster until they dive into a chimney to rest.[3] But do they feel the unity?

Their nervous systems seem to say so. Fish swimming in a school exhibit slower heart rates and calmer nervous systems compared to the single fish swimming solo.[4] Many mammals nuzzle, groom each other, and huddle together to reduce stress, calming themselves by releasing the neurotransmitter oxytocin. Honeybees and ants are, individually, not so smart, but collectively form an intelligent hive mind. Collective animal behavior and swarm intelligence confer evolutionary advantages for animals that behave together. Even the plant and fungi worlds are connected in ways we are just discovering. Mycologists discovered the "world wood web," a fungal network of shared resources between trees.[5] There are connections that we are just learning about, connections we don't understand.

Studying other animals through comparative anatomy gives us humans humility. We are not the best perceivers of sensory information, and other animals might have consciousness too. We might be missing what really exists out there; perhaps our central nervous systems developed a filter for Oneness along the evolutionary way. We are surrounded by ultraviolet light, but we do not see its emission from leaves. Likewise, we are surrounded by and imbued with Oneness, but do not perceive it because our DMN (default mode network) thinks of "I," "me," and "my." The question is, when we are in our default mode, paying attention to ourselves, are we missing something else?

We don't know what we don't know. My favorite neuropsychological term is *anosognosia* (an-nos-og-nos-ee-uh), which describes this perfectly. Usually applied to people with a neurological impairment to describe a lack of awareness of their symptoms and limitations, anosognosia applies to all of us. In mental health, anosognosia can be deadly. The symptom tells us that we don't have a mental health problem, and this lack of awareness can be a great barrier to seeking treatment. In spiritual application, anosognosia blocks our ability to consider other realities. We think we are perceiving the world accurately, rather than humbly acknowledging the constraints of our perceiving apparatus, our central nervous system. We think we know what reality is, but perhaps there are other states of awareness, other planes of existence. We think we are individuals, but there is a hive mind, a greater intelligence.

We are taught to ignore Oneness, groomed to think of ourselves as separate.

Legacy Burdens

In modern, industrialized societies, we have separated ourselves from our spiritual natures. Some cultures understand that every act is a spiritual practice, so they pray before they eat, make love as a form of spiritual connection, and honor the One in all their affairs. Yet, many of us have learned to see ourselves as separate entities and get entranced with seeking our well-being through material means.

What happened? How did we get so disconnected? Many developments silenced our inner knowing over the millennia. Farming happened. We began to work the land, developing the ability to feed thousands of people, and we gave up our connection to the wild. Religion happened. We gave to a select few the power to communicate with Spirit, and we gave up our ability to directly experience Oneness. Calendars happened. Nations unified under a shared understanding of time, and we gave up our connection to nature and her cycles, to the present moment. Technology happened. We developed tools for communication, weapons, and travel, and we gave up our satisfaction with the abundance of Earth's resources. Racist colonialism happened. We traveled the world clutching pieces of her to our chest in ownership, and we gave up languages, peoples, traditions, and thousands of years of Indigenous wisdom. Science happened. We observed, measured, and published our understanding of the material world, and we relinquished other ways of knowing and the understanding that some things are not directly observable. Capitalist materialism happened. We bathed in champagne and pearls, plastered our walls with digital displays, and we gave up our creativity, calm, compassion, and connection.

Richard Schwartz, founder of Internal Family Systems therapy, summarizes this cultural programming into four "legacy burdens": racism, patriarchy, individualism, and materialism. He describes how these burdens synergistically work together to "create the pervasive sense that we are all disconnected and on our own in a dangerous, dog-eat-dog world."[6]

In this analysis, no one culture is celebrated, and no one culture is denigrated. It is not our cultural background that determines our capacity for spiritual awakening, but rather our reaction to it. We are not victims of our time, place, and cultural location; on the contrary, we, as souls, have specifically chosen these opportunities as our classroom. However, in this moment in human history, we have missed the earlier, gentler signs, messages, and omens. Now facing the brick walls of climate change, mass poverty, and world war, we must choose to live a more conscious life or kill off everything around us.

Instead of burying our heads in the sand, we can ask ourselves, are we One, or are we separate?

We are both self and Self. We are at Home in the One and aware of the two.

To be in a state of Oneness requires us to calm our evolutionary programming, which seeks pleasure and more. When we begin to pay attention to our thoughts, to what we are seeking, we find clues to what part of us is running the show. Spiritual practice gives us the freedom to choose how we want to respond to the world.

What if I could switch from my oil-sputtering, gas-guzzling, self-seeking engine to a cleaner burn? People do this all the time; it is called prayer and meditation.

Willing to Search

I knew that my biggest stumbling block to staying sober was a relationship with a higher power. Instructed to get a sponsor by the treatment center, I warily looked around the meetings for a woman who "had what I wanted," which was anything unlike myself. My counselor, Dick, and I often attended the same sessions, where he would get busy as a matchmaker, introducing me to women who "worked a good program." In my mind, the word "sponsor" was a synonym for failure, reminiscent of my effort as a child to sign up neighbors as my sponsor to fill my UNICEF box with coins for the number of books I read, only to be so blown away by my brother's lengthy list of completed readings that the resulting shame prevented me from returning to collect any coins. In this case, Dick explained that a sponsor was like a guide dog: They don't direct, but nudge by sharing their own experience.

One woman stood out to me, like a spotlight shone on her during the meetings. Rosaleen, who joyfully described herself as a Cholla from the barrio, raised her hand and shared at almost every meeting. She emitted cool from the streets as she talked about her relationship with god: "Man, I was talking to god the other day, and I was like, 'What am I supposed to do with this mess?' and god was like, 'Just let go of the steering wheel. I got you.'"

Sitting next to her one night, I worked up all my courage to say, "I like your bracelet."

She turned toward me and gave me her full, luscious attention. "Thanks, doll," she said.

In the sunshine of her attention, I got braver and said, "I was wondering if I could call you sometime? I like how you talk about god."

I called her that night and asked her to be my sponsor. Every week, I drove to her apartment to read "The Big Book," a main Twelve-Step text, unpacking its outdated language and absorbing her explanations of the spiritual solution to the disease of alcoholism. Sitting on her couch, drinking from mismatched mugs, I soaked in the cozy comfort of the tea and cookies and her.

Still convinced that I was too different to have a relationship with god, I worried about completing the second step, where we "come to believe" in a power greater than ourselves, and the third step, where we "turn our will and our lives" over to this power. Rosaleen drove to my family's home to guide me through the second and third steps. We tucked into the back deck, protected from the wind by glass walls.

"Let's kneel," she said.

My anxiety spiked.

I asked her, "What if I haven't yet come to believe in god? What if I am not sure?"

She made a wide archway for me to walk through when she replied, "Are you open to the idea that there could be a higher power?"

"Totally," I admitted, as I obsessed daily with thoughts about whether there was a god or not.

"That's all you need, doll. An open mind."

For the third step, Rosaleen didn't ask me to turn my life over to this unseen force. Instead, all she asked was, "Are you willing to do the rest of the Twelve Steps?"

"Of course," I said, ever a good student.

"Just be willing, and god will meet you halfway." She pointed out the sentence in the Big Book that said that there are only three necessary ingredients: honesty, open-mindedness, and willingness.

I had already made an honest admission that my best thinking and problem-solving landed me here, all tied up in knots. I continued to be honest daily, telling on myself when I had sneaky thoughts about getting high again, how this time would be different, how I could have just one. I was open-minded to the idea that there could be a power greater than myself in the universe. And I was willing. I was willing to not suffer anymore, to not be depressed and alone, and to embrace all kinds of uncomfortable new behaviors to live sober. I was willing to reach out into the void, without any evidence, and ask for help.

I got on my knees and held Rosaleen's hands. We said the third step prayer together: "God, I offer myself to thee, to build with me and do with me as thou wilt, relieve me of the bondage of self, that I may better do thy will, take away my difficulties, that victory over them may bear witness to those I would help of thy power, thy love, and thy way of life."

I wrote that night in my journal, "You who push the mountains up and thrust the sea against them. You who have saved me from myself. The creator of beauty, love, and strength, in the image of yourself. A loving god, I have found you now."

And just two weeks later, I vacillated again, writing, "It is a trip how many people are CONVINCED of your existence, and yet it is so hard for me to believe."

I found a map and used it, only to forget and get lost again. Sometimes we are connected and pray; sometimes, alone and in the dark, we reach out despite our doubts.

CHAPTER 5

This Is Your Brain on Oneness

The next step in our spiritual awakening is to identify a new source of energy. After admitting we are unplugged light bulbs, we acknowledge there is a Source, and that we could be plugged in.

Research into the inner workings of our nervous system reveals that we naturally have the wiring necessary for this connection. While searching for this new source, we begin to use different neural structures and pathways that have been there all along. Through spiritual practice, "small mind" pathways in the brain deactivate, the ones that know separation and strive for more. We uncover the neural pathways of "Big Mind:" calm, presence, and unity. We choose to see the world differently.

We choose the filter of Oneness.

Missing an Outer Layer

As a raw, vulnerable, newly sober twenty-year-old, I resigned myself to not having friends. During the day in my college classes, I sat in hard metal chairs, feeling different from everyone around me. At night in Twelve-Step meetings, I sat in hard metal chairs in churches I disdained, entering and exiting alone.

I rented an apartment in a busy neighborhood because it was one block away from the local Alano Club. An Alano Club is a private non-profit organization that usually springs up around Twelve-Step communities. The club serves the function of helping us anti-social, self-centered, lonely addicts learn how to say hello and ask someone else how they are doing. The Alano Club on my block was a one-story dilapidated house; its battered condition reflected the people floating around it. Only the front porch was visible to passing cars, its smoking section constantly filled with hulking hordes of men and hardened women who had been there, done that. To attend meetings, I would weave my way through this scene, trying to hug as few men as possible as they reached out for me, and make my way inside to sit on the hard, wooden church pews that lined the walls. The meetings had a rhythm, a patter, starting and ending the same way, with the same set of periodic clapping and chanting, prayers, reminders, and sayings. I breathed deeply into this reassuring sameness, knowing that I was about to hear the instructions for how to stay sober that day.

Dick, the counselor from my treatment center, became an anchor. Months after I completed treatment, Dick continued to nudge me along in recovery, herding me like a sheep dog. "What are you doing this Saturday?" he asked when I ran into him at a meeting one week.

"Studying" was my rote answer to social invitations, when in reality I would watch TV alone.

"You've got to come to the Alano Club's Fourth of July barbecue. There is someone you have to meet."

"OK, maybe," I hedged, giving myself an out. Inwardly, I rolled my eyes at this probably very nice middle-aged woman.

Before I even rounded the corner into the grassy backyard of the Alano Club, I could smell the fat of the sausages and hamburgers dripping on the wide barbecue. I strategically chose my path through the clumps of misfits, cool guys, and former and present sluts, until I found Dick sitting with a group under a willow tree. I joined him, lit a cigarette, and put on my glossy veneer.

He jumped up when he saw her. "There she is!"

Light poured off her white-blond hair, and while she only had one week of sobriety, she was the most luminescent person in that dumpy backyard.

"Teri, this is Catherine," he proudly introduced me, "She's got great recovery."

Stunned by the role reversal—Dick was now introducing me as a woman with a strong program to a new member—I stammered, "Hey, nice to meet you."

Tall, gorgeous, and with style that effortlessly oozed out of her, Teri bubbled as she talked, so excited to be alive and grateful to be sober. In that moment, Teri did with me what she did with everyone: she opened her heart and collected me. It was in her heart that I first met god's love.

This Is Your Brain on God

Changing fuel sources takes time because it involves rewiring our brains. When we seek spiritual connection, we quiet the DMN's (default mode network's) constant analysis of how we are doing in the world. As our dopamine reward system becomes more sensitive, we learn to appreciate the taste of the apple rather than needing the apple fritter. We discover that, deep within us, we have the capacity for connection.

Western science first became aware of our brain's capacity for spiritual experiences through drugs. Just like a kid throwing wet wads of paper towels at bathroom ceilings to see what sticks, scientists give the drugs first, then later discover their action on the brain. For example, much of what we know about the brain's neurotransmitter communication systems we have learned through the effects of drugs on the brain. Through opiates, we discovered endorphins, naturally occurring neurotransmitters that block pain. Through antidepressant medications, we learned about serotonin's influence on mood; through marijuana, we learned about our own endogenous cannabinoids. And through the broad class of drugs known as psychedelics, we learned about our capacity to experience Oneness.

Psychedelics, as a group of molecules, defy our human attempts to categorize them. They are considered a subgroup of hallucinogenic drugs, even though some psychedelics do not produce hallucinations (e.g., MDMA, ketamine).[1] The Latin building blocks for the name of this class of drugs—*psyche* (soul) and *delos* (clear, manifest)—reveal our attempt to describe the expansive, non-ordinary states of consciousness these drugs provide. Further attempts at subcategories include labels such as "empathogens" (feeling within), "entactogens" (touching within), or "entheogens" (becoming divine within). Some are synthesized in a lab (e.g., LSD, ketamine, MDMA, MDA), and others are naturally occurring substances central to spiritual traditions (e.g., psilocybin, iboga, ayahuasca, and peyote). And one psychedelic is a compound experienced when you happen to lick the back of a Sonoran Desert Toad (i.e., 5-MeO-DMT).[2] (Side note: Please don't lick the toads. DMT can also be synthesized.)[3] The drug action of psychedelics does not even hang together as a group. While most bind with serotonin receptors, facilitating strong serotonin messages, others act on nicotinic and kappa-opioid receptors (e.g., ibogaine and salvia divinorum, respectively). Just as these molecules unzip us from our mental identities, so too do they unzip themselves from our attempts at categorization.[4]

While Western science has only recently discovered these "drug" molecules, they have been known to Indigenous wisdom traditions as sacred medicine for more than five thousand years. Anthropological evidence shows a worldwide history of psychedelic use for spiritual purposes. In Algeria, a cave painting shows a human figure covered in an outline of mushrooms, in Guatemala, stone carvings represent human-mushroom figurines, and carbon dating of peyote traces shows long-standing use by ancestral First Peoples in the southern United States.[5] In the present, these plant and fungi medicines continue to be central channels for some First Peoples' spirit communication and healing practices. These Indigenous wisdom traditions and sacred medicines unite the spiritual and the material in a basket woven of rich cultural context. The medicines are revered for their power, respected for their healing abilities, and used in intentional ceremonies. Within Indigenous wisdom worldviews, plant medicines are not "drugs" to get high from, but rather gifts from Spirit to connect us to Spirit.[6]

Psychedelics are also connected to the history of "Western civilization." The ancient Hindu text, the *Vedas,* refers to a drink called Soma, which may have had psychedelic ingredients. Additionally, there is a growing analysis of potential psyche-delic use in the Old Testament.[7] In *The Immortality Key*, Brian Muraresku proposes that some early Christian rituals used a psychedelic sacrament.[8] The evidence for this connection lies in the ancient Greek religious and cultural practices where early Christianity was incubated. Archaeochemists identified residues on temple artifacts and teeth in Greece as ergot, a hallucinogenic alkaloid found in the mold that can grow on wheat and barley, related to LSD but less potent. Ancient Greeks prepared sac-raments with this key ingredient for more than two thousand years and called it "the mysteries." Muraresku suggests that this sacramental drink was used in the early ritual celebration of the Last Supper, the Eucharist, and later suppressed by the Roman Christian Church. Additional evidence for entheogenic mush-room use in Christianity can be found in "frescoes, illuminated manuscripts, mosaics, sculptures, and stained-glass windows."[9] In Western-industrialized cultures, this history of ritual psyche-delic use was actively suppressed and then, in time, forgotten.

Meanwhile, Western science literally stumbled across the drug action of psychedelics. In 1943, Swiss chemist Albert Hofmann accidentally exposed himself to the chemical he had synthesized, LSD, before going on a bicycle ride that was initially terrifying, then evolved into "unprecedented colors and plays of shapes that persisted behind…closed eyes."[10] In the United States and Europe in the 1950s and 60s, more than a thousand research articles, published and presented at international psychedelic research conferences, demonstrated LSD as a helpful adjunct to psychotherapy and a possible treatment for alcoholism.[11] Bill Wilson, co-founder of Alcoholics Anonymous, was a strong advocate of LSD to induce spiritual experiences for alcoholics.[12] This early research showed promise for depression, anxiety, relationship issues, and end-of-life anxiety, as well as a strong indication of LSD's ability to provide lasting spiritual transformation after as little as one dose.[13]

One study from 1962, known as the Marsh Chapel Experiment, was designed by then Harvard theology graduate student Walter Pahnke (who later became a minister and psychiatrist) under his supervisors Timothy Leary and Richard Alpert (who later became Ram Dass).[14] In this double blind, placebo-controlled experiment with a small sample, the participants who received the experimental dose of psilocybin reported having profound, life-changing religious experiences, indistinguishable from "naturally occurring" spiritual experiences. Even twenty-five years later, almost all of the experimental participants reported they experienced "a genuine mystical nature and characterized it as one of the high points of their spiritual life."[15] Later, Pahnke and his colleague William Richards summarized the consistent and reliable mystical experiences psychedelics provided into a few categories: unity, transcendence of time and space, sense of sacredness, and deeply felt positive mood.[16]

In 1970, despite the overwhelming evidence of the healing potential of psychedelics, the United States Drug Enforcement Agency brought this research to a screeching halt when it classified LSD as a Schedule 1 drug, declaring without justification that it had the highest risk of abuse with no accepted medical use. We locked up drugs that open minds.

In the recent psychedelic resurgence, brain scanning research shows how psychedelics induce mystical experiences. Causing reduced activity in the DMN, parietal lobes, amygdalae, and hippocampi, psychedelics dissolve our perceptual barriers, shifting us from perceiving each object separately to experiencing the unification of all things.[17] Psychedelics also increase activation of other brain regions, flooding the thalamus and visual cortex with sensory information and allowing us to perceive the world differently in a way we remember (unlike alcohol and marijuana, which impair memory), as well as help our neurons make new synaptic connections by promoting dendrite growth.[18] Psychedelics turn on the brain's capacity for Oneness, with lasting effects.

And yet, we do not need psychedelics to experience unity.

Indigenous wisdom has long known other pathways to Oneness. In 1972, professor of religious history Mircea Eliade described shamanism as "archaic techniques of ecstasy." Techniques to induce "flight of the soul" include drumming, breathwork, meditation, chanting, trance dancing, vision quests, and fasting.[19] Although psychedelics can be a nice shortcut to unity and powerful agents of healing, there are many paths to mystical experience. We have an innate capacity for spiritual connection, and we can access expanded states of consciousness through many practices.

A Spiritual Docking Station

Brain scanning research shows that our brains are hard-wired to experience Oneness; people who meditate regularly show the ability to quiet regions that produce internal chatter.[20] While research participants meditate inside the tube of a whirling brain scanner, breathing in and out, the images of their brains on the screen transition from splotchy, active red to cool, relaxed blue. Over and over again, replicating research findings, we scan the brains of Carmelite nuns and Buddhist monks, finding a deactivation of their DMN and parietal lobes, which create a felt sense of the body. Brain researchers have constructed an understanding of the neurobiology of mystical experiences; these involve quieting our awareness of ourselves, where our bodies are in space, and the sense of our bodies as a separate entity.[21]

Lisa Miller, author of *The Awakened Brain,* employed MRI scans to compare people's brains when they remembered spiritual experiences versus when they thought of stressful experiences, then analyzed the differences.[22] A common theme in the stress narratives was "pedaling hard for control in the face of uncertainty" and the "terror of not having or getting what the person most craved."[23] The stressful stories activated the brain regions we would expect—the dopamine reward system in the frontal lobe and basal ganglia.

How Miller's participants described their spiritual experiences is strikingly familiar to research on psychedelic experiences:

> Physically, the participants felt warm, calm, energized, and more alive. Their hearts beat faster, their senses sharpened, their nagging thoughts disappeared. Emotionally, they experienced clarity, awe, openness, peace, and unity, and felt a powerful connection with, and sometimes an overwhelming love for, other people, a higher power, or their surroundings...[There was] a feeling of oneness with the environment or the divine; a sense of their own individual voice or identity

or presence dissolving into something larger around or beyond them. They narrated direct, felt experiences of oneness.[24]

These descriptions are reminiscent of Pahnke and Richards's findings on common themes in psychedelic experiences.[25] They are also similar to the Eight C's of Self-leadership as described in Internal Family Systems therapy: compassion, curiosity, courage, clarity, creativity, connection, confidence, and calm.[26]

But Miller's participants were not Buddhist monks or Carmelite nuns. Nor were they people induced to have mystical experiences through psychedelics. These were people like you and me, just telling stories, stressful and spiritual. The same brains activated different pathways. These MRI scans revealed spiritual pathways in the brain—a deactivation of the DMN and parietal lobe, and activation of the ventral attention network and the social-relational frontotemporal network. Miller and her colleagues demonstrated that we all have the capacity to choose. We can choose to activate brain pathways of desire and reward, or we can choose to activate Oneness. As Miller said, we all have a "neural docking station of love, unity, and guidance."[27]

Our *ventral attention network* (VAN) resides mainly in the right hemisphere of the brain. When humming away, it helps us to be aware of our surroundings, mindful and present to what is.[28] The VAN helps us to respond to unexpected events in our environment. This type of present, aware attention is called "bottom-up processing" to describe all the sensory information traveling from the "bottom" of our peripheral nervous system and "up" spinal cord channels to the central nervous system, which then processes information as it is, without judgment.

In contrast, the *dorsal attention network* (DAN) is our laser focus. The DAN allows us to filter out extraneous stimuli and only see what we expect to see.[29] The DAN prevents us from seeing life as it is; instead, we see life as we are looking for it. This "top-down processing" creates filters for our perception. Both attention networks are necessary for survival, and they operate together in a dance. Our VAN takes in the environment broadly, then sees a shiny object that lights up our DAN for further investigation.

Meditation, like weight training exercises, can strengthen both systems.[30] Different meditation practices can strengthen different neural pathways. For example, open-monitoring meditation practices, such as mindfulness exercises, where we allow our focus to be with what is, strengthen our VAN.[31] And as we would expect, focused-attention meditation practices, such as the use of a mantra, pump up the DAN. We can use prayer and meditation as spiritual exercises for our brains.

Remove the Filters

When we calm the DMN and our grasping dopamine reward pathway, we restore ourselves to perceiving what is real. Perhaps we are not the separate selves we think we are. We are not our anxieties and worries, and we are not in space and time; instead, we are in undifferentiated Oneness. As Miller says, it is our normal capacity to "consciously connect to the life force that moves in, through, and around us."[32] Instead of altering our experience of reality, perhaps psychedelics help us to remove our filters to experience what is real. Ralph Metzner, psychologist and pioneer of psychedelic research, described psychedelics as "perceptual instruments" that "allow us to observe phenomena at a scale or reality to which we don't have access in our ordinary, functional waking state."[33] From a perspective of Oneness, life is a unified experience that our brains continually chop up into what is "me" and "not me."

Underneath all the mental chatter—the to-dos, the wants, the desires, the feelings, and the thoughts—is our beingness. When we rest in the timelessness of our being, our walls of separation dissolve, our need to achieve becomes a cosmic joke, and we arrive home where we belong and feel secure. Our unity is our true default mode, our original resting place. Just like the flocks of swifts that ripple together in a wave and the Labradors that sleep in the same sickle, so too are we able to join the wave and rest in togetherness. We just happen to have very capable and busy minds that evolved on top of our beingness. Spiritual practices like prayer and meditation can quiet the mind and restore us to the truth of who we are.

Restoration to Sanity

The second step in the Twelve Steps offers a declarative statement of belief in a spiritual solution: "We come to believe that a power greater than ourselves could restore us to sanity." Many people overlook the last clause, the idea that there is a sane version of ourselves to which we can be restored. This simple statement—that a part of us is ever-present, unchanging, and always connected— is the hallmark of many religious traditions. It refers to the god inside of us, the Atman in Hindu traditions, the awakened one in Buddhism, the Big Mind in Religious Science, the Christ within us. We already are what we are seeking to find on our spiritual paths. Waking up is really the process of uncovering and letting go of the lies that keep us from knowing our own divine nature. Being restored to sanity means being restored to the truth of who we are.

This second step is a visioning process. When facing a problem, we can ask ourselves: What is it that I want to be restored to? What does sanity look like to me in this situation? Even when we are on our knees, combing through the shag carpet, looking for the rock of cocaine we dropped, even when we are stuck in the bath house, even when we see ourselves getting hit again by our lover, even at our lowest moment, our highest Self is present, watching, ready to step in with care.

Recovery is not about the first thought we have in a situation (fear, shame, blame), but how long it takes us to arrive at the recovered second thought (faith, acceptance, compassion). I still have my first thoughts, but my second thoughts, where I pause and experience my unity, the sanity I want restored, arrive faster every year.

I have spent the last thirty years searching for a higher power and trying to understand what this sanity looks like. I found one answer for both questions: Oneness. This transition—from being the chemist trying to control her own puppet strings, to surrendering control to some unknown outside force, then finally coming Home to rest in the One—has taken me a lifetime.

My pathway to love was blazed first by my friend. When I was an unplugged lightbulb, she turned on the light for me.

Don't Postpone Love

Teri's smile betrayed her at times, so large that it showed her gum line. She had a special superpower: she could put on lipstick in the morning and have it last all day. She learned this surviv-al skill in her conservative Orange County upbringing: how to be fabulous even when raised by ordinary humans who think they are helping you when they forbid makeup. Teri was a mil-lionaire by her mid-twenties, a successful young artist painting original works of art on clothing. She developed a catalog and sold her clothing line to department stores and boutique retail-ers. "Teri Wear" gave her money to play hard. She broke bones on mountain bikes, stayed up all night on cocaine, and relocat-ed to Hawaii. When her marriage ended in domestic violence and bankruptcy, she arrived on her brother's doorstep in Marin County, at rock bottom, ready to start anew.

Teri was ten years older than me, and yet we were kids to-gether, raw in our recovery. She made more friends in her first week of sobriety than I had in my first year. In our rambling conversations, we poured over everything we experienced and brought it all back to our relationship with god. Somehow, we were both filled with self-loathing and would commiserate on what we didn't like about our gorgeous young bodies. We were tramps together, moving through relationships, trying to find our soulmates in broken-down jalopies. I brought all my ques-tions to her, but somehow, she would end up writing what I said on small pieces of paper all over her house. She would ask me, "How did you get so wise so young?" and I would honestly reply, "I don't know."

I'd say sophomoric things like, "The only way out of this is through."

"Oh my god, I'm salivating," she'd exclaim. "That is so bril-liant. I have to write that down."

That would egg me on to come up with more insights: "It's like I want him to fill me up, but I need to learn how to fill myself up."

She started cracking up before she even said, "That's what dildos are for!"

But it was Teri who had poetic bumper stickers flowing out of her pen:

"Don't postpone love."

"I want to grow out of inspiration, not desperation."

"I'm here to thrive, not just survive."

Meanwhile, my skeptical mind floated between doubt and conviction that I was not good enough. In my relationships, I created chaos and drama, replicating on the outside what I felt about myself on the inside. Blind and numb, I couldn't see or feel god.

Recovery members told me that my mind was a "dangerous neighborhood" and "don't go there alone," so I brought Teri with me into every dark alleyway. Teri poured words of praise on me, sticky tar to the inner terrorist trying to kill me. In the aftermath, she brought bandages, gauze, and god's delight in who I am. Loving me back to myself, Teri gently picked me up and stayed with me to clean up after my messes. In the dark quiet, Teri helped my hands find the golden thread pulling me Home.

Meera's Message: The Path Home

Come close, Best Beloved. I invite you into the temple that is your soul. Your soul is worth dedicating your time and attention to.

On the road Home, back to Source, there are infinite opportunities for you to turn down different paths. At times, you fret over this decision, unsure of which path to take. You might seek the "right" answer. In the timelessness of the soul's journey, there is not one right answer, and there is no preordained choice. You always have free will because you are a co-creator of this experiential learning. When you say yes to one path, you are also saying no to others. The question is not how to make the "right" choice, but how to make the choice that frees you. There is no one straight line Home.

Some decisions are like treading water for the soul. They generate a lot of movement, but really do not move you. Getting lost in the material world and its trappings is expected and by design. The goal of the soul's journey is to get lost and find oneself again. In this experiment, we are all finding our way Home; indeed, we are already there. Some people might experience temporary states of Oneness, perhaps when in love or in nature. And then they get kicked out again because the relationship gets real, or they head back to the city. Time passes, and the show is over.

Ultimately, every experience is an opportunity for awakening. Opening your heart in the face of loss is a rich experience for the soul. You can trust in the process of grief and use it for your awakening. Everything, every moment, is an opportunity. Open your heart with compassion to your experience right now.

We each have our own path Home. There is not just one way. Just as we have individual tastes and preferences that please us, so too do we have individual ways to awaken. There is a myriad of paths to the One.

Eventually, even the method that you practice for awakening will be examined. True liberation means freedom from any attachment, even to a practice that brings freedom. You can meditate daily or not meditate daily; either way, you are Love itself. Oneness is already yours.

The lessons you are learning in each life are about love and nothing else. The truth of who you are is revealed to you each day through your choices made in free will.

We are here to know and experience ourselves as Source.

Let's go back to the beginning, Best Beloved. Before there was time, before this relentless projection of matter out into the farthest reaches of space, before all that, we existed, including you and your consciousness. We were all One, and there was no separation. There was no light and dark, only a roaring fire of bliss, only the fullest knowing of love, unity, and peace.

That awesome raw power of the One is inside of you. You want to change the world? Love. You want to lead people? Love. You want to achieve, build, create? Love, love, love. This is the practice that we wish to instill in you.

PART 2

How to Get Home

What is in the way, is the way.

– Margaret O'Malley

In Part 2, we jump tracks from the material to the spiritual. I put on my reverend hat, and we start broad, considering how the spiritual and the material interact, then zoom in to how Spirit interacts with the body. Along the way, we see that Western science continues to leave the door open for an understanding of our spiritual nature. As we continue in this spiritual awakening, we come to see that our soul has its own unique path, designed by our greatest life challenges. We consider how the soul transforms over lifetimes, especially how it learns from relationships and from our ultimate teacher, the body. We all have our own individual path Home; finding it is our life's work. Rather than relying on self-seeking through material means, we can seek our own answers within.

My spirit chose rich compost to grow in. I was born into a perfect ecosystem to foster the core belief that I was not good enough: a loving family with extraordinarily high expectations. When I had a near-death experience at nine years old and had my first spirit communication, I looked to the scientists who raised me to make sense of it. I could have interpreted the visitation to mean I was held lovingly by Spirit. But no, instead I learned that I could die at any moment, so fuck it.

CHAPTER 6

How the Spiritual and Material Interact

Let's lift the veil that separates the material world from the spiritual world to understand the journey one soul embarks on when it takes birth. In a spiritual understanding of the universe, there is only the One. The One experiences itself by creating material forms. Each soul is part of the One, pretending to be separate. Souls take physical form to learn the lesson that we are already at Home in Oneness.

We are conscious awareness, we are here in the present moment, and we experience love. We originate from conscious loving awareness, we are born into bodies capable of conscious loving awareness, we awaken into conscious loving awareness through lifetimes of suffering, and we die into conscious loving awareness.

As a soul, I knowingly stepped into the suffering of this lifetime's karmic lessons, like stepping into shackles as a paradoxical pathway to freedom.

A Ripe Follicle in a Ripe Compost of Karma

My parents were both raised in the Midwest on corn, ham, green beans, and shame. My mother grew up in the stereotypical American heartland; her small, idyllic town in Michigan was named "Heartland." Her genome hails from Germany, and when I visited their castles and saw the painted portraits of young princesses, I saw my mother's oval face there—brown hair, beautiful, deep-set eyes, a significant yet cute nose, and full pink lips. Her parents met while teaching high school. My grandmother was in despair and on the verge of quitting her overwhelming job teaching English to a classroom of sixty kids when she met him, the strong, handsome football coach.

My mother, the youngest of three, was celebrated as the first female child born to my grandfather's family in fifty years. I look at my mother's childhood—riding her horse with her best friend, practicing her flute, and reading Jane Austen—and wonder just how she learned she had to be the best at everything, or she was worthless. She had a gift of imagination, like most clairvoyants do. She dreamed of creating worlds as a writer of fiction, like her idol, Henry James. But my grandmother, hoping to prevent her daughter from repeating her mistakes, gave my mother two options: "You can either be a doctor or a lawyer. And you can never be a teacher (too hard), a nurse (bedpans), or a mortician (dead bodies)." My mother, looking for herself in the approving eyes of others, gave her valedictorian graduation speech and set off to college to become a doctor.

My father was likewise the youngest of three. His mother described herself as a "Shakespearean," and his alcoholic, chemist father was always at risk of blowing things up. Born gay, my father was raised at a time when homosexuals were jailed and beaten by police, condemned as riddled with sin, and sent to psychiatry to be cured. The good son, he sublimated these desires into academic excellence. He approached life like a master chess player, his rook sweeping pawns off the board while hiding his king's shameful secret.

There is only one reason that my improbable parents ever procreated: They were both trying to claw their way out of the same "not good enough" tarpit at the same time. My parents met in college and later reconnected in medical school, where they were both churning out accomplishments in the academic achievement-reward system. They celebrated their intellect and rising bourgeoisie with cigarettes, classical music, and games of bridge. On the surface, they were a golden couple, two young doctors, bringing to fruition a hundred years of colonizer ambitions and dreams. My father, deeply insecure about his clinical skills as a doctor, pursued a career in pharmacological research. There, he dominated in the realm of clinical trials on human subjects and covered his closeted orientation with the Band-Aids of workaholism and drinking. My mother, so focused on breaking glass ceilings for women in medicine, never saw her own imprisonment in academia, nor the shards of glass that would tear at her family.

In this ripe compost of karma, my brother was born while my father was serving in the army in Korea. My mother paused her career trajectory to enjoy her son's beauty, along with the hordes of local Korean women who swarmed around his blond curls. My father loved being a dad. My father so wanted me, he snuck bottles of milk to my brother so my mom would ovulate again.

I imagine myself as a soul looking down on this family system and thinking, *This is it! This family, a ripe follicle full of family pride and love, yet seething with addiction and shame and self-abandonment and fear, is the exact right family for my personal liberation.* I think about that egg and that sperm coming together, and all the other possible combinations that did not make it. I got my father's blond hair, my mother's oval face with deep-set eyes, and my grandmother's small body and gracile limbs. The genes for creativity, sensitivity, and communication came my way; the genes for playing chess and remembering facts got flushed down the wastepipe.

I imagine why my soul chose to be born at this time. Human cultures are at maximum technological development, our factories so hot from churning out material goods that we will see the afterglow for centuries. With our faith in the material at its apex, we are witnessing an emerging spiritual crisis. Straddling the analog and digital divide, we can meet our desires for connection and validation with elixirs, possessions, and thousands of "friends." After hundreds of lifetimes, my soul is not fully free yet; I have more to learn before I am unified with the One. I am getting close, though, and I have something unique to offer on our collective journey of awakening. I ready myself to slip into unconsciousness again, forgetting the truth of who I am. I pull on my individual spacesuit and lower the shield over my eyes.

My birth was a planned cesarean section delivery set for two weeks before Christmas so as not to inconvenience anyone's holiday. My father was allowed in the operating room because he was a doctor.

"She looks like she needs to go back in the oven," he said.

My mother's first words were, "She is so ugly."

Coming to my defense, the doctor said, "Aw, come on, give her a chance."

Day one in a female body, and I am judged for my appearance. In photos, my eyebrows are furrowed up to a peak, my large eyes closed to a squint. I look worried.

It is an intense experience to have a body again. I received a sensitive body for this lifetime, a body with a Ferrari of a nervous system capable of communicating with energy on a higher plane of consciousness. I was sensitive to sounds, to touch, and to what my mother ate and fed me. Sleep was difficult, and my stomach was often irritated; I was diagnosed with colic. I was not the "easy baby" my brother was, and my mother wrestled with me and with herself, questioning her abilities as a mother. My detailed baby book compiled by my mother, the pediatrician, contains her complaints about my fussing and irregular eating and sleeping. As a child, I drew on more resources than she had to give. My changing nature, vulnerability, and need for her roused frustration and despair. A "difficult" baby, I had to earn love with my behavior.

My parents were inspired to have it all—high-powered careers and a family. When I was two years old, my mother returned to complete her medical residency. At the time, only 10 percent of doctors were women, so there was no space for flexible schedules. My mother devised a way to share a residency with another mother, resulting in a schedule where she worked one month on and one month off. Any student of psychology knows the infant's early years are centered around attachment and bonding. When my mother returned after a month's absence and picked me up for a hug, I pushed her away, confused by her appearance and disappearance. Then I would rebuild my attachment to her in that month—and poof, she would disappear again. My small heart broke again and again, leaving me with deep questions about my worth.

From my soul's perspective, I chose this path to heal rejection and abandonment by seeking others' approval and love. This same motor that has driven me to addiction and abusive relationships propels me forward on my spiritual path. In this way, my greatest suffering has become my biggest gift for spiritual awakening.

Having internalized this story of my brother being the easy baby and me being the difficult child, I set about earning my parents' affection. I compared myself to my older brother in every way—learning to write our names, riding bikes, playing games, reading. This competitive spirit haunted me like a hungry ghost. My report cards came in: not good enough. My parents laughed at his jokes: not good enough. My grandparents tested us on spelling: not good enough. By the time I was five years old, I knew the truth of who I was: not good enough.

Material, Causal, and Astral

To understand the soul's experience, we must first understand the structure of the material realm, astral plane, and causal plane, and how these all relate to the One. The words "plane," "realm," and "world" are used interchangeably here. We are limited by human language to describe, in spatial terms, something that takes up no space.

The *material plane* is where we are now, reading this book, aware of our body's movements, our location in a physical place, and our perception of the world around us. We are spirits in bodies in the material realm. If you want to experience the material realm, just pinch yourself! Or better yet, ask someone for a hug.

The *spirit realm* exists in a separate reality, infusing the physical realm. In and through everything you see, hear, touch, taste, and smell is the spirit realm. Imagine it as a holographic image superimposed on the material realm. Science is on its way to explaining this; string theory and the concept of multiple universes are trailheads to follow.

The spirit realm consists of the causal plane, the astral plane, and Home, Oneness.

In Oneness, there is no separation. As souls, our starting and ending point is at Home in the One. Here, there are no desires other than what the One desires. There is no time, nor any unmet needs. There is only the ever-present, rapturous bliss of loving union. In Oneness, we experience total fulfillment, satisfaction, and peace.

The *causal plane* in the spirit realm represents the highest form of consciousness before Oneness. Like 11:59 on the clock, the awarenesses on the causal realm are as close to Oneness as possible while still expressed as unique, differentiated forms. The causal plane exists in thought only; it consists of pure conscious awareness. Here, it is easy to create. From a simple thought or desire, form can emerge.

As souls advance in awakening, they take on more responsibilities in the spirit realm. There are different words for these souls, such as angels, spirit guides, master teachers, enlightened beings, and so on. They have stepped out of the cycle of birth, death, and rebirth because they know where it is all going. There is no need to learn it again. You can only play Candyland so many times. Spirit guides help us navigate our karmic course, helping us see the boulders up ahead and step to the side, or caring for us when we get smashed on the rocks. These guides and angels are dedicated to the awakening of all.

The next subdivision in the spirit realm, the *astral plane*, represents forms of consciousness that are more differentiated and denser than those on the causal plane, still finding their way Home to the One. We go there as spirits when not bound by a body. We hang out in the astral plane before birth and return after death. We can take a day trip to the astral plane when day-dreaming and at night when asleep. Children connect easily to the astral plane and express this through imaginative play. The astral plane is a playground for us as spirits released from the limitations of our bodies.

If you were to visit the astral plane right now, you would see colors that are more vibrant than here on Earth. Nothing im-pedes expression on the astral plane. You may be able to intuit or feel communication from other spirits, rather than hear it or see people move their mouths, because it does not require physical effort to communicate. On the astral plane, we are free from the laws of the material universe, such as space and time. Just with intention, our spirits can travel freely, flying, running on air, or simply teleporting where we want to go. We can be transported from one spot to another as quickly as we can think of it. Our consciousness can connect via a web of love to others, and death is never a form of separation.

The densities of consciousness of the spirits on the astral plane can vary and have been described as low, medium, or high.[1] Spirits of more expanded consciousness, more awakened, are of lighter density on the astral plane, while spirits of denser consciousness still have healing and awakening work to do. As we will explore later, just because a spirit is on the astral plane does not mean you want to ask them for directions.

God in Drag

Ancient yogic philosophy helps us to understand how Spirit manifests in the material world. Yoga is not a form of exercise, nor a set of poses, but rather a path to enlightenment. The Sanskrit root word for yoga is *yuj*, which means "to join," "to yoke," or "to unite."[2] Yoga teaches us how to achieve inner peace by uniting the layers of self. Of its eight branches, one includes physical postures (asanas). By bending, twisting, and stretching the physical body, we release and move the energy in the layers beneath.

According to the *Vedas,* the oldest Hindu texts dating to 2,000 BCE, there are only two states of being, *Purusha* (formless) and *prakriti* (form). Purusha is the Sanskrit term for whatever your image of god is. It is the highest form of consciousness, which is always in a state of flow, always present in everything. Some religions refer to this godhead as the Atman, Yahweh, Allah, Father Sky, Big Mind, Christ Consciousness, and even emptiness. Purusha, pure consciousness, expresses itself in form, which is referred to as prakriti. As the creative energy of the One, it is the force that pushes the formless to express itself as form. Tyson Yunkaporta describes this as the foundation of Indigenous wisdom, explaining, "Nothing is created or destroyed; it just moves and changes, and this is the First Law."[3]

Why would Oneness do any of this? In the face of violence, starvation, pain, and loss, we look up at the stars and ask, "Why?" These kinds of questions are the backbone of spiritual inquiry. I offer here the results of my explorations. One friend shared after a near-death experience the understanding that to the One who has all power, "limitations are sexy." From the perspective of a digestor of karmic lessons, limitations *are* sexy. I can delight in my struggles.

The material world is made up of prakriti. Many Indigenous knowledge cultures revere the creative aspect of god as female, for instance, Mother Earth, Corn Mother, and First Woman. To understand how Purusha manifests itself as prakriti, we consider the origin of the universe. Imagine a fraction of the first second of the Big Bang. The entire universe, as small as a peach and incredibly hot, expands outward in a phase called inflation. A few minutes later, cooling begins, and the first elements, hydrogen and helium, begin to form. But before that cooling process, the universe was just made of quarks, the foundational building blocks of atomic nuclei, and gluons, a subatomic force that binds quarks together. We can understand prakriti as quarks and gluons, the building blocks of the material world.

Prakriti, form, also includes mental images and the mind. Consider that the human mind is capable of various levels of consciousness, let's call them low, medium, and high. In states of lower consciousness, thoughts have form. For example, I'm thinking that my dog needs to be let out, or how to write this paragraph, or (more often) what my next meal will be. In meditation, we achieve a medium level of consciousness, where we may feel connected with all things and intuit information from the spirit realm. In states of higher consciousness, we are Oneness, reunited with that everywhere-present state of beingness. We are in the flow, Love itself. At the highest level of consciousness, our thoughts can be formless, rejoining the flow of Purusha.

Likewise, souls on the astral plane and spirit guides on the causal realm have form and so are made of prakriti. Behind it all, and through it all, is the One, the Thing Itself. In the cycle of birth-death-rebirth, form is expressed over and over until it returns Home to formlessness.

Three additional yogic concepts help us understand the relationship between the spiritual and the material: maya, dharma, and karma.

Maya is the cosmic illusion of physical manifestation. All form does not really exist; what really exists is the One behind it all. This illusion is described as a veil that shrouds our awareness, causing us to forget the truth of who we are and instead believe in the separateness of our individual forms.

Dharma refers to the truth of who we are when we live according to our highest purpose. Every form has its own dharma; we each have our own essential way of being, our purpose. In Hindu scripture, the *Bhagavad Gita* describes our human dharma as selfless service, living with universal love and devotion for all.

The last concept, *karma*, can only be understood in the context of the One. Karma is defined as deeds, actions, or something that is done. If the universe is only one unified experience, then an action in one corner of the universe will cause an effect in another. As Newton theorized, for every action there must be an equal and opposite reaction, which is especially true given we are all One. Karma is our teacher. As we make choices and act in the world, we experience the consequences of our actions. Over time, over many lifetimes, we learn from our karma, and we move toward living according to our truth, our dharma.

To summarize: Purusha (the One) expresses itself as prakriti (the many) using maya (the veil of illusion) in order to learn through karma (consequences of actions) how to live according to Its dharma (truth). Said another way:

- Your soul is god dressed up in drag, pretending to be a separate thing.[4]

- Your soul enrolls in school, completing a grade with each life as it learns from karmic lessons, and

- Your soul is on a path to enlightenment, with all roads leading Home to the One.

Multiple Locations at the Same Time

It is hard to believe in our spiritual natures. Invisible, undetected energy. Souls that learn through lifetimes. Chakras that move energy through the body. Spirits that communicate with us. A higher power, Oneness, somehow behind and through everything. These remain beliefs, held in suspension, dangling out of reach.

This is the line.

Many of us cannot step over the requirement of faith.

It took me my whole life.

Scientists who have investigated the material universe have discovered a "both/and" solution to our burning questions.[5] Let's review some of the current findings from physics, which show that the door to a spiritual understanding of the universe remains open.

Our material reality is interconnected. Scientists have directly observed how two subatomic particles separated by space remain connected and share information, such that if one spins or rotates, so does the other.[6] This interconnected nature is labeled *quantum entanglement*. Cardeña states, "Entanglement means that the quantum states of such particles are not independent but part of a system."[7] Albert Einstein described this behavior of particles as "spooky action at a distance."[8] Yes, it is spooky, all right, and that is just the beginning.

These subatomic particles, the building blocks of our universe, are both waves that have movement and particles with fixed locations. This property is called *wave-particle duality.*[9] Physicists break down the material world into smaller and smaller units by hurling subatomic particles at each other in colliders, waiting to see a tiny burst on a screen. But the particles don't play the game fairly. They cheat. For example, when scientists try to find out a particle's location, the little trickster shows up as a fixed speck. Like a Where's Waldo picture with his red and white striped shirt and matching hat, waving at us, "Here I am!" But when the scientists switch their intention and want to measure the movement of the particle, the little trickster now shows up as a wave, not a speck. A wave exists in multiple locations at the same time. Imagine Waldo stretched like Gumby breakdancing as a wave. The building blocks of the universe are particles that are also waves, which means that everything is a particle and a wave: you, me, bacteria, and the stars.[10] String theory provides one possible unified explanation for these findings, that Waldo is an energetic string with a specific vibration. Waldo is energy. Matter is energy. You, me, bacteria, and the stars: energy.

Our inability to measure location and movement at the same time is called the *uncertainty principle.* Not knowing is baked into the system. Not only is matter uncertain, but it also seems to engage with our consciousness. There is an interactive quality to this expression of the material, which changes when we place our attention on it. When we search for the particle's location, it is Waldo, but when we study its movement, it is Gumby.[11] In

1979, physicist Bernard d'Espagnat challenged our fundamental understanding of nature, stating, "The doctrine that the world is made up of objects whose existence is independent of human consciousness turns out to be in conflict with quantum mechanics and with facts established by experiment."[12] As Miller summarized, "Our attention collapses the wave of possibility into a single point . . . our attention changes reality."[13] The material interacts with consciousness.[14] To summarize, matter is interconnected, has a dual nature, and is possibly energy vibrating.

Now let's expand our perspective outward from the micro and quantum mechanics to the macro and a grand scale of the universe. Where there are large, unseen gravitational and expansional forces at work.[15] Physicists are discovering that all the physical, visible matter in the universe—stars, planets, galaxies—is a tiny slice of the pie. Western science is just beginning to understand the nature of our physical reality.

There is so much we don't know.

We often let our confirmation bias limit us by affirming what we currently perceive and believe.[16] Yet this material reality is "spooky" and "uncertain" and "entangled," not always willing to play by its own rules. Entangled particles that interact with our consciousness, energetic strings, and dark forces and energy all point to an unseen, interconnected web.

Indigenous knowledge systems have long known about the interconnectedness and entanglement of consciousness and matter. Tyson Yunkaporta notes how Indigenous wisdom has long respected unseen powers:

> We yarn [talk] about the sentience of stones and the ancient Greek mistake of identifying "dead matter" as opposed to living matter, limiting for centuries to come

the potential consciousness and self-organizing systems such as galaxies . . . Theories of dead matter and empty space meant that Western science came late to discoveries of what they now call "dark matter," finding that those areas of "dead and empty" space actually contain most of the matter in the universe.[17]

Why is it hard to answer our questions? Why can't we know, with certainty, about the integration of the spiritual and material, the existence of Oneness? Why all the smoke and mirrors and obfuscation of such a foundational truth? We are hampered by our limited ability to perceive, measure, and observe. In this particular universe, we are bound by laws of physics that keep us from experiencing other planes of existence. We are bound by the limitations of language.

We are bound inside our minds.

Perhaps the ancient Aramaic language that Jesus of Nazareth spoke was closer to the truth in its ability to merge the spiritual with the material. The Lord's Prayer, as traditionally translated from Greek to English, begins, "Our Father, who art in Heaven." A lot of assumptions are made in this translation, including gender and location, but the main mistake is in providing a single translation. In ancient Aramaic, the original phrase, *"Abwoon d'bashmaya,"* can be translated in a multitude of ways, given that each word has multiple meanings. Neil Douglas-Klotz noted that the interpretation of "Father" from *Abwoon* ignores the fact that *woon* is literally the root word for "womb" and has a female/birthing meaning.[18] In another example, the translation of "heaven" from *d'bashmaya,* with its root *shm* or *shem,* ignores its meaning of "light, sound, name, or atmosphere."[19] Similarly, the ancient Aramaic word for "spirit" is the same word for breath, air, and wind. Therefore, another possible translation of the ancient Aramaic "Abwoon d'bashmaya" becomes "The Birther, the Mother-Father, from whom the breath of life comes."[20] Douglas-Klotz states in this analysis that "the duality of spirit and body, which we often take for granted in our Western languages, falls away."[21] Our language shapes our mind's perception of reality.

Oneness (Purusha) dresses up as strings and particles, and also thoughts. Formless (with a capital F) manifests itself as form. Therefore, how could we possibly use one of the forms—our mind and its creation, science—to understand Formless? Rupert Spira describes this predicament, writing, "The finite mind will always superimpose its limitations on everything that it knows . . . so the finite mind can never know who or what we truly are, and what we are is simply pure awareness."[22] We each find our own way Home to Oneness, but none of us uses the mind to think our way there.

It is here that the uncertainty principle and the dual nature of matter unite with the yoga of the soul's journey. Just like those tricky particles can be interconnected and exist in multiple places at once, so too can our consciousness. We step into our spiritual nature by breathing into our pure awareness, right here, right now. We can exist in our bodies, and our consciousness can also exist out of our bodies on the astral and causal planes. When we understand that we signed up for specific, challenging life lessons as souls, then we are empowered to step into the strong, intelligent, co-creative, sovereign beings that we are.

Awakening to my spiritual nature began when I almost died at the age of nine and had my first experience with a spirit who was not in a body. At this young age, I sowed all the seeds necessary for my awakening. Into the compost of karma, suffering, separation, maya, and illusion was planted love, dharma, and truth.

Not Good Enough

When I was nine and still able to do anything—cartwheels, handstands, bridges, anything—I came down with strep throat. No, it was diagnosed as mono. At home, I vomited violently, and we went to the emergency room. No, it was appendicitis. At a world-renowned medical school hospital, I had a routine appendectomy just a few days into July. The bright and shiny hospital floors were staffed by young, bright and shiny doctors, just a few days into their first residency rotation. As I recovered from surgery, my mother slept by my bedside, a privilege for her status as a full professor at the medical school. She noticed an odd color developing around my incision, a blue warning that signaled emergency. My mother brought in the new doctor to examine me. He arrived, cute in his white coat with his name in curlicues on the lapel, full of sophomoric knowledge.

"I think my daughter has an infection. You need to page your attending surgeon right away," she said. With just a few days of clinical experience, he dared to defy my mother. Not wanting to bother his supervisor on the Fourth of July holiday, he said, "She will be fine until the morning."

My father, also a doctor employed at the same medical school, shifted the hospital's gears directly from first to fifth. Working his Rolodex, he called the infectious disease specialist and the chief of surgery, who received the page while standing with his son and birthday party friends in a movie theater line that wrapped around the block to see the premiere of Star Wars.

"I'll take your son to Star Wars," my dad said to the surgeon at the pay phone, "and you come see my daughter."

Necrotizing fasciitis (fash-ee-i-tus), the "flesh-eating bacteria," raged a firestorm through my abdominal wall, killing every cell it touched. This extremely rare form of streptococcus is memorable due to gruesome news stories of body parts being cut off to save lives.[23] Fascia, a thin, white tissue that encases every muscle, bone, blood vessel, and organ, is now known to be innervated and sensitive, like skin, carrying messages of pain and sensation. Like a chicken breast being prepped for the frying pan, my fascia was cut off, first around the site where my exploded appendix previously was. As the infection raged on, so did the surgeons, cutting into my lower abdomen, upper abdomen, side body, and even the top of my pubis. And then I did what most people with necrotizing fasciitis at that time didn't do: I survived.

In 1982, the same year of my infection, a study was published with a whopping twenty-seven cases of necrotizing fasciitis, where 73 percent of patients died.[24] The speed of the firestorm was so fast for these patients that a delay of more than half a day before starting surgery resulted in death. I had a mother who diagnosed me in the morning, and a father who paged the chief of surgery in the afternoon, and I was in surgery that evening. While 87 percent of patients who had more than one surgery to remove tissue died, I had seven surgeries in nine days and lived. So many surgeries that they stopped sewing my belly closed in between. Just gauze and tape kept my innards from the world.

Lying in my hospital bed for weeks, I looked past the hundreds of get-well cards and out the window to the cityscape of San Francisco. Unable to eat, I hallucinated about hamburgers and milkshakes. In and out of consciousness, I floated in and out of my body. When the television was off, a man in the black box talked to me, keeping me company. During the height of my illness, when I had surgery every day, he visited me daily. I don't remember what he said, but I remember his kind, watchful presence. At home a few weeks later, I got brave enough to ask my mom how this was possible, and she explained to me that hallucinations were a side effect of morphine. I somehow knew she couldn't understand this communication; the realm of spirit was outside her purview. So I stopped talking about him and pretended to accept her answer. At nine years old, I knew when to stop asking questions.

After my return home, my invisible scars ran deeper than the ones on my surface. I was now officially different from other kids. I had seen death and wanted to taunt it further by doing everything upside down, fast, and early. As a teen, I gave myself to boys and then to men, looking to be made whole again. I sought release from myself by trapping myself inside 40-ounce bottles of alcohol and the narrow chambers of my pipe. I drove fast, racing along the edge of cliffs, racking up accidents and moving violations. But the peace and equanimity were short-lived. I always crashed back down into the bitter cold of my own mind, with its arctic messages of "not good enough . . . not enough . . . just, not."

CHAPTER 7

Our Spiritual Nature

Scientific research still struggles to explain how conscious awareness happens. The mind-body relationship has been "the hard problem" of science for more than four hundred years.[1] Western psychology believes that all conscious experiences arise from brain structures and functioning (i.e., materialism). Psi research exploring near-death experiences, end-of-life experiences, past-life memories, and afterlife communication suggests non-material explanations. The academic disciplines of psychology and philosophy are breaking apart at the seams, ejecting new "post-materialist" disciplines.

Meanwhile, spiritual traditions have sidestepped this debate by declaring we have a spiritual and a physical nature: We are spirits in bodies. In this chapter, we explore a spiritual explanation for our capacity to change our energy. We consider how the energy around us affects how we run the energy in our body through the chakras. The words "aura" and "energy" both describe the same thing—our spiritual self. Who we are, our consciousness, interacts with our body, but is not the body. We can use our spiritual energy to change our physical experience. We have the power to change how we feel.

As spirits in bodies, we are never actually stuck.

My first psychic class was a big step. One foot planted in materialism, I stepped across a chasm of doubt, skepticism, and stigma to see myself as a spirit in a body.

Psychic School

In the fall of my first year of recovery, we spilled out from the middle school gymnasium into the night at the end of the Twelve-Step recovery meeting. Clumps of humans topped with mushrooming clouds of smoke formed under the cover of the schoolyard walkway, where we all measured ourselves against an invisible yardstick—in or out, hot or not. I had already noticed Lisa. On the surface, we were similar, short with long blond hair and youthful cheeks that were buoyant when we smiled. Yet her leather jacket, short flower-print skirt, and hearty laugh conveyed that she was ready to play. Lisa was on her way to go dancing to live music at a bar. Although she didn't know me, she said, "You should come!"

Under twenty-one and lacking a valid ID and self-confidence to get me in the door, I stammered, "I have to work tomorrow."

"You know, Catherine," she said, turning to direct her gaze at me, "It's important to have fun in sobriety. As the Big Book says, 'We are not a glum lot.'"

As I lay in bed and wrote in my journal that night, recounting what this invisible god had put in my path to keep me sober, I noted the lightning bolt she so casually offered. I searched for any place in my life where I was having fun and saw how I had assumed that the price of being sober was the loss of joy. She was clearly having fun, always in the center of the meeting's afterparty outside, smoking and drinking coffee, living in a funky, grand old Victorian mansion flophouse with roommates, even playing bass guitar in a band. Lisa worked her recovery program with this same level of enthusiasm, preferring the raw, gritty meetings at the local, dingy Alano Club, where she often raised her hand to share. She quoted the Big Book like the religious studies major she was, describing how the Twelve Steps and a relationship with god had "released her from the bondage of self." I'm pretty sure others in that room visualized Lisa in bondage and wanted to keep her for themselves. I watched her the way a kid presses her nose up against a toy store window. I wanted to quote the Big Book like her, make the group laugh like her, and be free of myself, like her.

When Lisa casually told me over coffee that she was taking classes to develop her psychic abilities, I was both stunned by her brazenness, admitting something so taboo, and crazy curious.

What I didn't know at the time was that I was psychic too.

We all are.

I pelted Lisa with questions about this psychic school, looking for evidence that would justify me locking the idea away again. I learned that she attended weekly classes at a center called Aesclepion (pronounced "a-sklep-ee-on"), named after the ancient Greek healing centers. Patrons of these centers sought healing from Aesclepius, god of medicine and healing, son of Apollo. They received spiritual treatments to promote physical health, including sleep treatments that placed importance on the visions seen during dreams. As in most Indigenous cultures, communication with the spirit world was fully integrated into an individual's health and wellness in ancient Greece with no separation between physical and spiritual healing. At the time Lisa shared this name with me, I just thought it was odd.

This psychic school in a suburban enclave of the San Francisco Bay Area taught psychic skills as if it were a normal thing to do. Although Aesclepion refrains from telling its origin story and presents its teachings with neutrality toward any religion, everything is located in a cultural, political, and social context. Like many countercultural establishments, Aesclepion began in Berkeley, California, after individuating from the Berkeley Psychic Institute (BPI). The BPI was founded in 1973 by Lewis Bostwick, who grew up seeing auras and became a lifelong spiritual seeker, studying with the Masons and Rosicrucians, and later identified as a "psychic Christian."[2] Yet, their connection to Jesus was typical Berkeley-radical in their stance that, "Psychic freedom creates no ideologies, no isms, no dissenting philosophies which divide, corrupt, and destroy communication between human souls."[3] In 1985, John Fulton founded Aesclepion, an education center that promoted skills-based learning to explore our spiritual abilities, as well as a church for spiritual healings.

In that moment, I didn't know any of this. I didn't understand whether Aesclepion was a school or a church. I asked Lisa, and she replied, "Both." My fear clamped down upon this information. I needed to know the church's dogma and if they would try to get me to eat their wafers. Lisa described the two separate entities. There was the education center downstairs, where people took classes to learn how to be in better body-spirit communication, by running their own energy. She described the second story of the building as dedicated to healing work like hands-on healing and trance medium healings, where advanced students learned to work with these outside energies to bring themselves and others into greater body-being communication. There was no drive to recruit students, no marketing or outreach. The information was simply offered, and people chose for themselves if they were interested.

"OK, but what about this church upstairs?" I inquired. "Do they believe in god, and whose god?"

"You can choose for yourself," she said. "You have the freedom to choose which energies you want to work with on any given day. These can be spirits, master guides, or the Supreme Being."

Still not satisfied, I asked her point-blank, "Do they believe in Jesus?"

With a knowing Mona Lisa smile, she replied, "Well, just like we do at the beginning of every Twelve-Step meeting, at Aesclepion they invite the Supreme Being in at the beginning of healings, but they don't tell you who that power is. It is up to each student to choose for themselves."

This is really what I needed to know, to address my inherited fears that people would try to take over my mind and convert me. I wasn't sure if Lisa sidestepped my question when she described how we can learn to sit in the middle of our head, remove other people's energy from our space, and see for ourselves what is true about god, master teachers, and spirits.

Knocked back, I wondered who was in my space—my mother, the ardent scientist, or my father, who could only enter, like a feral cat, a church that wanted nothing from him in return. In that moment, I was aware that I had been so busy running other people's scripts that I didn't even know what I believed.

The Mind-Body Problem of Consciousness

It is confusing. How can I have a body and be a spirit? How can I have thoughts that are tied to the structure and function of my brain, and yet my consciousness somehow also lives on outside of my body?

First, let's clarify the terms "mind" and "consciousness." Consciousness relates to our subjective qualitative experiences, such as our awareness of sensory perceptions, feelings, pleasure, pain, and self, while mind describes cognition, such as our thoughts, memories, and intelligence.[4] Consciousness is the container that is aware of and holds mind.

This question of the mind-body relationship predates the dawn of psychological science. At the rise of the Enlightenment Era in the mid-seventeenth century in France, French philosopher René Descartes conducted human dissections to discover how the mind, which is not in form, acts on the body, which is in form. He settled on the pineal gland, a small structure in the brain that did not have a left or a right counterpart. Here, he thought, the soul must interact with the body. Anyone who has taken supplements to help them sleep will appreciate the important role of the pineal gland as part of the endocrine system that secretes our own endogenous melatonin.

In his philosophical inquiries, Descartes discarded all previously held beliefs and asked, "What am I?" He determined he was not a body, writing, "I am not that structure of limbs and organs that is called a human body; nor am I a thin vapour that permeates the limbs—a wind, fire, air, breath, or whatever I imagine."[5] Descartes concluded that he was a thinking, feeling, experiencing, aware being, which he succinctly summarized with the words *Cogito, ergo sum*. I think, therefore I am. Descartes's belief that the mind and body are separate is called *dualism*. Dualism holds that consciousness is not localized in the brain and could potentially continue after physical death.[6]

Current neuropsychological theory is based on *monism*, the belief that the mind and consciousness arise from the biological structure and processes of the brain. In this framework, structural or functional changes within and between neurons cause every thought and feeling. For example, when we think of an oak tree, neurons responsible for seeing the shape of an oak tree send electrical signals to release their neurotransmitters to their next neighboring neurons responsible for color and other neurons connected to memory, and so on. Brain lesion research strongly supports the monist theory. When pieces of the brain are removed, we can observe a causal decrease in cognitive functioning.[7] Neurobiologist Robert Sapolsky summarizes the current view: "Few dualists are out there anymore, for whom our mindness floats pristinely above all that nuts-and-bolts biology of cells and organelles and molecules."[8]

Indeed, the mind is not held to be simply of the brain. It is also of the body. That is, the mind is fully embodied. Neuroscientist Antonio Damasio states that this embodied view of the mind includes the most "refined" aspects of our experience, including that of our soul.[9] Psychologist Paul Bloom said that while we are naturally dualists with an inborn inclination to think of our souls as separate from our bodies, "our souls are flesh."[10] In this monist perspective, "when the brain dies, so does the consciousness."[11]

Brain functioning is related to consciousness, but does the brain cause consciousness?[12] Descartes's search for brain regions responsible for mind and consciousness continues, but "To date, there is no evidence, not even indirect or circumstantial, of a single brain region, area, organ, anatomical feature, or modern Cartesian pineal gland that takes charge of this mysterious job of 'producing' or 'generating' consciousness."[13]

In 1995, philosopher David Chalmers dubbed this the "hard problem of consciousness." We can describe the brain's relationship to perception and function all day long, but we cannot describe how our experience of perception and function occurs.[14] Indeed, as Phillip Goff summarized, "physical science has a dismal track record in explaining consciousness."[15]

The philosopher Thomas Nagel, in his 1974 paper, "What is it like to be a bat?" questioned whether it is even possible for us to understand consciousness through reductive materialism, the philosophy that all mental experiences can be explained through physical processes.[16] Nagel later expanded on this idea to suggest that nature is made by consciousness, rather than the other way around.[17] In this reverse psychology proposition, the brain does not make consciousness. Rather, the immaterial consciousness makes the brain.

Some evidence suggests that brain activity is not the sole cause of consciousness. Research into awareness separated from brain function falls into four categories: near-death experiences (NDEs), end-of-life experiences, past-life memories, and afterlife communication via mediums.[18] After forty years of studying NDEs, professor of psychiatry Bruce Greyson has determined that physical factors alone do not explain the cause of consciousness after death.[19] For example, cardiologists in the Netherlands compared patients who experienced cardiac arrest and had NDEs after resuscitation (18 percent) with flatlining patients who did not. The NDE was unrelated to physical explanations, such as the length of cardiac arrest and experience of cerebral anoxia (lack of oxygen to the brain).[20] Greyson concludes, "The enhancement of mental functioning at a time when the brain is physiologically impaired, as well as the paranormal and otherworldly experiences, are not easily explained by materialistic models."[21]

Secondly, there are common cross-cultural experiences at the end of life, including death-bed phenomena such as pre-death dreams and visions, visitation by loved ones, and clocks that stop at the time of death.[22] A third line of research has explored young children in different cultures around the world who report past-life memories from around the ages of two to three.[23] Finally, highly controlled laboratory studies on mediums' ability to connect with the consciousness of deceased people have yielded consistent support.[24] Yet many Western scientists struggle to consider these lines of study neutrally.

Psychology once valued the importance of the individual's reported experience in qualitative research. In 1879, the first psychological research lab, established by Wilhelm Wundt in Germany, used a research model he called trained introspection as a method for systematic self-reflection.[25] By the mid-twentieth century, funding prioritized quantitative experimental design that compared groups of people. Ram Dass explained this philosophical shift in the field of psychology: "We got so frightened of Introspectionism [. . .] that we got fiercely into Behaviorism and we ruled out the possibility that a person could be the observer of his own behavior, without having the subjective fallacy as the experimenter."[26] Funding formulas for research have prioritized comparative samples and quantitative research to the point of devaluing people's stories.[27] Yet, studies on consciousness and the mind particularly benefit from self-report methods:

This is because, unlike other physical processes, in which both causes and effects can be observed from a third-person perspective, in consciousness studies, one is confronted with a cause—the brain activity—that [. . .] produces an effect [. . .] which can be apprehended only from a first-person perspective. This 'perspectival asymmetry' makes consciousness [. . .] alien to any attempt at conceptual causal and ontological scientific reduction.[28]

If we want to understand consciousness and the mind, then we must value our own internal experiences again.

Even ardent rational materialists report having extraordinary human experiences. When a random sample of scientists and engineers was surveyed, 93 percent reported having "exceptional human experiences," such as telepathy, precognition, and clairvoyance, with frequencies similar to both a normal comparison group (94 percent) and spiritual enthusiasts (99 percent).[29] As with NDEs, the sample of scientists reported their anomalous experiences to be positive and life-changing. Sometimes, our own lived experience helps us to be open-minded.

Just because brain cells and brain activity are correlated with thoughts, feelings, and behavior, that does not mean that the brain creates consciousness. Miller described this as "the place where psychology had become stuck [because it was] bound by three limiting assumptions: (1) that the brain creates thoughts, (2) that all meaning is interpretation, and (3) that we can feel better by rearranging our thoughts."[30] She posited an alternate hypothesis: "But what if the brain didn't create thoughts so much as receive them? What if our brains were less like idea generators and more like antennae or docking stations for a larger consciousness?"[31]

This theory of the brain as an antenna for consciousness is similar to William James's theory of the brain as a transducer of consciousness, such that if the transducer is broken, it does not mean that the transmission of consciousness has ceased.[32] James used the analogy of a prism to show that "this should not lure us into the logical correlation-causation fallacy that the prism 'produces' colored light."[33] The Windbridge Research Center expands on this idea:

> A relationship clearly exists between the physical brain and the mind/self/consciousness (what makes you *you*). When the brain is injured or damaged, the mind functions differently. However, this does not prove that the cells and chemicals of the brain *make* mind. Correlation does not equal causation. Alternatively, mind may be like a signal and the brain like an antenna. Without the antenna, the signal can still exist.[34]

Perhaps our nervous systems are not even great transducers. Perhaps we do not perceive reality all that accurately. Steve Taylor, author of Spiritual Science, agrees, "Indeed, higher states of consciousness . . . reveal a more expansive reality which suggests that materialism is a very partial view, created by the limitations of our awareness."[35] Perhaps what we perceive is only relatively real. As Ram Dass said,

> We grow up with one plane of existence we call real. We identify totally with that reality as absolute, and we discount experiences that are inconsistent with it as being dreams, hallucinations, insanity, or fantasy. What Einstein demonstrated in physics is equally true of all other aspects of the cosmos: *all reality is relative.* Each

reality is true only within given limits. It is only one possible version of the way things are. There are always multiple versions of reality. To awaken from any single reality is to recognize its relative nature.[36]

Revisiting the debate between dualism and monism, we currently know only that consciousness and mind are related to brain activity. We do not know the cause.[37] It will require an integration of our best qualitative and quantitative, scientific and philosophical, material and spiritual understandings to discover what causes consciousness and mind. Some philosophers and researchers are beginning this work. Psychologists Imants Barušs and Julia Mossbridge wrote the first textbook on consciousness published by the flagship American Psychological Association. In it, they allow that non-local consciousness, separate from brain functioning, is possible.[38] A new wave is forming, causing some to break free from long-held ideologies. They are calling it *post-materialist psychology*.

But what if it weren't an either/or debate? What if there were some other explanation that sidestepped this dichotomy? What if everything were consciousness? Philosophers and physicists are exploring this possibility. Called *panpsychism*, this theory posits that consciousness (non-material reality) gives rise to the material reality.[39] Consciousness, rather than the output of brain processes, is who we are. Consciousness is what everything is.[40]

Indigenous wisdom traditions from around the world have known this for thousands of years. We are Spirit. We are the One expressed as the many. Rather than debating dualism versus monism, ancient wisdom traditions state that all exists in *nondualism*.[41] Nondualism states that there is no mind-body separation, nor any hard problem of consciousness, nor any separation between material and spiritual, because all is One.

We exist in Oneness. Our physical nature (our material form) and our spiritual nature (our aura, energy) are one and the same.

And we have the power to use our consciousness to change how we run our energy.

We are Electrical, Energetic Beings

Western physics defines energy as having the capacity to do work. Our body is made up of cells surrounded by exterior membranes, which expend energy to create electrical gradients. At rest, the inside of the cell has a different electrical charge (negative) than the outside of the cell (positive). We eat food and expend cellular energy to maintain this electrical charge within every one of our cells. Communication between two brain cells starts with an action potential, when an electrical charge flows across one cell's membrane. All of our thoughts and actions are based on electricity. We are electrical beings. We are energetic beings. We have the capacity to do work.[42]

The cells of our nervous system communicate through electrical and chemical messages. Sensory information travels up the spinal cord from *afferent* (approaching the brain) nerves in the peripheral nervous system to the *central nervous system*. The brain sends commands (such as motor movements to pick up a cup of coffee) through *efferent* nerves (exiting the brain) down to the spinal cord. The *peripheral nervous system* has two branches: the *autonomic nervous system* and the *somatic nervous system*.

The autonomic nervous system is responsible for the automatic, nonconscious control of our organs and body, including the *sympathetic nervous system* (fight/flight/freeze), the *parasympathetic nervous system* (rest/tend/befriend), and the *enteric nervous system* (digest).

We used to think that we had no conscious control over the autonomic nervous system. We breathe fast when running from a tiger, or we rest under a tree while digesting a big meal. Now we know that we can consciously change our experience. For example, we can directly engage our internal relaxation response, the parasympathetic nervous system, with deep, slow breathing.[43]

For thousands of years, Indigenous healing traditions have centered on changing the flow of energy to improve health. Ayurvedic medicine supports the flow of life force, *prana*, through thousands of tributary channels called *nadis,* which flow into the seven *chakras*. In the ancient Chinese tradition of acupuncture, these chakras are known as acupoints, which connect to meridians. Traditional Chinese medicine manipulates the flow of our life force, *qi*, through meridians to treat physical and emotional ailments.[44] More recently, Western medicine has demonstrated that acupuncture is helpful for nausea and pain,[45] and that meditation is beneficial for stress, pain, insomnia, high blood pressure, depression, and other mental health concerns.[46] What is novel to Western science is old news to Indigenous healing traditions.

Our capacity to change our energy has a spiritual explanation: Our spirit is in reciprocal communication with our body as well as the energy around us. We can heal our bodies and minds by changing our energy.[47] We have this spiritual ability to heal ourselves because there is a hierarchical relationship between the two. Our spirit runs our body.

The Spirit Runs the Body

Our aura is our spirit, surrounding and infusing our body. It is the same as our qi, our life force. Here, the following words are synonyms: aura, energy, spirit, and spiritual information.

Our spirit and physical body are in constant communication with each other. Indeed, the physical body is the manifestation of the flow of information in the spiritual body. Just like any other transfer of information, that flow can be fluid and fast or slow and bogged down. Our spiritual body flows most freely when we run our own information, when the energy in our space is our own. Conversely, when we absorb the energy of those around us, run our energy to meet others' expectations, or allow other people's truth into our aura, our energetic body becomes stuck and sluggish. Our physical body will express this as muscle tension, pain, and dis-ease. Mentally, other people's energy in our space can feel like depression, anxiety, self-criticism, and telling ourselves what we "should" do. In Twelve Step, that's called "should-ing on yourself." We might describe this as feeling stuck, "not feeling like myself," or being in pain. With practice, we can learn to run our own information, allowing the information in our energy body and our physical body to flow freely.

Our spiritual body exists before we are born, and it will continue to live on after the body dies. It consists of a rainbow of energies of different wavelengths that are constantly in motion. If technology allowed us to take a picture of the spiritual body, we could see a snapshot of where our energy is running smoothly and where it is bunched up in pain and suffering. It is not necessary to focus our attention on the stuck parts. This is a little like watching efferent waste go down the toilet. Instead, it is helpful to focus our attention on the image of what it looks like when we are in flow, in full communication with ourselves.

Learning to run our own information, to stand in our truth, is a miracle. When we run our own energy, we heal generations of trauma, bringing to a stop the pain and suffering handed down through our families. When we own the space around us, we stand in our own power, fully sovereign, reigning supreme as co-creators with the loving, creative energy of the Universe. When we move through the world grounded, we walk with purpose, and others respect our physical space. When we run our own information, our words come out clearly, succinctly. We speak our truth because we are in our truth. People do not push back on our statements because they see there is nothing to push against. And when we are in our truth, we naturally allow other people the opportunity to be in their own space. The ripple of benefits extends outward, offering all beings the opportunity to say hello to the miracle that they are.

Stepping out of my good girl conditioning, I trampled over my family's beliefs to receive my first psychic reading.

Crossing the Street

From the outside, Aesclepion looked like a nondescript office building. No banners with bright colors indicated you could be saved here, nor were there any crystals or dream catchers in the windows. The inside was as familiar to me as all the dingy Twelve-Step meeting rooms I had spent so much time in, with its dated carpet, mismatched office chairs, and donated couches. What was different was the brightness of the "Hello!" I received from the young man who greeted me. I felt seen for who I really was. I sat in the waiting area intently eavesdropping on the murmured preparations in the next room. Laughter rose, and a lightness of being floated through the thin walls. Invited into the room, I sat in a chair facing a line of five other people. They sat with their eyes closed, feet on the ground, hands palm-up on their laps.

Happily, I saw my friend and now security blanket Lisa sitting in the second chair from the left and waited for her to break role and acknowledge me. Her eyes remained closed, lightly fluttering. I felt hesitant with her lack of validation. Behind the line of clairvoyant students stood another person, who, like a conductor, was guiding the seated line of people engaged in the reading. This person introduced her role to me as "the control." She told them to "blow roses" for my expectations and to "sprinkle some amusement." The line responded by yawning and giggling. She asked them to look at how open my rose was, and the person in the center chair said 93 percent, which, being the college student I was, I interpreted to mean I was getting an A at something. She cautioned the readers to keep in mind my vulnerability and openness to being programmed. I felt as if I had already done something wrong.

The psychic reading began with the student in the center chair asking me to say my name three times. She said, "I'm going to read you from a light pink."

My favorite color! I thought.

She used a rose to describe me as a spirit, the color of the light pink petals representing my seventh chakra, a summary of what I was presenting to the world. She described my rose's position under the sun as "a little off to the right," meaning I was slightly off on my spiritual path. She saw two leaves on my rose, which I was told, "represent baby beings in your space that you are looking at agreements about giving them bodies."

I was amazed they could see my future children.

She described the length of the stem and how its roots stretched to the earth, indicating the great number of past lives I had lived.

The control person asked the members of the seated line what they were looking at. One by one, each person spoke and offered me a bit of information.

Lisa went next. Clearly an advanced student, she read me with confidence: "There is a dark blue energy in your heart and lower belly. This energy is heavier than yours and represents male-control energy. It looks like it is your father's energy. He has a way of using his resources to get people to do what he wants."

Other students were more tentative and offered a sentence or two. I was able to ask questions, of course, about my boyfriend, which they answered with colors and descriptions of whose energy was in my space. I could have stayed there for hours, asking for insights into my life, but the control person brought the reading to a close, and I was led out of the room.

I waited in the lobby to walk out with Lisa, like an excited puppy ready to go back and smell all the spots we had just visited. As we walked to the coffee shop around the corner, Lisa was calm, centered, and somewhat disinterested in the details that came through in my reading.

"That was so cool!" I bubbled on. "I never knew about those hooks of other people's expectations in me."

"Yeah," Lisa demurred, without interest. I felt the conversation hit a wall that I couldn't see. She refused to reenter a psychic reading space and kindly explained, "We just had an awesome 'clean out,' where we blow up any remaining 'matching pictures' in our space from the reading."

In between sips of coffee and drags on our cigarettes, Lisa got to the point, "You know what's really cool?"

"What?" I was on the edge of my seat.

"The amazing ability is not being psychic and seeing into other people's spaces." She waved her hands, gesturing to the people around us. "Because we all do this naturally. We are all reading all the time."

I looked at the people in the coffee shop and tried to see the color of their auras, but only saw the color of their clothes.

She went on, "The freedom comes not from being psychic, but from using our psychic tools to clear out other people's energy from our own space."

Misunderstanding everything, I said, "I can't wait to come back for another reading."

Lisa fetched me up sharply. "Do you really want to keep coming back to have other people see for you, Catherine? Or do you want to see for yourself?"

As I walked away from the coffee shop, I knew I was crossing more than just the street. I had crossed over a chasm in my beliefs, leaving rational materialism behind. Keeping it secret from my family, I enrolled in Aesclepion's entry-level meditation class.

I entered my first class at Aesclepion as a true beginner in psychic kindergarten. My teacher was the same young man who greeted me during my first reading. With his red hair and beard and college student attire, nothing about him said, "I'm psychic." He asked the five of us sitting in the circle, "Have you ever learned to ride a bike from someone telling you how?"

Heads shook left and right.

"Right, so I can't tell you how to ground your body and run your energy. You have to try it yourself." He went on, "The most important thing is to keep your amusement and have fun.

Approach this class like you did kindergarten. Play. Be silly. Taking yourself too seriously is not good for you!"

I chuckled knowingly. I thought of Rule 62 from Twelve Step, which says, "Don't take your self too damn seriously." Seriously, I should get that tattooed somewhere.

Our first lesson was in groundedness. We learned what happens when the spiritual body is not grounded in the physical or natural body. I watched myself being ungrounded, walking into walls, getting spacey while shopping in large box stores, or making impulsive decisions. I practiced, discovering how different it was to be grounded, and I learned how much I enjoyed feeling connected, stable, and in control. We played with our grounding cords, making them any color or material. I tried feathers, a striped straw, and even a cement tube when I really did not want to lose my space. Sometimes I struggled to see my grounding cord; the bottom faded out of view, or it billowed in the wind, unattached to the center of the earth. Other times, I would obsessively hunt back and forth, making sure I was connected at all points. Simply seeing the cord from the center of my head, from my imagination, rather than forcing it to exist with effort, took practice too.

Tools are only as useful as you pick them up and use them. I only permitted myself to dip my toes in, feeling the sting of stigma that prevented me from wading deeper into psychic waters. Instead, I attempted to work a perfect Twelve-Step program, then cried through my core issues of inadequacy and abandonment in therapy. The harder path of sitting in meditation and practicing energy-clearing skills required me to break too many family taboos. It was too woo-woo. I still needed validation. I had to earn a degree, get a job and the all-important health insurance my mother was so focused on, and find someone who would love me better than I could love myself. Being psychic remained Lisa's thing, and healing in psychotherapy became my thing. Together, we shared the recovery from addiction thing.

Learning Through Relationship

We belong to a web of interconnected relationships. When our souls select our karmic intentions for a birth, we also select traveling partners, other souls that will be embodied with us during this lifetime. Our soul family, whether liberating or binding, painful or loving, nurturing or abusive, is our key to freedom. We find and heal ourselves through relationship.

The dominant Western, industrialized narrative has instilled false ideas of self-sufficiency, self-reliance, and independence. Self-reliance is seductive—we want to believe in our own self-determination—yet it only validates the veil, our sense of ourselves as separate from Spirit. The amount of time we spend thinking we are solo voyagers is the precise amount of time we spend cut off from spiritual resources, the food, water, and sunlight our souls need.

Even when I thought I was alone, I wasn't. In recovery, I found my soul pod swimming next to me.

Fluorescent Yellow Dots

Along the way of our recovery journeys, we collected other women to our pack of "litter mates," spiritually born at the same time, new in our recovery together. Michele arrived fresh out of rehab, still trembling, to a raucous Friday night newcomer's meeting. Just twenty-four and strong from slinging boxes of vegetables at an organic grocery store, she arrived still wearing her steel-toed work boots and jeans. Michele's crystal-clear blue eyes and dark brown hair captured me. We shared the luxurious burden of coming from privilege. Having had all the doors opened for us, we struggled to find our own inner compasses.

Our fledgling group was an amoeba that kept changing shape as new women joined. I was always the shortest, always the youngest, always listening to the loudest rap. At chip meetings, where hundreds of alcoholics walk down the center aisle to receive poker-like chips to celebrate lengths of sobriety, Teri would start to vibrate next to me in the metal chairs. Her excitement gushing, she had to jump up and hug people as they made their way down the aisle to get a chip. It was superfluous and completely appropriate when Teri committed to being the person who stood at the front of the meeting, handing out chips and hugs. Hundreds of people, self-conscious yet beaming, walked, skipped, and danced down the aisle to celebrate in her jubilant arms.

When god was unfindable, my sober sisters were fluorescent yellow dots showing me the outline of love. They taught me to be kind to myself, pray for others, let go of my unspoken expectations, act as if I believed, clean up my side of the street, speak my truth, let go of the outcome, and be grateful. Daily, I would drive my relationship jalopy into their spiritual mechanic shop, crying about the awful noise the engine made, although I was only willing to change the oil. Catherine, the chemist, was still titrating, through self-will, doses of love and sex to bind together a broken heart. Patiently, they heard the same story over and over, with different names on different days. They celebrated when I felt loved and listened compassionately, the next day, when I felt abandoned.

For more than a decade, Teri taught me what it would be like to love myself. She picked me up off the couch, moved me out of his apartment, read me poems by Hafiz and Rumi, and cooed her love for me into the phone. A psychic told her that, in a previous life, we were both nuns, spending our lives together, married to god, teaching His children. She thought that was so awesome, adding, "But this time we get to have sex!" She was always my last-ditch phone call, that person I could call regardless of self-loathing and shame. She always reflected my own preciousness back to me.

"There is no place that god is not," she would say.

"Really? How do you know?" I doubted.

She replied sweetly, "Catherine, you are a precious child of god. God's got you in the palm of His hand, holding your sweet, tender heart. He is with you right now, in this breath. Breathe into that."

"Okay," I breathed deeply.

"I love you so, so, so much, and I'm just a human! Can you even imagine how much god loves you?

"In this life, we get to be our own heroes. I'm so amazed at our humanity, at our precious, hard-earned, fine-tuned, lifesaving ability to receive every ounce of the Love that is all around us. Beautiful, wise, brilliant Catherine, you are such a miracle. God sees us being so brave, putting our big girl panties on in this life!"

When I met Teri under that willow tree, I met my traveling partner. Perhaps I should have known, given how hard Teri played in this life, how vibrant she was, gushing with creative energy and love, that she had just a few years to live. Perhaps I should have known that she would guide me Home even after her last breath.

Born to Bond

Even before we are born, we are ready to bond. Fetuses prefer their parents' voices, remember speech patterns, and relax when touched through their mother's belly.[1] After birth, babies prefer to gaze at faces—especially their mother's—and are calmed by their mother's smell.[2] Early skin-to-skin contact, called kangaroo care, promotes brain development, weight gain, and sleep.[3] Likewise, loving touch is essential for neurological development.[4] In the first year, the rhythm of caregiver-infant interactions develops into a duet of immediate, synchronous responses to each other. You coo, I respond. You point, I look.[5] The caregiver repeatedly tells the infant, in a thousand non-verbal communications every day, "I am here with you; we are one." Together, our brains swim in the neurotransmitter of connection, oxytocin.[6] Our survival and optimal development depend on relationships. The good news for us parents is that we do not need to be perfect. We just need to be "good enough."[7]

Our early experience of bonding becomes wired in our brain as an attachment style.[8] If our caregiver is consistent in their attention, responsiveness, synchronous mirroring, and touch, we develop a secure attachment style. We trust that our caregiver is a secure base and will be there for us while we explore the world.

Our nervous system regulates stress by seeking comfort from our loved ones. Furthermore, we develop a positive self-concept because we know we are worthy of love. If our caregiver is unable to respond to us, perhaps due to personal or health limitations or environmental stressors, we internalize an insecure attachment style. We become either desperately afraid our caregiver will leave us (*insecure-approaching*), or hope that they will indeed leave us alone (*insecure-avoidant*), or a mixture of both (*disorganized*). With inconsistent, abusive, neglectful, or stressed caregiving, we learn that people are untrustworthy, the only person you can rely on is yourself, and there is something wrong with us that made us unworthy of our caregiver's time and attention. And just to complicate the picture, you can have a picturesque early childhood and still experience an attachment disruption later on.[9]

Early in life, we use our primary attachment relationship to determine how we will respond to stress. Securely attached infants develop an internal barometer that says, "Uh oh, the shit is about to hit the fan, but I got my loved one next to me, so I'm going to be okay." And they successfully engage in attachment seeking behavior: moving toward the one they love, seeking tactile comfort, and asking for help (crying). This stress-response warning system becomes coded in the body, where securely attached infants release less cortisol, the stress-response hormone, into their blood than insecurely attached infants.[10] We perceive and experience the world differently based on our early childhood experiences of love.

As we develop, this internal barometer continues to give us readings of "I'm going to be okay" or "I'm not okay," but instead of pointing to an external loved one, we develop an internal representation of this security.[11] Stan Tatkin, in his book *Wired for Love*, describes how our early attachment style affects our adult relationships and relabels the different attachment styles as anchors, islands, and waves.[12] Securely attached adults are the anchors. Anchors feel safe in intimate relationships. When presented with stressors, anchors can regulate their nervous system by trusting they will be okay, engaging in loving self-care, and seeking comfort from loved ones.

The islands are the insecure-avoidant adults. They are independent, self-confident, and often accomplished. Islands want connection, but they also can feel threatened by intimate relationships when there is high emotionality, relational stress, and demands. Islands learned through traumatic experience that loved ones can take over with their emotions and needs, and so they cope with the stress of a relationship by retreating into solitude. Due to the instability or absence of their caregivers, islands learned to regulate their nervous systems by self-soothing. Although they want connection, they also enjoy the privacy and secrecy of their islands. Islands can react to emotions as if they are nuclear waste: Don't go there. For islands, the spiritual work is learning to go inward and be present with their own feelings, so they can be vulnerable and present for others. Vulnerability takes great strength.

Waves represent adults with insecure-approaching attachment. Waves deeply desire connection; they hunger for true intimacy. But due to either being abandoned by their caregiver or engulfed by a caregiver's needs, they learned to regulate their nervous systems by seeking connection with others. Like the coming and going of a wave, people with an insecure-approaching attachment style will act in unstable ways, moving from seeking connection to creating conflict, from clinging to distancing. Waves expect to be abandoned and neglected. They long for the security of the anchor.

My insecure-approaching attachment style is my secret superpower and greatest challenge. I developed a highly sensitive nervous system that pays acute attention to the non-verbal behavior of others. I am deeply attuned to connection—when it is present and when it is absent. My vagus nerve is a superhighway of emotional information. I am an expert at my own internal experience and always have words to describe how I feel. My relational acuity has benefited my career as a psychologist, teacher, and leader. For me and others with insecure-approaching styles, the spiritual work is to relate to myself. My challenge is to learn to calm myself and love myself, rather than seeking my worth through others' reflections.

Attachment theory helps us understand how we are wired to learn from relationships. Tatkin states we can use our awareness of our attachment style to build secure, functioning relationships. He argues it is not possible to learn to love yourself first, then engage in relationship. Rather, we learn to love ourselves by being in relationship:

> Is it really possible to love yourself before someone ever loves you? Think about it. How could this be true? If it were true, babies would come into this world already self-loving or self-hating. And we know they don't. In fact, human beings don't start by thinking anything about themselves, good or bad. We learn to love ourselves precisely because we have experienced being loved by someone. We learn to take care of ourselves because somebody has taken care of us.[13]

Similarly, I was told early on in recovery by sober women, "Let us love you until you can learn to love yourself."

Securely or insecurely attached, we have all experienced pain in relationships. We all have wiring in our default mode networks that makes us self-conscious in social situations. We have all experienced shame, that adaptive social survival tool that tells us when we might get kicked out of the group.[14] So this is the karmic work: learning how to be in relationship with ourselves and others, and ultimately Spirit. Many of us would rather sidestep the mess of relationships and try to rise above our karma. But karma cannot be outrun or outsmarted. It only waits for us, for the next lifetime.

Traveling Partners and Past-life Agreements

As we prepare for the next life, we choose to hammer out aspects of our soul on the anvil of experience. When a soul prepares for a birth, it considers which soul pod members to journey with. Just like strings of various lengths produce pleasant harmonic sound vibrations when they have a similar frequency ratio, soul vibrations can emit similar frequencies. Said another way, souls have an affinity to travel together. Like souls attract like souls while in the material world. Our biological parents and caregivers are our biggest teachers because they pass their karmic lessons and genetic information on to us. That said, many of us create a chosen family as the most loving thing to do for ourselves when the karma of our biological family is not healthy for us.

Souls travel in packs consisting of biological family members, friends, and community members throughout various lives, which together weave a fabric of lessons. New souls have smaller pods of about twenty individual souls. As we live life after life, we make new connections. Our soul pod grows in size to more than one hundred members for a middle soul, to more than a thousand connections for an old soul.

Before birth, we make agreements with some beings, which become our strongest connections. Sometimes an agreement serves both parties equally and is mutually beneficial; sometimes, like a parasite, the agreement benefits one and drains the other. Past-life agreements explain why we instantly like someone when we meet them, a sign of a positive past-life connection, or why we feel immediate mistrust, remnants of a past-life betrayal largely out of our conscious awareness. Examples of agreements include sharing some of our personal healing energy, shutting down communication, or not running our creative energy at its fullest to prevent others from feeling bad about themselves. An agreement is not necessarily good or bad, but it is worth examining and choosing if we want to maintain it.

Accepting our past connections and using them productively, as information, helps us heal and consciously awaken. Using our relationships as teachers is like being inside a library with shelves filled to the rafters with important archaeological information—information we have learned and cultivated in previous lives. We can choose whether we want our past-life karma to run us, or if we want to bring our agreements into the present moment and heal, let go, and forgive.

Discussions about karma and freedom might seem to be concerned with an individual's journey. But we are here to help other souls awaken, too. One soul awakening is a drop in the ocean; a group of souls awakening together is a powerful wave. We can feel the power of the group flow while we sing in church, meditate with our Satsang, or sit on a metal chair in a church basement trying to stay sober. Together we can raise our consciousness higher, lifting each other up. Our social networks make us infinitely stronger.

The lessons that we sign up for in this lifetime are wrapped in relationship.

It was at the moment of Teri's death that she validated for me my greatest life lesson: I am a spirit in a body.

Things with Wings

Teri could not be contained. Her spiritual path eclipsed mine in our recovery. She was more open-minded to spiritual movements, while I was skeptical and cautious. She would start to follow teachers, then later quietly admit in a private conversation that maybe it was a cult. When she started following one teacher, bringing her flowers, and acting like a humble servant, I watched and waited. She suddenly had new friends, and I was suspicious of the new language she was speaking, how reverent she was. She revealed to me the spiritual awakenings she was having, direct experiences of oneness with god, and I felt left behind and, again, not good enough.

Teri began to refer to herself as "god's Teri," audaciously signing all her emails and professional correspondence that way. That seemed a bit much to me. I coped by chuckling, the way you do at a crazy aunt. That I was studying clinical psychology and her chronically unstable mother was diagnosed with schizophrenia did not help my judgment. She continued to create and sell majestic artistic creations, moving homes frequently. Her finances flowed in spurts. Teri had crossed over the line where everything reflected god's love for her. I was still playing the game—get an education, get a job, get a home loan, get married, get kids. Meanwhile, she enrolled in an interfaith ministry program, and in her studies, a calmness grew. She learned how to listen deeply and stopped talking over me. She became Reverend Teri. At her ministry ceremony, she glowed in her white dress, finally marrying the man of her dreams, god.

Teri flew from Marin County to Sedona, Arizona, on her wings and a prayer. She landed on the red rocks of Sedona and opened her first store, Things with Wings. Walking into her store was the same as walking into her heart. It dripped with her hand-painted creations, angels, and jewelry. She greeted each customer like a long-lost friend. Talking to her on the phone was almost impossible during this time, as she was always oozing over someone in her store. The hose was unkinked for her now. She was on her way to making her second set of millions. We still poured our hearts out to each other in our phone calls, but I was on a different treadmill, having kids, working, and being married.

Like a sugar crystalline dome, it all crashed down just at the height of expansion. As Teri breathed life force into her store, her body blasted out breast cells. Young, vibrant, and fully connected to god, of course, she would beat it. But cancer beat her, and no amount of yoga, nutrition, prayer, or healing by shamans and doctors would stop the karmic train coming to claim her. She sold everything she had, found homes for her many dogs, and moved to Byron Bay, Australia. On her way there, she visited my house, riddled with cancer. She giggled as she switched between her blond and brown wigs, to the delight of my children. Descending on this beachside town, Teri somehow did it again. She opened a store, rescued a puppy, and met "her man," telling no one of her cancer. Six months later, she was admitted to the hospital for intense pain. Pounding her pillow in anger, she faced the end of her fabulous body. Her girlfriends did her hair and makeup, and she slipped away in three days. Her new community hand-painted her coffin, sending her out in brightly colored Teri-style.

In grief, Michele and I went to Aesclepion, the same psychic school where I had just dipped my toes in years before, to receive psychic readings. It was unlike any reading I had previously experienced. When I sat in front of the line of readers, the temperature in the room rose, and the readers broke out into a sweat. I physically felt Teri's fingerprints touch my heart, leaving behind an indelible tattoo that persists to this day. I wasn't intellectually receiving information from that reading like I had in the past. No, I knew Teri was in that room. I knew she was also in the room next door with Michele. No amount of Western education or socialization could get me to deny the experience. That night, as we stepped into the parking lot to share our experiences, I knew Teri's body had died, and yet her spirit lived on. I knew my body would die too.

So, how was I going to live?

Within the month, Michele and I organized a memorial for Teri at the same Alano Club where we met nineteen years before under the willow tree. Unbeknownst to me, performing her service would be my first act as a minister. We adorned a table with her artistic creations, scarves, poetry, cards, and jewelry. We hung lights, lit candles, and read her words. The bright light that Teri was for all of us shone in that musty Twelve-Step meeting room. As we left, we carried her light in our hearts, out into the night.

Unconsciously, I said goodbye to being a psychologist and trying to live up to normative ideals. Desperately hungry to honor my spirit and do what the psychic readers did in that reading, I enrolled in a year-long clairvoyant training program.

I had crossed the line to living a Spirit-guided life.

CHAPTER 9

Psychic Abilities

There is a myth that some people are psychic and some people are not. This is like saying vision is all or nothing, when we know this sensory ability has many facets. There are degrees of color perception, depth perception, nearsightedness, and far-sightedness. While we all vary in visual ability, we don't think less of those who need to wear glasses. Similarly, the ability to read other people's auras, perceive beings that do not have a body, travel outside of our bodies, heal auras, and communicate with Spirit can vary from person to person. Our psychic abilities exist alongside our other senses—vision, audition, touch, olfaction (smell), proprioception (knowing where our bodies are in space), equilibrium (balance), vestibular (movement), and likely even magnetoception (perceiving changes in the geomagnetic field).[1] We wait for science to explain these experiences, labeled "extrasensory perception" more than a hundred years ago.

We all intuit information, and we all have the capacity to read people. Indigenous wisdom traditions have quietly known for thousands of years that intuitive abilities develop through spiritual practice. While some religions have promoted fear-soaked messages against psychic abilities. Discovering ourselves remains a revolutionary act.

It was just when I learned how to use my clairvoyance abilities that everything in my life came undone.

Clairvoyant School

The setting of my first clairvoyant training class was oddly similar to the thousands of Twelve-Step meetings I had attended. The bottom floor of the two-story office building had been converted into a psychic education center. Leftover office furniture and used family couches lined each room; posters and inspirational sayings dotted the walls at random heights. The decor conveyed either a lack of resources or that external appearances were not the priority. I walked past the room where I had felt Teri's fingerprints on my heart and remembered how her spirit had filled it just a few months ago. Down the central corridor, I passed the teacher's office, with the familiar large presence of the lead teacher, John, at his desk, running the show.

As people arrived, the center became a beehive of activity. Teachers greeted clients arriving for readings and guided them to the right room, and students started soft conversations with each other. Yet everywhere I looked, someone was sitting, eyes closed, in their own space. A beautiful Eastern European woman with an open smile said "Hello" in such a way that I felt my entire unique self was acknowledged and validated. She introduced herself as Katrina and welcomed me to take a seat in the main room.

Exactly at six o'clock, John strode in and started class with a declarative statement: "I want you to close your eyes." His Texan drawl matched his ownership of the room. I half expected him to be wearing a cowboy hat with a silver star pinned to his chest. He led us into a meditative trance, revisiting the skills we had practiced in the introductory class—owning the room, grounding our bodies, and running earth and cosmic energy. I tried to raise the earth's bright orange energy through my feet and up my leg channels, but logjams were blocking the flow. I changed the picture to see the earth's energy flow like lava, bursting through those narrow spots, pouring through my leg and joint channels. The lower half of my body became heavy, stable, and cleaned of the detritus of my day. Light, effervescent cosmic energy descended channels in my back, then rose up channels in front of my spine. This running of earth and cosmic energy caused my organs to rearrange themselves and my spine to undulate. My breathing became regular and slow. Meanwhile, my mind was running around, frantically checking to make sure the energy was flowing and my chakras were spinning, wondering, *Am I doing it right?*

All of this I had practiced before, but with John's clear words and commanding voice, I dropped into a deeper trance than I ever had before. He brought our attention up to our sixth chakra at the center of our head, just behind the eyes and in between the ears. My attention bobbed like a cork in water. I arrived at the center of my head, then the sensation of lead in my stomach pulled my attention back down. John, reading the room, simply said, "Come back to the center of your head." It was a game of ping pong for me. I traveled with great effort up to my head, then got captivated by the feelings in my body.

John explained, "We are spirits in bodies. Our spirit communicates to us in pictures. The body communicates in feelings. Both are valid forms of communication. The body deserves to be listened to and respected. But to be in greater body-being communication, we sit in the center of our head. We use our natural clairvoyant abilities to see."

I sat there in the circle of students and doubted myself. Was I in the center of my head? How would I know?

The body registers some fear when we first start to bring our attention to our sixth chakra. "The body's job is survival," John said. "Up to this moment, it may only be familiar with your spirit leaving when you sleep and in death. The body's job is to live, so when raising your consciousness to your sixth chakra, the body may respond by opening the first chakra, the one responsible for survival, or the second chakra, where feelings live, or the third chakra, by making you think you need to do something." John instructed us to communicate with the body by sending it a picture of our first, second, and third chakras, partially closing like a dial. With clarity, he said, "See it. I want you to do that now."

My lower stomach felt pregnant again, carrying the weight of my children who were at home while I was in class, my students with psychological disabilities whom I supported at work, and my husband, who didn't understand any of this. As I got lost in these pictures, a heavy weight pulled me down, back into these many problems.

With lightness, John said, "Notice when you are stuck in a picture. See that picture out in front of you and give it a read." He asked us to see a color associated with that picture and then look to see which part of our body lit up with that color. My second chakra was a train station with passengers passing through every day, and a hotel that housed some people overnight. They gave me their psychic energy, asking me to heal their problems. I was busy trying to be OK by making everyone around me OK, striving for their thanks and validation. I was clogged up.

John's commanding voice forced me to claw my way back to my sixth chakra, to find some space, some distance between me and this tidal wave of pictures pulling me under. He instructed me to put that color in a rose out in front of me, allowing it to pull that person's energy out of my space. We moved those roses farther away from us, outside of our auras. Then, with the commanding voice of a general, he said, "Blow that rose up. Blow that image. Put a bomb underneath it and light it up." Silent explosions radiated around the room—*boom, boom, boom.* Like Wiley Coyote, I put a box of TNT under my rose and lit the fuse. I watched the spark travel up to the box and then, boom! My eyes flinched, and my body reflexively tightened as a nuclear mushroom cloud developed and dissipated where my rose was. Afterward, my head felt clear, my lower belly light.

John reassured us that clearing these pictures was the point of being clairvoyant. We were not there to do psychic readings, but rather to clear our own space. The more we read others and cleared pictures, the more we ran our own energy. Getting stuck was an opportunity to see the energy, give it a read, and blow it up.

As clairvoyant students, we regularly traded psychic reads with each other. John would create exercises and pair us off. For example, he might say, "I want you to trade reads with your partner. Look at the word shame and see what color it is and where it lights up in their space."

Sitting in my chair, I blew roses for my performance anxiety and for effort. I blew roses for my children and their dad, who peered into my space. Shutting down my lower chakras, I arrived at the center of my head. I saw a blank screen in front of me, and fear raced up my spine that I would see no information. Following John's instructions, I would find my amusement and just let the images come. I asked my partner to say their name three times. As they said their name, I held out in front of me an image of a clear rose and allowed a color to flow into it. Like a snapshot in time, that color represented the summation of all their chakras. Once I had that color locked, I could then read what chakras were lit up with different colors, representing the energy they were releasing and what they were bringing in.

Those chakra colors came with details that I learned to state neutrally. "I see olive green in your heart. This is your father's information. His way of moving through the world is much narrower than yours, like he is following the rules of a military. He has judgments in your space about what behavior is acceptable or not. He is showing me tools . . . he has some kind of mechanical job? He is showing me that he is a problem solver, likes to fix things, and does not understand you as a spiritual being. His information is affecting how you see yourself."

My partner validated what I said. Yes, her father was in the military. Yes, he was a mechanic. And laughing, "Yes, he doesn't get any of this." Little by little, I began to trust what I was seeing. John called this having certainty in our clairvoyance abilities.

I learned to own my sixth chakra, to clear out people who wanted to borrow my clairvoyance and see the world through my eyes. I saw how many people were trying to jump into my body and drive it like it was their car. Now, when I welcomed my students into my office at work, I saw the edge of my aura and understood where my students ended and I began. I saw my students who were diagnosed with schizophrenia differently. When they struggled with auditory symptoms, I saw their difficulty regulating the traffic jam of energy in their space. While I was there to help, I was no longer there to take their energy into my space and heal it for them.

At home with two young children, I used my psychic skills to parent differently. My children naturally and playfully jumped in and out of my space bubble like hopscotch. I wanted to be connected to them, and also run my own energy and replenish my aura, rather than letting my children suck me dry. I learned to give them a special place at the edge of my aura, a rose for each of them, a special hello that said, "We are as close as can be. I'm going to run my own energy and give you the space to run yours." As parents, we often want to jump into our kids' space, silently telling them what to do. I lightened up, allowed them some space to own their bodies for themselves, to feel their own natural energy flow. I validated their ability to see the world for themselves, not just through my eyes.

I had no way of knowing then that running my own energy, standing in my own information with certainty, would cause all my agreements to crumble—and with them, my life.

We Know Things Without Knowing Why

In the dominant Western-industrialized worldview, psychic abilities are stigmatized and shamed. And yet, most Americans have reported having psychic experiences.[2] On the other hand, people biased against mystical things might feel perfectly comfortable talking about their "gut feelings" or "going on instinct." How is it that we are comfortable acknowledging our intuition but have outright disdain for psychic abilities and mediumship?

We know things without knowing why, but science and religion have unknowingly colluded to obscure this. Hundreds of years of Catholic doctrine have disconnected us from our inner knowing. The Christian church sought to consolidate power by separating whole cultures from their Indigenous (so-called "pagan") rituals, beliefs, and practices, replacing them with dependency on their priest to communicate with god. The Christian calendar subsumed celebrations tied to the seasons. As givers of life, women had previously been the connectors between the spiritual and material, but they were forcibly removed from their long-held roles in religious rituals as ceremonial drummers, keepers of ritual secrets, and healers.[3][4] The Inquisition's bloody rampage enforced Church doctrine with swift violence, as did the centuries of witch hunts that followed, which have been described as a psychological war on women that instilled fear and shame.[5] Western cultures are still healing from the trauma that severed us from nature and our inner knowing. We still don't trust what we intuitively know.

The scientific method is an exceedingly helpful way to build a body of knowledge. It relies on asking questions and testing these questions through direct observation and repetition of these tests. The scientific method has been so helpful in building a body of knowledge that we revere it. As philosopher of panpsychism Philip Goff said,

> The success of physical science in the last five hundred years is due to the fact that Galileo narrowed its scope of inquiry . . . The argument from "Physical science has been extremely successful" to "Physical science will one day explain the sensory qualities of consciousness" is

not supported by the history of science. Let me repeat for the sake of clarity: I'm not saying that this proves that physical science cannot explain consciousness. But it does undermine arguments that try to show that it inevitably will.[6]

However, the scientific method is just one way of knowing things, and like the Catholic Church, Western science has blood on its hands too. How many Indigenous ways of knowing did it trample, invalidate, and discard? Science and religion have been the left and right hands choking out cultures of color. We lost whole cultures and languages. We lost Indigenous wisdom about the connection between the spiritual and the material worlds and how to honor it with rituals and ceremonies. My own northern European ancestry had Indigenous knowledge at one time. But we don't brew those potions anymore. We don't know how those plants and animals can heal us. Instead, we swallow little white pills.

Scientific racism has subjected thousands of bodies of color to disease and cut out body parts without consent to study them. Scientific racism sought to demonstrate white superiority and created the eugenics movements that Nazi Germany maximized into extermination camps. Only recently, in 2001, did the American Psychological Association finally admit and apologize for more than a hundred years of "failing to challenge" racial superiority.[7]

Just as "silence isn't neutral," neither is science. What it doesn't study is just as important as what it does.[8] Leaving women out of medical research wasn't just convenient for controlling confounding variables: It was lethal.[9] Science is not neutral because its experiments are designed and carried out by people who are biased by their cultural context of time and location.[10]

Science has its own belief system, called positivism. Positivism asserts that there is one true reality that can be known. Science relies on directly observed empirical evidence to demonstrate this one true reality and rejects other ways of knowing, such as introspection, intuition, metaphysics, and theology. A positivist says, "There is one reality, and I can measure it."

But what if reality is relative? Would science know?

At its best, the scientific method is a difficult tool to prove that we have psychic abilities. Experiments can only tell if there is a significant chance that we don't *not* have psychic abilities, as experiments are designed to either support or reject the null hypothesis that psychic abilities do not exist. This limitation of the scientific method was described more than a hundred years ago by Hyslop in his book, *Enigmas of Psychical Research*.[11]

From its inception, the scientific discipline of psychology has struggled with its own identity—whether it studies psychic phenomena or not.

Gnashing of Teeth

In early formations, like gaseous nebulous clouds forming in a star nursery, there was no separation between the scientific disciplines of psychology and parapsychology. "Para" means alongside, beside, or resembling something. Indeed, parapsychology has been alongside the field of psychology since the beginning. In 1885, the academic leaders of the time formed the first professional psychological association, the Society for Psychical Research.[12] Its membership included the most famous early American psychologists, still taught in every introductory psychology class: G. Stanley Hall and William James. Using new methods to test the validity of the mediums and séances that were popular at the time, G. Stanley Hall sought to debunk parapsychology, while William James found it worthy of investigation.[13]

The split between the emerging fields of psychology and parapsychology came early; since then, the two have been like eagles with their talons entangled. The division arose in 1892 when Hall broke away to form a "new psychology," the American Psychological Association. William James laid the foundation for an open-minded study of human spirituality and religiosity with his tome, *The Varieties of Religious Experience*.[14] He famously critiqued material scientists' readiness to discard psychic phenomena in 1896 when he said, "To upset the conclusion that all crows are black, there is no need to seek demonstration that no crow is black. It is sufficient to produce one white crow. A single one is sufficient."[15] And yet, no matter how many people have seen a white crow—seen apparitions, or intuited information—no matter if even a group of people come forward reporting they all saw the same white crow together, the field of psychology says there is no proof. And collectively, the eagles plummet.

And yet, shockingly, the US Army and the CIA have funded research on psychic abilities.[16] The US government thought that the Russians might get the upper hand by developing psychic intelligence resources, and so for more than twenty years it funneled more than $20 million into about eighty separate research studies to investigate if "anomalous cognition" was possible. One specific facet of anomalous cognition studied was the capacity for "remote viewing," where one person, "a beacon" or "sender," in a remote location sends to the "remote viewer" details about the physical landscape. The CIA then funded a meta-analysis of more than eighty experiments, which concluded that overall, there were significant findings that could not be explained by chance alone. Yet, we are still left wondering what the thing is that makes this anomalous cognition possible.

Parapsychology has attempted to answer these questions. Where psychology is limited to studying material realms, parapsychology is willing to consider the possibility of an as-yet-unexplained factor in sensory perception. This factor is named *psi*, a letter from the Greek alphabet and the beginning of the word psyche, meaning "mind" and "soul." Since the two eagles locked talons in the mid-1800s, parapsychology researchers have attempted to legitimize their field of study, while others have poked every hole possible, critiquing their methods. And rightly so. The debate over methods, scrutiny of results, and demand for replicability of research findings make the scientific method a valuable tool for building knowledge.

Over the years, the field of parapsychology got downright paranoid about its research methods. In fact, when it comes to blinded protocols, where the researcher does not know which condition or group each participant has been assigned to, parapsychology was found to blind their researchers the most (79.1 percent of published studies) and physical sciences the least (0.5 percent).[17] Meanwhile, the field of psychology employed questionable research practices as the norm and integrated racial bias into the very fabric of its peer-reviewed publications.[18]

Psi research flies over two main territories: (1) *Anomalous cognition*, which includes non-inferable reception of information through means other than the senses and more accurate than chance through *telepathy* (being influenced by the mental state of others at a distance), *clairvoyance* (receiving information from a distance, including remote viewing), *precognition* (knowledge of the future), *retrocognition* (knowledge of the past), and *mediumship* (perception of survival of consciousness after death); and (2) *psychokinesis*, the influence on physical objects by mental actions, referred to as *non-local consciousness*.[19] Non-local consciousness is defined as awareness that can be experienced separately from the body, not bound by space or time; it may occur intentionally or unintentionally, and/or during other states, such as dreaming.[20]

In 2018, one veteran eagle allowed itself to be vulnerable. The flagship journal of the American Psychological Association published a paper by Etzel Cardeña summarizing and legitimizing parapsychology as a field of inquiry under consciousness studies.[21] Cardeña integrated the findings on psi research from multiple meta-analyses, or studies of studies. Meta-analysis systematically compares research findings across multiple studies using standardized statistical analysis.

Cardeña determined that, overall, these meta-analyses have supported the psi hypothesis more often than not.[22] The greatest effect sizes (the biggest effects) were seen in those studies that used free-response stimuli (e.g., large photo storage database) rather than forced choice (e.g., deck of cards) and studies that included "psi gifted" participants, participants in a non-ordinary state of consciousness (i.e., deep meditation), or just open-minded participants. Cardeña concluded the overall support of psi was stable across time, across different protocols with increasing rigor, greater than chance, and "cannot be readily explained away by the quality of the studies, fraud, selective reporting, experimental or analytical incompetence, or other frequent criticisms."[23]

Other studies have repeatedly shown what Cardeña saw: This shit works. A meta-analysis of eleven separate research studies on non-local consciousness investigated whether we can heal others with only our intentions. [24] This study summarized the findings across 576 remote healing sessions, where one person (A) sits remotely and directs their attention to person (B), who is focusing their attention on a neutral stimulus, such as a candle. While critically comparing the quality of the research methods across these studies, Schmidt determined that focused attention from a distance "more clearly indicates the existence of genuine interactions between distant people" that affect both the human body and behavior.[25]

A second meta-analysis of remote healing was even more stringent. Researchers removed human participants from their comparisons of the studies.[26] They controlled for the powerful placebo effect by selecting out studies where humans were either receiving the healing (treatment group) or placed in a control group. Instead, they focused on remote healing of tissue samples and animal subjects; tissue samples are much less susceptible to bias. Again, they found that remote healing had a positive effect, supporting the possibility of non-local consciousness.

Even a stanch critic of psi research, Thomas Rayberon, acknowledged:

> The psi studies, viewed as a whole, suggest that a kind of "direct" interaction (conscious or unconscious) between individual humans and their environment is possible. This interaction concerns events or objects situated at a distance in space and time (Mossbridge and Radin, 2018). It can take many forms (gut feeling, behavior, mental representation, etc.) with different intensities (e.g., a small or a strong emotion). It can be perceptive (from the environment to the person) or projective (from the person to the environment).[27]

Is it all so clear-cut? No. Comparing findings across multiple research studies can yield more murky water than clear springs. Sometimes a small positive effect size is found, but the methodologies are so poor that the finding is not considered reliable, such as meta-analyses of intentional healing on simple non-human and human living systems.[28]

But even if parapsychology were to publish solid research findings, would we believe them? Research has shown that we would not. When the same findings are dressed up as "neuroscience research" versus "parapsychology research," we are more likely to see them as valid and reliable.[29] Our stigma and confirmation bias against parapsychology are so strong that we become the eagle tearing out its brethren's feathers. The debate rages on, and feathers flutter to the ground.[30]

Parapsychology is no longer "fringe" science. It is here to stay, and it might even teach psychology a thing or two about research methods. It happens like that, doesn't it? As Radin described, "History shows that as the scientific frontiers continue to expand, the supernatural evolves into paranormal, and then into normal. During the transitional periods, there is much gnashing of teeth."[31]

What if religion permitted us to see for ourselves, and Western science allowed itself to study all of our human experiences?

Divorce as Spiritual Experience

While I was developing my clairvoyance, my husband and I were engaged in a rescue operation for our marriage, crumbling under the weight of stark disagreements. Weekly, we attended couples' therapy in an old Victorian building crowded with mismatched furniture and clients coming and going. I sat on our therapist's leather couch and practiced "owning the room," clearing out all the previous clients' energy. I saw myself connected to the earth, with a grounding cord at the base of my spine and my feet chakras open, soaking up the earth's energy like a cloth next to blood.

I showed up to my weekly clairvoyant class laden with a suitcase of pain to process, sending lead chunks of grief down my grounding cord. One night, John asked me to sit in the middle of the circle and trade a reading as a demonstration. I broke down in tears and said, "Can I pass this week? I can't get in the center of my head." I registered sympathetic looks around the circle from my classmates. They could see that I was struggling.

John did not flinch as he said, "You have a long history of using your tears to manipulate men. I want you to know that I see that, and you do not need to do that here. Here, you can be senior to other people's energy in your space."

Taken aback by his refusal to let me have my victim role, I simply nodded.

He softened as he continued, "Your body is moving energy by processing the pain with tears. I want you to close your eyes." Using this as a teaching moment for the class, he said, "In fact, everyone, close your eyes. Find your space, see that grounding cord connected to the center of the planet. I'm not talking about feeling something or sensing it with your body. I'm talking about seeing a picture and letting that picture be a command from your spirit to your body."

I followed his words like a dog being fed kibble, one pellet at a time. I found my way up to the center of my head. Down below me was the nuclear wasteland of grief that I was moving out of my body. The black tar stuck to my ovaries, wrapped around my guts, and started to drip out of me, making its way down to the earth, where it could be cleansed and used again. I found that I was able to see, to be clairvoyant, while my body processed pain. With practice, I found that I could clear this pain much easier and faster energetically than my body could by crying. While I was moving through my divorce, the grief would settle into my stomach like an anchor as I sat at my desk at work. It was difficult to breathe, and my thinking slowed down, trapped in a foggy enclosure. Closing my office door and turning off the fluorescent light, I practiced running my energy and moving the grief out. The skills I learned long ago in that first meditation class—owning the room, grounding cord, bringing in golden suns—saved my life.

When I finally said to my husband that we had gone as far as we could go, I had already cleared so much of my pain and grief that the decision was simple, but not easy. I had never felt clearer about a decision in my life. It was a spiritual experience to honor my truth as more important than everyone else's thoughts and feelings about my truth. Sure, sometimes I wallowed in the mud and wondered if it would be possible for anyone to love me again. Those thoughts became roses to blow up, old ideas to let go, examples of someone else's judgment in my space.

To cope with the sludge-like pain and grief, I ran my energy every chance I got. While attending a Twelve-Step meeting, I sat in my metal chair and closed my eyes. I made my way to the center of my head, rising above the emotions I was healing for others in my second chakra and the to-do list in my third chakra, past the signposts of defeat and failure in my fourth chakra and the words I wanted to scream out in my fifth chakra—all the way to the perch of my knowingness in my sixth chakra. In a deep trance, I saw myself on an airplane to Hawaii, flying high in the stratosphere above the earth, the ride smooth and peaceful. Looking through the small oval window down on the water below, I was able to see crinkles on the surface of the ocean's expanse. I knew that to be on the surface of the water would be to experience life-threatening giant waves. From my vantage point so high up, the ocean looked calm and glassy. I could see the curvature of the earth. Returning to my body at the end of the meditation, I came back with the knowledge that my divorce could be like this. I could sit high up in my sixth chakra in meditation and neutrally move the grief out of my body, restoring me to my own truth. Or I could ride my life raft on the surface of the water, sliding down the steep face of the waves, taking on everyone's pain into my body, like water in my boat. There was no choice. In survival, I tethered myself to my meditation practice.

As I drove my car to school drop-off, work, and the grocery store, dutifully fulfilling my roles, I would sometimes pick up my phone and pretend to call Teri. One day, pressing the phone up to my ear, I said hi, asked how she was, told her I missed her, and then talked about god and boys, as always. I paused in between confessions and waited for her to respond. Seeing the road in front of me, I heard her giggle and remind me, "There is no separation" and "You are love Itself." Tears rolled down my face. I smiled and thanked her for the spiritual quest that her death ignited in me.

Teri began to visit me in my dreams. In one, my cell phone rang, and I saw her name on the screen. Michele exclaimed, "Oh my god, I can't believe her phone still has service on the other side!" In another dream, we were having a party at Michele's house. It was chaotic and messy inside, and I was worried about her house. Teri was dancing, being her full fabulous self, strutting her stuff on the dance floor in her hot pink feather boa and leopard-print something, her bright, shining smile showing all her teeth.

Each morning, before the house of teenage hormones would stir, I did the hardest thing of all: sit down to meditate. With a cup of coffee to entice my body, I developed my own routine of burning things (sage, incense, frankincense), settling into a cross-legged position with a vertical spine and cleansing breaths, and writing affirmative and supplicative prayers. From the center of my head, I would own the room, create a grounding cord, see my protection rose, run earth and cosmic energy, and heal myself with golden suns. Daily, I cleared out what was not mine and restored myself to my own creative energy.

One morning, Teri was with me. I felt her fingertips on my heart, just as I had years before, after her passing. It was a physical sensation, reminding me I was a spirit in a body. I didn't think she was present; I knew she was. I was so excited, but she was even more so. Bubbling over, she talked to me in a very fast, high-pitched voice that I could barely hear. Teri was always effusive, but as a spirit she was bursting. I rose up out of my body to join her on the astral plane. We hugged and danced and smiled and looked into each other's eyes. She had the same straight blond hair and big toothy grin, but she wore a patchwork quilted cloak with golden threads that connected each gilded green and blue square. My soul sister had returned to collect me.

I asked her, "Can you please slow down? I want to hear you." Briefly stepping back into my body, exerting the least possible effort, I opened my journal to record the moment.

"I'm so excited you can finally hear me! I've been trying to talk to you, but you act like I'm a mosquito," she said, laughing.

"I'm so sorry," I said.

"You found me!" she said. "We meet today on the astral plane, where your loved ones are helping you. There is another plane waiting for you with more powerful beings, and I will take you there. I am always your soul sister, traveling with you on this journey. There is so much love in life, so much love in Spirit. Let's go!"

I felt her love for me and thanked her.

She prayed for me, "Precious Catherine, you are a light beyond measure. You radiate light and see it reflected back at you in others' faces and in their gratitude for you. They feel more connected, listened to, and validated because of who you are and how you walk in this world. That is your service, that is your awakening, that is your path to god and enlightenment. Boldly be you! Celebrate you! Cherish you! Embody Spirit's love for you and know that you are always connected. I say these words to you and know it is already done. And so it is."

I came back to my body and sat looking at my journal, stunned. I saw her words on the page and bowed deeply in gratitude for her visit. A doorway opened. And I told no one.

CHAPTER 10

Our Body, Our Greatest Teacher

Having a body, being alive, is our greatest opportunity for expansion and awakening. And yet, we often struggle and disagree with our bodies. Fueled by lies taught to us by our cultures, we want our bodies to be different from what they are. Social programming is a powerful force that teaches us to value narrow ways of being in the world. Turning toward ourselves with loving care to learn how to run the body is a necessary step on the spiritual path. It turns out, the body is the perfect vehicle to get us Home to freedom.

Life on Life's Terms

We climbed the forested hills surrounding our hamlet, traversing crooked fingers that delivered us to glorious coastal vistas. My sober sister, Michele, loved road cycling, her strong, trim frame wrapped in black cellophane, her calf muscles, thighs, and backside sculpted for this sport. For her, endurance cycling was a celebration of what her body could do post-baby, post-breast cancer, and in the present moment of recovery.

After answering people's questions all week as the dean at our local community college, I was happy to let Michele be the expert in cycling each Sunday. She taught me how to scan my bike and gear before each ride, moving through a safety check-list—tire pressure, brakes, water bottles, nutrition, eye protection, helmet, and gloves. Any missing piece made us vulnerable and made others responsible for our well-being. She taught me how to yell out "Car back!" and silently use hand signals to communicate "pothole," "gravel," and "stopping." She navigated around potholes and cars by slightly flicking the angle of her bike with a twitch of her abdominal muscles, balancing as if on the head of a pin, while I veered off the road when I took a sip from my water bottle. We strapped heart monitors to our chests and attached devices to our wheels, celebrating our miles and elevation gain each ride. We spun through our lives as we spun past mustard flower blooms in vineyard rows and under the protective canopy of wise old oak trees, living life on life's terms.

I could never have predicted then that the simple, sometimes dull, repetitive motion of pushing pedals would propel me into the spiritual stratosphere, or that I would have to land on my face first.

World-famous cyclists climb our local hills. Fans spray-paint their names—"Go Jens"—and their slogans—"Shut up, legs"—on the road. Once a year, I would walk from my house and join others on the corner ringing cattle bells to see first the pack of motorcycles with cameras and spare tires, then the team vehicles racked with spare bikes, followed by the tour riders who easily chugged their legs up 18 percent gradients. The area is known for its expansive coastal views that reward riders at the top of punishing climbs. We are also known for our crumbling pavement; the road strata are constantly broken up and subsumed by the earth's crust.

Michele and I rode Sunday after Sunday, breathing heavily as we unpacked recovery, parenting, work, relationships, Teri, and god, hill after hill. Michele loved to push herself with 100-mile so-called "social rides," which were tests of personal endurance rather than timed races. Like a cult follower, she encouraged me to join her, exclaiming how great the snacks were at the rest stops—baked potatoes with oil, salt, and pepper, banana halves, and the best part, Oreos. I fretted about my first century ride for months, and rightly so. On the day of, I learned about both the points of pain that come with sitting on your bike seat for seven hours and the accomplishment that comes with crossing that finish line, even when no crowds are applauding, even when not one person is watching. Inwardly, you know: You did it. You survived a century ride.

My bike was a vehicle for exercise, for sightseeing, for a break from parenting and work, for pushing my body, and for seeing how much suffering my mind could endure. Sitting on the edge of rural roads with no cell signal, in tears, attempting to repair flat tires, I learned how to scan the road for glass, nails, screws, and sharp edges of payment. I learned how to avoid "bonking" (those horrible moments when your legs have no juice, the ride sucks, in fact, everything in your life sucks, and you somehow have to make it home) by creating "hot" water bottle mixes with electrolytes. I learned how to fuel my body, discovering the joy of a baked sweet potato in my back pocket or a peanut butter and jelly sandwich at the top of a two-hour climb. Over a few years, my riding improved, and people started to comment on how I was a good mountain climber or how I confidently leaned into turns. My preparations for nutrition, hydration, and endurance paved the way for moments of flow where I knew I was in the right place, doing exactly the right thing, my body and mind one united mechanism, my heart reliable, my muscles responsive, my mind calm. With the flick of an abdominal muscle, I too could navigate the holes in the pavement, balancing my bike as if on the head of a pin.

Before our next ride, I tried to excuse myself due to lack of sleep. Like everything, the hardest part of riding is getting on the bike. But Michele was willing to go to a Sunday service with me first, so I acquiesced. The service lifted me up. I felt my faith in Spirit and humanity restored despite the terrible shootings in the news. Chatting in between breaths as we climbed the hills behind her house, I felt sluggish but pushed on, buoyed by my favorite matching outfit (a "kit"), riding my new bike with my best friend. Floating downhill, we enjoyed the respite of the rollercoaster that rippled us onward after all the climbing. My body finally warmed as we entered a patch of sunshine, and I entered a moment of flow. My gratitude for my life spilled over, my body felt perfectly balanced on all its contact points with the bike—sit-bones, feet, hands—and my breath and heart rate transitioned from disjointed to rhythmic pumping, sending me resources just where and when I needed them. I was at One.

Michele and I spaced ourselves apart on the road wordlessly, giving each other enough space for a mishap while communicating to cars to see us as one unit. As the left side of my body soaked up the morning sun, I thanked god for this moment, this life, knowing there was no separation between me and the I Am.

The country road meandered under the protective bent arms of watchful oak trees whose leaves created hexagonal shadows on the road. I didn't see it until my front tire disappeared into its red alligator mouth. The split second of reaction time only offered me the chance to pump my brakes once. The front of my tire was completely swallowed by the gaping pothole, instantly bringing all my bike's forward momentum to a stop.

The Gift of Having a Body

Being born into a body is an opportunity for the greatest expansion and awakening. Souls without bodies on the astral plane would love to have this opportunity to learn, heal, and grow. This is only possible while in a body because the suffering of separation is only possible when in a body. Our next incarnation comes at a confluence: when we have completed the healing from our last life, when we select the genetic and karmic lessons for our next life, when we have reset our agreements with our soul pod, and when the Creator cares for the right timing of our birth. Life is the greatest miracle.

To accept our body exactly as it is and exactly as it is not means to accept the teachings of the One. Our soul's journey is to use these lessons for our awakening. Our body is our teacher.

We can ask ourselves, "How can I love who I am in this moment?"

The answer is to deeply accept, down to our bone marrow, our unique manifestation in this life. We are here to lovingly care for our body as our sanctuary and teacher.

Run the Body

Proper spirit-body communication means allowing your spirit to direct the flow of energy in your body. The body exists in the gross physical plane, as energy waves manifested as form. The spirit is subtle energy expressed as consciousness. Because our spirit (consciousness) is not held captive by form, it is capable of perceiving more information and imagining more expansive possibilities. Which of the two would you prefer to run the show, the spirit that can see everything and be anything, or the body that is just one thing? There are three simple steps to bring our spirit into right relationship with our body:

1. Use our spiritual control panel in the sixth chakra to direct the flow of energy in the body,

2. Care for the body's needs to maximize energetic flow, and

3. Practice radical self-love.

Our Spiritual Control Panel

We learn to sit in our spiritual control panel by bringing our attention and awareness up to the sixth chakra. The sixth chakra, located just behind our eyes and in between our ears, is like a dashboard where we see ourselves and the world, and where we have our higher spiritual abilities, such as clairvoyance.

Sitting in the center of our heads is like being the only patron inside a large movie theater. The expansive screen rises before you as you relax in your seat in the center of the middle row. If the movie screen is too close or difficult to make out because it is far away, you can simply move it to a comfortable viewing distance. With our imagination, we can look at anything we want by seeing it in the center of our screen. From our sixth chakra, we consider the body's energetic communication. It helps to visualize an image of our body, such as a chalk outline or an image of our body's current position. It takes practice to reduce the flow of energy in our lower three chakras and rise to our sixth. At first, it is common for our awareness to dip down into our body and start feeling things rather than seeing them as energy. Catching ourselves and bringing our attention back to the movie screen, we learn to see what our body is communicating to us. With practice, we learn to run the energy in our body from the sixth chakra, rather than let our bodies run us.

From the neutral perspective of the sixth chakra, we see what parts of our body are lit up, where energy is flowing, or where energy is stuck. Colors appear—reds, purples, greens, and blues. Sometimes energy is stagnant and coalesces into pools of black, gray, and brown. We can ask ourselves simple questions like "Where am I in fear?" or "Where is someone's energy in my space?" and see on the movie screen what part of our body lights up in response. We can, with practice, move out other people's information and restore ourselves with our own healing energy and that of the One.

Some people enjoy escaping their bodies to spend time in their higher chakras. While a useful skill, this can sometimes be a form of self-abandonment or "spiritual bypass."[1] When you sit down to meditate, offer your body several deep breaths and your gratitude for all that it does. Being on a spiritual path does not mean denying our bodies. Part of spiritual awakening is opening ourselves to the magic and mystery of having a body, and learning to tend and care for it.

Our bodies are always in the present moment, communicating with us through feelings and sensations. The first step in loving ourselves is to slow down and listen. It can be helpful to sit or lie down, with one hand on your heart and the other hand on your belly. Take three deep breaths, allowing the exhale to be longer than the inhale. Long exhales activate the parasympathetic nervous system, communicating to the body that we are safe and relaxed. Notice your body. It can be helpful to do a body scan, allowing your awareness to start at one end and travel to the other. But the body is always communicating something to us, for example, with laughter, tears, and pain. The simple and revolutionary act of pausing long enough to listen is all it takes to begin to transform. Being a spirit in a body means both honoring the body's feelings as a communication system and learning to use our spiritual tools to process them.

Care for the Body

We maximize our body's ability to move energy by giving the body what it needs: water, nutrition, movement, and sleep. Although the fastest way to move energy is from our spirit, the body also moves energy through rest, sleep, food, laughter, tears, sensual touch, and exercise. Energy movement is essential for a healthy life; living is energy work.

Life requires water. When scientists roam their attention around the galaxy looking for evidence of life, the first thing they look for is water. Bodies function with water. Our blood is made primarily of water, and our digestive system only functions with water. We can live for a month without food, yet only three days without water.[2]

We need to drink water regularly in order to run our own energy. Our central and peripheral nervous systems are electrical communication systems. Cells require water with electrolytes (sodium, potassium, and magnesium) to send these electrical messages. If we want to run our own energy and move other people's information out, then drinking water will help the body to process this change and become a clear vessel of energy perception. We drink water so that our body can manifest the changes our spirit is calling into existence.

The digestive system regulates energy flow. The type of food and substances we put in our bodies also matters. Clean eating helps the body perceive higher vibrations of energy. I'm not anti-food or anti-drugs. Our bodies can process and enjoy anything in moderation. However, faced with the modern diet—and the supermarkets that make all foods available all of the time—we must make informed, conscious choices about how we feed our bodies.

The digestive enteric nervous system is now considered the "second brain."[3] The gut produces most of the serotonin and dopamine in the body (95 percent and 50 percent, respectively).[4] This "gut-brain axis" consists of bidirectional communication between the bacteria in the digestive tract and the brain. This two-way highway of information impacts not only digestion (top-down commands from brain to gut), but also mood, motivation, and higher cognition (bottom-up driven information, with the bacteria driving the bus).[5] Western science now validates that we do indeed feel through our stomachs. We are so deeply interconnected with nature that the microbes in our gut communicate directly with the emotional regulation centers in our brain, the amygdalae.[6] Therefore, it is important to tend to these microbes, feeding them fiber and greens. The fact that our bodies are made up of more microbial cells than our own cells reminds us of the oneness of it all.

Some people begin eating a clean diet out of necessity. My friends living with Lyme's Disease and Multiple Sclerosis reduce symptoms by avoiding sugar, gluten, and any artificial additives. The same day I am writing about food and clairvoyance, my friend Joy calls me, upset. She tells me about the disturbing visions she is having, how she is soaking up like a sponge other people's suffering. She says, "I think it's my clean diet. It's like I'm being given these psychic abilities. But I feel overly sensitive, and it's scary." After celebrating and validating what she is perceiving, I remind her that she has spiritual tools. She reminds me that we can nurture our sensitive natures through clean eating.

We can also be mindful of what we feed our mind, which is fertile ground, especially first thing in the morning and last thing at night. What we do when we first awaken can program our thoughts for the day. Likewise, we can influence our dream state with what we expose our minds to right before bed. We have known since 1961, when Stanford psychologist Albert Bandura first showed children a video of an adult beating up an inflatable "Bobo doll," that the media we watch changes how we behave.[7] The Shipibo communities in Peru prepare for ayahuasca healing ceremonies by practicing the *dieta* (like diet) before and after each ceremony, careful of all that they consume physically, mentally, socially, and spiritually. We can choose to plant the seeds of gratitude through practice, prayer, and meditation, or we can choose to consume violent, adrenaline-pumping media and negative news stories. In time, the desire to be entertained by hijacking our sympathetic nervous system will likely slip away.

Many physical practices, in addition to meditation, can move energy out of our bodies. Exercise that gets your heart pumping is a great way to push energy through your system so it flows freely. Cardiovascular exercise opens our lower chakras, moving energy out. When I run up a hill or paddle on a surfboard, I open my third chakra in my solar plexus to be more energized. Yoga, ecstatic dance, and martial arts systematically open chakras and move energy through them.

Sex is simply energy play. Our sexual energy is our creative ability—how we create new life. We also use our creative life force energy in varying doses in our careers, art, music, and dance. Sexual energy originates in the lower chakras and can rise up the central channel. Orgasm builds as that energy reaches our sixth chakra. At the peak of orgasm, waves of our creative energy can flow up our spine. We can use our orgasm to clear out chakras that may have been blocked. If we heal other people's information, judgments, shame, and sex negativity from our space, our sexuality will have more freedom to be playful, pleasurable, and positive. People who practice sacred sexuality intentionally create with orgasm, a spiritual practice called "sex magic." This is one of the many tantric yoga methods that honor the body and desires as a path to liberation. We all absorb cultural conditioning around sexuality. There is much healing to do. When liberated, our creative lifeforce energy becomes a powerful ally in all that we do.

Likewise, good sleep is necessary for energy work. Our bodies operate on a rhythm tied to the earth's rotation. Most of us do not give our bodies enough sleep; instead, we pay in sleep for our entertainment and social connection through electronic devices.[8] When we do not give the body the seven to nine hours of sleep it needs, we put a ceiling on our attention, concentration, memory, judgment, and planning. And guess what, we need our full cognitive abilities for spiritual awakening. Honor the rhythm of healing darkness every day. Honor your body's need to heal—to remove waste products, store energy, and release needed hormone communicators. When we shorten our sleep cycle, we reduce the REM sleep stages where we dream and where our spirits travel on the astral realm. In the triad of our well-being—sleep, diet, and exercise—our achievement-oriented culture often overlooks sleep. The good news is that we can use a few simple sleep hygiene practices. We can remember that caffeine has a six-hour half-life and ask ourselves if we want half that cup of coffee or tea in our system six hours from now. Just as we look forward to vacations and retreats, we can appreciate our body's daily rhythm and need for rest.

As we remove energetic blockages and restore our own energy, we will be freer to create, to destroy, and to perceive information through clairvoyance, clairaudience, and clairsentience. With our body freed up to run our spirit's energy, we communicate, love, heal, and teach authentically. We experience more certainty, inner knowing, and conviction. Allow yourself to be sensitive. Spend time in nature, allowing your feet chakras to be rooted to the earth. Honor your body as worthwhile and deserving of this time and attention. In this way, body, mind, and spirit all embark on the journey of awakening. No part of us is left behind.

Radical Self-Love

Our bodies are our greatest spiritual teachers because they teach us to love ourselves radically. Most of us struggle with our bodies. I know this karmic lesson well. Simply walking past a mirror elicits automatic negative messages for me: too much here, not enough there. I tug at skin and compare myself to some imagined other, the ever-present invisible her who is perfect. She is a shapeshifter, changing over the years with the cultural mores—thunderous breasts one decade, a lithe and lean gazelle the next—only to morph into a swayback hippopotamus. I lie in the sun to tan, then laser the skin off my face when I wear out its elasticity. I inject fat into one location only to sweat it out in the gym in others. I know self-abandonment.

We all have the power to transform and heal ourselves; we use it when we begin to honor our bodies. Loving our bodies is a necessary step on the spiritual path. But this life lesson is never complete. As long as we are alive, the body will continue to be our teacher, and we its loving caretaker. Treating ourselves as sacred aligns us with truth: We are sacred. In *The Altar Within*, Juliet Diaz teaches us that worshipping ourselves is "an even more powerful way of connecting with Spirit. It is not replacing your God. It is adding to your worship the most important link: you."[9] We worship ourselves and the One through the tender care and respect we offer our bodies.

Some of us experience excruciating pain in our bodies. The suffering that results from physical and emotional pain is difficult to bear; daily survival is the hardest work. Emotional and physical pain activate many of the same brain regions and therefore trigger the same coping response.[10] Suffering caused by pain is another opportunity for spiritual practice, energizing our souls into greater communion with god. We can ask ourselves, "Can I trust the signals my body is sending to me and respond to meet its needs?" "Where do I feel connection in the midst of so much pain?" "How am I willing to be cared for, and where can I ask for help?" Even when in pain, we are still on a spiritual path. As the Buddha said, everyone suffers. Every life is exposed to both light and dark. We can rest in the timelessness of the soul and the temporary nature of this body. The body's suffering will end at some point, just as all our lives will come to an end.

But our soul, this beautiful, unique, radiant energy of consciousness, always lives on.

Indeed, our soul is the only thing about us that is never broken, diseased, injured, or sick. Death is a spiritual transition, where we step out of the body and fully into our spirit. For some, the work is to stay in our body, one breath at a time. Nothing is permanent. Our experience always changes, and we are never alone.[11] Whether we stay to breathe or end our lives, we are our consciousness. Our set of karmic lessons will remain. We have support in our friends, family, trusted professionals, and healing guides. We can soften our hearts to soak in the acts of everyday kindness that are present in our lives.

Sovereignty comes when we heal other people's messages about our bodies, removing the "too much" and "not enough."[12] We act as sovereign beings when we pay attention to and heal our past traumas, learning to regulate and love our sensitive nervous systems. We unknowingly absorb harmful messages throughout our lives from our family, our culture, and the media. These messages program us to neglect and criticize our bodies.

Self-love is a revolutionary act.

Self-love disarms any barbs thrown our way and communicates our invincibility to others. Sovereign self-love overthrows the racist, sexist, homophobic, colonist overseers we inherited and internalized. Sovereign self-love creates the opportunity for us to reclaim our Indigenous identities, tied to the seasons and the rhythms of the earth. We are good stewards of our bodies when we lovingly tend to them and speak our truth. Self-love, radical self-acceptance, and deep self-cherishment are synonymous with spiritual awakening.

I am still learning today that there is but one source of love, with many forms. I am still learning to welcome the smallest, most vulnerable part of myself into the deepest realm of my heart, to cherish her even when she has needs, see the miracle of my own existence, and be for myself that kind, loving presence that I so often seek from everyone else. I consider how I would move through the day if I deeply accepted and honored myself, how much more energy I would have to offer others. It is a tightrope walk from self-abandonment to self-acceptance. False perceptions and unattainable comparisons pull at me. Every day, I wake up and again pick up the balancing pole, mindfully sliding my feet forward toward the platform of love.

The Gravity of My Karma

My back tire skipped, lifting off the pavement, sending matter into motion. Brand new carbon fiber bike, water bottles, my favorite kit, safety gear, rider, dean, sober sister, daughter, mother, body—all moved through the space time continuum. Time slowed, and I wondered which direction I would fall, to the left or maybe to the right. My body kept going past my bike, flying through the air, headfirst. I thought, *Oh, this is how I'm going to fall, head over heels.* My arms, pinned to my sides by force, didn't have time to open into wings. I flew in this lifetime, sailing past bike, past pothole, down the midline of the road with invisible tick marks. Five feet, ten feet, I flew on. Fifteen, twenty, twenty-five feet before the gravity of my karma grounded me.

I moaned face-down in the pavement, my hands pressed like dove wings under the weight of my pelvis. Michele was busy spinning golden threads into a network of resources: the woman praying over me, the wilderness EMT assessing my vitals, the 911 dispatcher, the neighborhood firefighters streaming out of their homes after seeing an emergency alert on their phones, the firetrucks and ambulance, and family and friends driving to the hospital. This second time, when death greeted me, I knew. Teeth scattered in the grass, gravel embedded into my face, blood flowing in a pool on the pavement—I knew that the Oneness I felt on the bike moments ago was still there. I knew that I was loved, looked after, and cared for. The golden net cradled me, its fibers carried in the mouths of eleven white swans with crowns on their heads, carrying me to yet another emergency room.

In the back of the ambulance, my body rhythmically rattled the metal gurney. My primitive nervous system took over as I drunkenly drifted in and out of consciousness. I was not in the ambulance, nor on this earth. I traveled in space, moving through a tube wrapped in the colorful fractals of the northern lights. Singular words popped up unconnected to thought. I was the witness to the show and applied the clinical term to my experience, "word salad." A hydraulic press machine forced me back into my body, my head flattened between its large metal plates. I escaped again to the colors where I was fully free, unencumbered by the physics of this world.

The loud metal shaking of the gurney brought me back inside the ambulance, and I thought, *This is what fish do when they die.*

The paramedic touched me and said, "You are going to be OK."

Meera's Message: Only You Can Give it Away

As you move down the path of transformation, through birth, death, and rebirth cycles, you collect along the way, like mushrooms, tools, skills, and abilities. You learn from your experiences. This flow of your information through time and physical space is the crux of the learning process. You are a spirit in physical form; the body is but a precious shell covering who you are. I have no intention of dismissing the body as your teacher. Please do not misunderstand me. The spirit, your soul, is the collector of your experiences, the one who ripens in the sun, learns from your choices, and moves on to the next opportunity to open into more love.

Being ego-identified causes you suffering. To the precise extent you grip onto your attachments, you will feel discomfort. Let it all go. The seeking, the grasping, thoughts of comparison, trying to be different than what you are. Your body is what it is. No one can possibly steal your light or your power.

Only you can give this away.

You are a being of Light. You can unzip from your current karmic predicament at any time and step out of it. You can choose to use suffering as a lesson, like an amuse-bouche. And how amusing it is to believe that you are stuck, that you are alone, that you are separate, that you are lost, when actually all you are is connected to Source.

Your soul concocted this experience for your own growth and awakening, so you can find your way Home to what already is.

Look at your liquid Light Self—fluid, flexible, able to create in an instant. Is something in your material experience dying? Good. Let it perish. Come Home to the One. Come Home to your divine Self, who is already drunk in love at this very moment. Allow the layers of your identity to dissolve, the robes you have been wearing to slide off your back. See what remains. Experience the you that has always been present, aware, loving, conscious. Your conscious awareness is your connection to Source. It is from this place that you create and manifest in the material.

You, as a spirit, exist on the most subtle plane—consciousness. You create and destroy with your thoughts. Your thoughts matter. The visions you create in your mind matter. You are, always, a powerful being, a spirit capable of operating your body and mind.

Create from a foundation of love and peace. Create from Spirit.

Arriving

Let's review. We honestly admitted we have been stuck. Relying on the self-seeking engine, we were going nowhere fast. We realized that we could switch fuel sources by running our lives with our spirit at the center. We understood that we are spiritual beings in a physical body, and how Spirit and the material world interact.

Here, in Part 3, we find that we have been at Home in Oneness all along. Underneath the layers of our identities, we uncover who we are. Our spiritual path always leads us back to our true nature, our soul. We have always been Spirit-guided, because we are Spirit.

The bicycle accident launched me into the air—and into spiritual transformation. The resulting brain injury removed my identities and responsibilities one by one. Resting in an unprotected energetic heap, I received my first communications from spirit and met my spirit guide. Healed by love, I discovered that everything I ever wanted is here, now.

CHAPTER 11

Uncovering the Soul From the Layers of Identities

We have been at Home in Oneness all along. Oneness wrapped itself inside a soul; that soul got to have a body; that body was born into a culture and time that shaped a mind; that mind was raised inside a family and became a person; that person learned it had likes, dislikes, and identities. And now, all those layers, like Russian nesting dolls, keep us from resting in our true nature. Through various methods, such as spiritual practice, psychedelics, and even healing from trauma, we can step beyond our identities and lean back into Oneness

For some of us, the transition to living Spirit-guided can be messy. Ignoring all the gentle hints the Universe sends us, we continue on our fear-based self-seeking journey, trying to achieve and attain until we hit a brick wall.

I had to get completely knocked out of my head to find myself.

A Major Pause

My metal gurney and I were wheeled down halls and into x-ray machines and CAT scans. Molecules of medicine flowed through my IV and relieved the painful pressure in my head. I had hours of clear thinking that day, like the left hemisphere of my brain knew it needed to download all its information. I made lists of all the things I needed to do at work and pelted asteroids of texts and emails out into the world, discharging responsibilities, saying, "I'm going offline, riding this comet for I don't know how long." Visitors flowed by—Michele, my kids, and their dad. I reassured my son that we would ride bikes together again. I held my daughter's hand and tried to speak words of comfort, but instead spat out bits of tooth into my crumpled hand.

In time, doctors wheeled my gurney and me into surgery, where they flushed out the road rash on my face, sewed the rips under my eye, and repaired the break in my jaw. During the night, the mania of my to-do list unfurled in my mind, dot matrix-style.

The next day, my mind gave out, and I retreated to the land of dark quiet. Fluorescent lights and speech were the enemy, quiet darkness a comfortable womb. Thinking hurt. Reading hurt. Watching TV hurt. Listening to podcasts hurt. Talking hurt. There was nothing to do, no way to be. I could only rest and try not to think about resting. Meanwhile, the celestial bodies set in motion carried my life forward. Kids, pets, mail, medical decisions, work—everything my mind held was lovingly taken by others.

I engaged in the spiritual practice of receiving help and letting go.

I woke up with a new brain and a new reality. Words were not there when I looked for them. When I tried to speak, my brain, hunting like a dog for a bone, instead retrieved metaphors. I spoke like my grandparents. Colloquialisms rolled off my tongue, and I was unable to get directly to the point. Memories of what I did that day or even thirty seconds ago were shrouded behind clouds. My need for quiet was so intense that I became irritable when doors were not shut mindfully. I crawled into the cave of my room and drew the blinds. My kids tiptoed to keep the humming of our home to a low murmur.

My front teeth and the surrounding bone had stayed behind somewhere on the pavement. I thought about looking for them, but could not figure out why. Grateful for my surgeon's skill, as represented by her tiny blue stitches on my face, I still felt sad at the simultaneous loss of my intelligence and beauty when she said I had facial paralysis. I sat in the unknown of what would be restored.

Instead of my usual busyness of thinking and talking, I lived in feelings, swimming in a cistern full of gratitude for my life. In the week after the accident, I wrote thank yous to everyone who assisted, compelled to tell people how grateful I felt for their presence and the gifts they brought to my life. Thinking and planning for the future was a forest. I got lost in it. In defeat, I returned to the present, aware and feeling. Bright television, computer, and phone lights seared my eyes. The bass notes in music thumped like a carpenter inside my skull. Conversations were exhausting. The simple act of tracking what someone said, waiting to respond, and planning what I wanted to say drained me of life force. When answering phone calls, I would bend my head to the side, expose my tender neck, and allow the energy vampire to drain me. Reading, normally a restorative pleasure, went into my cognitive bank account and bounced checks. I was a puddle of a human, dripping from my bed to my couch and back again in the hardest treatment plan of all: doing nothing.

Somehow, out of all the sensory information in the world, my brain gave my kids a hall pass. They were allowed inside the quiet, polished halls of my mind. They returned this privileged access by knowing just when to give me space, when to be quiet, and when I needed something. I reaped their attunement to me, harvesting the sweet nectar of all the seeds of love previously sown.

Spheres We Inhabit

Let's uncover what lies beneath our layers of identity. We can imagine our identity as a ring of concentric circles, layers of spheres we inhabit. We can build on Urie Bronfenbrenner's Ecological Systems Theory, which proposes that children develop within interactive systems, represented as circles. The smaller subsystems of family are nestled within the larger circles of community, culture, and environment. We then internalize these layers of circles within our identity.

One way to think of the order of the circles is to consider how a child develops their identity. First, a child develops a sense of themselves as separate from their caregiver. Then, they become aware of having a name, their position in the family, their gender, and so on. These early-to-develop identities might be the core inner rings of who we are; as we develop, we continue to add on more distant identities. For example, the layers of my identities might move from core to outer identities like this: I am Catherine, a daughter, a sister, a cisgender female, a mother, white-identified, a psychologist, a teacher, a writer, a yogini, from California, and so on. The largest outer circles are those identities that we hold loosely; we easily let them go if we move or focus on other priorities. Closer to the center are the identities we hold more dearly. These inner identities may relate to our roles and social belonging in our family, church, or work. Each of us will prioritize our rings differently. Some of us will place work as a more central ring than family, others will center their group affiliations. These rings of identities continue to evolve over a lifetime—fluid, never fixed. Having layers of identities is natural and healthy.

However, our attachments, desires, perspectives, and cultural programming about our identities can be blockades to spiritual awakening. We want others to see us, to validate us, and to recognize our skills and abilities, and so we run around performing for their applause. Even something as beautiful as gender identity (how we express ourselves) or sexual orientation (our desire for others) can become complicated with all the cultural shame added to it. So much of who we are and how we live our lives is based on fulfilling the programming that others have given us. It is difficult to separate which attachments and perspectives are ours and which are not. Spiritual awakening involves loosening our grip on the reins of our identity, giving ourselves the freedom to run freely. A soul attains true liberation when, first, we are fully in the game, attached to all these layers of identity, and then choose our spirit and finally the One Spirit as the most important identity of all. We block knowing our true Self when we cling to our identities.

From a soul's perspective, the layers of our identities are merely dress-up; in the next life, it will be something different. The soul knows it is always connected to and returns to Oneness.

Therefore, at the soul level, life experiences are just sand that we throw around in a sandbox, a way to experience ourselves. Our struggles for self-discovery become opportunities to grow, learn, and dance. We can delight in the *leela*, the Hindu concept of divine play, where god dresses up as us, forgets that this is all an act, then remembers again.

A unique identity experiencing itself as separate, our soul is motivated to learn and grow through lived experience. Life after life, in a body and not in a body, the soul desires to be at Home in Oneness. Still, as an individual identity, we are asleep. When we finally wake up and step beyond our identity as individual souls, we come Home to our true nature: Oneness. We are conscious awareness. We are peace. We are in love, the true nature of our being. Ecstatic bliss for this raw life force constantly explodes inside of us. We see clearly: There is no separation between us and anything else. From this side of the veil, we have deep compassion for others still trapped in form, hiding behind their identities. We rest, knowing we are connected.

The brain injury ripped my identities from my grip. I had to lose my intelligence, my beauty, and my career to awaken to my true nature.

Catapulted From Form

I found comfort in one activity that required no memory and no tracking. His words flowed over my body, rippled over my curves, and formed eddies in available bends. When I had energy, I swept my floor and listened. When I didn't, I lay down and rested in the timelessness of his message. Just as my kids got a free pass past the concussion and into my brain, somehow,

I could drink in the deep, soothing voice and self-deprecating humor of Ram Dass.

I was first introduced to Ram Dass as a spiritual teacher while in graduate school. Born Richard Alpert into an upper-class Jewish Boston family that controlled railroads and created universities, he was raised on the same feedlot grain of achievement and external validation as me. Like me, he played the game, only with greater success, becoming a young professor at Harvard, playing cello, driving sports cars, and flying airplanes. Like a hungry ghost, he flew around fast, doing ever more to consume the empty food of approval. And then one day, Timothy Leary invited him on an adventure in Mexico, where he ingested a plant medicine that allowed him to receive a mainline hookup to Oneness. As he frolicked in the waves in Mexico, the bright dome of the night sky enveloped the earth. There was neither up nor down, hot nor cold, young nor old, nor any form to be attached to. He could live or he could die, and he would be the same either way. Through complex chemical concoctions, he left his Richard-ness again and again, stepping behind the veil into the bliss of the One. He became an expert in this psychedelic method, too, practicing and perfecting doses, initiating others, getting fired from Harvard, jumping again and again on the trampoline to peek over the fence into the abyss, only to bounce back down into his incarnation, the limitations of his body, and the small, tight shoe of his mind.

Reading the *Tibetan Book of the Dead,* Ram Dass learned that formlessness could be approached more like a recipe in a cookbook—now turn around three times, take three deep breaths, and die—rather than the mystery it was in the West. He went east to find these teachers, who knew how to stay high. After a circuitous route through India, he found his guru, divine love in the form of a small old man wrapped in a blanket. After a lifetime of becoming and arriving, he unbecame Richard Alpert and arrived nowhere, resting in the train station between form and formless. He became a servant of the One: Ram Dass.

When I was introduced to his teachings on cassette tapes in my mid-twenties, he was at the height of his Ram Dass-ness, filling auditoriums, advising presidential cabinet members, leading retreats, and publishing books. At that time, I listened to his tapes as I cleaned my apartment, busy sweeping up the detritus of my life, the crumbs from writing a dissertation, trying to acquire approval through the letters p, h, and d. He described how he had stepped off the game board, how he wasn't passing "go" to collect $200 anymore, but I was too much in the game to hear it. What Ram Dass offered remained a curio, an interesting knick-knack that lived on my shelf, something to dust off and admire from time to time.

Twenty years later, as I cleaned my house, wiping up the crumbs of motherhood and gluing together the pieces of me scattered after the bike accident, I saw Ram Dass peeking out behind his form, like a friendly leprechaun, inviting me in for tea.

He said, "As long as you identify with that part of you that is in form, you are merely a lawful happening."[1]

I wondered, *Is this concussion just a lawful unfolding?*

He continued, "Do you want to be the victim, or the Creator? Because as long as you are the incarnation only, you are the victim. You are being had by the law. And you feel yourself caught in stuff that is just happening to you. You didn't ask for it, if you think you are the form. Ah."[2]

I took a breath, drinking it in. I asked myself, *Do I think I am my form, that I am all these layers of identity?*

Catapulted from form, from my roles of dean, psychologist,

mother, woman, I could finally see how Ram Dass stepped out of his roles and rested in freedom. He knew pain and suffering, ego and achievement, attachment and loss. He had played the same academic game that I attempted. He had searched through the drugs and love relationships. Ram Dass had the same self-seeking engine, pistons pumping away, a messy, oil-sputtering combustion engine driving us up the same hill.

And yet, Ram Dass was farther down the road. He sat at the top of the hill in a lotus position, waving a cheery hello, encouraging me onward through the muck of it all. He invited me into the divine play as he rested in Oneness.

He planted a signpost: "But as you begin to acknowledge that part of you that is not in form and even to rest in it, you begin to experience what it feels like to be That which created yourself."[3]

I tried to imagine. *So, I created this bike accident, this opportunity to look at all my identities and become willing to surrender them?* I wanted to use this opportunity to come into more awareness and love.

He encouraged me: "And there is only One of It and It creates. It is Creation by its nature. You could call it God, you could call it Creation, and you are it. And standing nowhere means you are both the Creator and the created."[4]

Ram Dass snapped me out of my current predicament, drunk with identity. He taught me that every experience is grist for the mill that grinds up small mind so we can awaken into the greater One. There was no victimhood—Catherine lying on the pavement that day, missing teeth, the brain she lost, the job she desired, or even the love she craved—there was only this moment to soften into. I surrendered all my identities, all the forms I created, so that I could awaken into my ever-present connection in Oneness.

He went on, "The paradox is when you stand back and you look at the forms of the universe, and you see law. You see the law of karma—or whatever you want to call it, that is one way of calling it—the law of the unfolding of cause and effect, in which everything is related to everything else in the universe, every blade of grass bending is related to everything else. And you stand back, and you are awed by it, and you see your body, and your personality, and your family, and your history is all part of it. And you appreciate the perfection of the unfolding of it all, including the suffering."[5]

I wondered, *Can I bow in gratitude for the suffering I have experienced?*

The suffering and near-death experience of the bike accident made me grateful for the opportunity to place my spiritual connection and my children at the center of my solar system. I parented like tomorrow was not promised, taking them to musicals, creating travel adventures, and moving them through my motherhood bucket list, which sometimes overlapped with their wishes. Meanwhile, I consistently lost what we needed for the journey: passports, driver's license, keys. I delighted in their becoming. In the car, my son would dig his heels into his opinion, then reflect on his part in the conversation and apologize on his own. When, fatigued by the concussion, I snapped at my daughter, only to apologize a moment later, she would respond with sweet forgiveness. I was amazed that my kids were normal.

Work was still like Jupiter, almost a second sun, and over-bloated in my psyche. I was impatient to return to work and felt overly responsible for the whole college. For the first time in my life, I experienced what it means to sit on the sidelines of life, angry and bargaining with god to put me in the game. Although on medical leave, I secretly sent out missive emails, paying for it with nausea and extreme exhaustion. My attachment to work and achievement was evidently greater than my own well-being. Being a dean was a perfect karmic role to play in a game of external validation set on the chess board of academia—neither a knighted teacher, nor the king president, nor queen vice president, but rather a pawn, a highly paid, over-educated pawn, moving forward one step at a time, taking blows from all sides.

Ram Dass drove me home: "The interesting question is who did [lay the suffering on them]. And the answer . . . is that the suffering that I am having, I laid on myself. I am the Creator, and I am the created. I designed my game, and now I am living it out. And now the question is, when I am living it out, do I forget that I designed it?"[6]

A month after the accident, I replaced the skin on my face and had the last pebble cut out from my chin. I saw a chiropractor and a massage therapist and stood up straight again. Fitted with fake teeth, I returned to work. Although I could work, it came at great expense. I spent hours lying down in my office, crying in moments of exhaustion. I handed my power over to my supervisor and colleagues, wondering what people thought of me, wondering if they noticed a difference, wondering, still, after all these years, if I was good enough.

CHAPTER 12

Learning from Experience

Souls transform over lifetimes with the goal of coming Home to the One. The concept of a soul age describes this transformation process along a continuum of new, young, middle, or old souls. We learn from experience, using the darkness to appreciate the light.

Stripped of my identities, recovering in the dark, I found the light of my spirit. My spirit guide stepped forward and claimed me.

Floating Downriver

A year after the accident, I noticed daily what I had lost. I missed my brain, my fabulous coping, remembering, planning brain. I remembered being able to remember—whether I had brushed my teeth or not, instead of feeling the surface of the bristles for confirmation, or why I went into the garage, or if I had seen a movie, rather than having my kids roll their eyes saying, "You watched that with us, Mom." I missed recognizing people by face rather than voice; I missed knowing when I had already met someone, rather than awkwardly saying, "Nice to meet you." I missed being able to navigate a grocery store in an efficient, linear fashion, rather than zig-zagging across the aisles, retracing my steps, unable to visualize the store in my mind to plan my approach.

My sensitivity to sounds changed the trajectory of my life. Instead of letting background conversations at restaurants fatigue me or plugging my ears during the incessant clapping at Twelve-Step meetings, I drove home and sank into the quiet of my couch. Memory was not a given; I worked at it with rehearsal and compensated by becoming the de facto notetaker in every meeting. Emails from myself filled my inbox, as I wrote down every phone call, every conversation, every meeting—an external extension of the memory that used to live in my brain. I struggled and thrashed daily in my job as a dean, but showed up anyway. I knew it was not good for my health, but didn't know what else to do.

I got comfortable sitting in the unknown.

The concussion made me so sensitive to other people's energy that it became essential for me to sit in daily meditation to run my own healing energy. I wanted to wake up. I wanted to use the precious time I had been given to awaken to my own magnificence. I wanted to know myself. I moved through my day as if everything was a spiritual experience, as if the One was always right there, communicating with me through signs, symbols, and omens.

In the sleepiness of my brain, my intuition and clairvoyance woke up. Sitting next to a friend, I saw a bubble of protection around her and knew it was her deceased love. With some nervousness about how it would be received, I leaned over to whisper, "He loves you so much and is sending you a bouquet of daffodils."

Stunned, after a moment, she said, "I can't believe you said that. Someone left me daffodils on my front door today."

In my dreams, I had my first experiences of astral travel. In one dream, I jumped into the sky to fly Home, feeling the wind currents going one way on the surface of the trees and then another direction higher up. I caught a fast stream of air, rushing me in the right direction. Although I was flying fast, I felt stable. When the wind pushed me slightly off course, I dropped my legs down like a rudder. Then my alarm went off, and I tumbled out of the sky and into my body. The landing was so fast, my legs hurt as I lay in bed. I felt the weight of my body, the temperature of the room, and my crushing to-do list.

I collected these experiences as touchstones and placed them in my pocket to remind me that I am a spirit housed inside a body. At night, when I couldn't settle my mind to sleep, I created a vision to relax. I visualized a wide, flat stream in the center of a high desert valley, with purple peaks rising on either side in the distance. For this nighttime voyage, I envisioned lying peacefully in a canoe to look at the stars overhead. I allowed myself to let go and float downstream, feeling the water ripple the edges of my boat. I left my worries behind in parcels bundled on the edge of the shore and noticed the empty landscape, the trees silent witnesses to my journey.

Night after night, I lay down on my boat to float to sleep. I began to see figures on the shore; first outlines, then details emerged of old, wise beings. Our shared ancestry and their gentle, careful watch over my journey were palpable. Night after night, a familiar face emerged, an older woman. As she came to the water's edge, her long gray hair hung over her robe. Her eyes were as black as the expanse of the night sky. I sensed she was there specifically to guide me on my journey. I began to look for her each night and found her in the front of my canoe, paddling gracefully.

I didn't know who she was. But silently she steered me wherever it was that I was going.

Baked Into the Design

Let's consider souls in terms of their age—new, young, middle, or old souls that gain more wisdom, compassion, and capacity for love over many lifetimes.

A soul's journey starts before the dawn of birth. Before each birth, preparations take place in the causal realm. A council of spirit guides and the soul consider the soul's age, previous experiences of love and connection, and next karmic lessons. Each birth is intentional; nothing about who you are is an accident. The council weaves together the conditions, genetic makeup, biological family members, and chosen family members. The individual soul gives consent, and the Supreme Being blesses all life. You have been specifically chosen for this life. Indeed, your soul chose it.

We can compare these cycles of birth, death, and rebirth to the minute hand on an analog clock, dividing the clock into four stages to explore soul ages:

- Twelve o'clock, when we depart from the One as new souls,
- Three o'clock, when we are young souls,

- Six o'clock, when we are middle souls, and

- Nine o'clock, when we are old souls.[1]

There is no value judgment attached to where a soul is in its transformation process, just like the apple blossom is no better or worse than the ripe apple. As Ram Dass said, "We are all god in drag."[2] Older souls see themselves in the antics of young souls and think with compassion, *Been there, done that.* We are all finding our way Home.

Here is the good news: We always awaken to the truth of who we are. Being born is equivalent to enrolling in a class. Our soul is signing up for experiential learning. Once born, we forget we made this choice and get lost in our life stories. At certain points, we may get hints, signs, reminders, and nudges that all is not as it seems. We remember and we forget. Over and over, life after life. But we also live, learn, grow, and love, life after life. Awakening is baked into the design.

Karmic Kindergarten

New souls are just starting on their path to enlightenment. When the minute hand first launches from twelve o'clock, our vibration, that signature light/sound/breath that is us, is embedded in physical form. Pop, we take birth.

When we first start taking bodily form and engaging with the material world, it is disorienting to us as spirits. We forget everything. The veil is firmly in place between the spiritual and the material world. The sights and sounds of this material plane are mesmerizing, like a slot machine with many flashing lights, pumping out cash. We stand there, mouth agape, transfixed. We are deeply driven to figure out how to pump out more cash.

New souls are in karmic kindergarten (in fact, we all are), yet they do not feel safe to make mistakes and learn from them. Pain, loss, and death feel final. As new souls age, they may acquire religious views about life after death, often bifurcating everything into good or bad. For example, some people go to heaven and others to hell.

New souls learn to form basic relationships, which are more black-and-white, all-or-nothing. Driven by the body's urge to procreate, they often give birth to children who are older souls. The new soul will struggle to understand these children and is vulnerable to parenting with criticism and abuse. In this way, new souls become the karmic teacher of older souls. The spiritual challenge for new souls is to build trust with their social group—social clubs, organizations, ethnic groups, and tribal affiliations—with which they strongly identify. Eventually, new souls learn about the importance of relationships and community; belongingness to the group is key to survival.

As the minute hand marches on toward three o'clock, the soul experiences birth, death, and rebirth. The young soul focuses on mastery of the material world, motivated to acquire material possessions, make money, and rise in their careers. They have found their creative energy and can manifest in the material world with abandon—all in service to themselves.

Young souls may pursue spiritual or religious activities because they look to gain something favorable or avoid something unpleasant, and may even be fervent attenders of religious services, memorizing all the right prayers and performing them dutifully. Their religious devoutness can be so sincere that they reverently build and donate, but, motivated by external approval, they will put their family's name on it. Young souls can have a brittle form of spirituality. The "right" line to walk is narrow, and they tend to see others who can't make it as heathens.

As souls move through lifetimes, a new awareness is born. There might be something more. Middle souls have mastered the previous lessons of belongingness and creating in the material realm. They now stand on the precipice, terra firma underneath their feet on one side (materialism), and a foggy unknown across the abyss (spirituality). Just past six o'clock, middle souls experience their first glimmer of spiritual awakening as they stand on that cliff. They look across the chasm and see people holding hands, living in peace and harmony. Middle souls wonder how to get that joy and mistakenly throw themselves harder at material success. A nagging sense of doubt creeps in; they wonder, *What is my purpose?* Mystical experiences may occur, but middle souls doubt to whom they should attribute the experience. Middle souls feel the pressure of time, that there is something here for them to figure out, but are unable to answer their questions.

As middle souls live more lives, approaching seven and eight on the clock, they try to solve this inner spiritual problem by exerting change in the material world. Their intent shifts from building their own empires to acting in service to others. If only I could move this mountain, arrange this peace treaty, provide food for my family and community, all would be well. Repeatedly, middle souls think this loving relationship, this honored title, or this social justice revolution will meet their spiritual needs. They are tireless once they start their quest. Goals and ambitions get loftier, accentuated.

However, material transformation comes to an end when spiritual transformation takes over. Tens of births later, the soul arrives at nine o'clock, now an old soul. At this moment, souls awaken into a birth that is on fire, in a state of spiritual emergency. Old souls attempt to play the material game according to its constricting rules that deny our true spiritual nature. However, the old soul experiences a state of disconnection from its true nature, a dark night of the soul, characterized by depression and despair. These souls can come unraveled early on, unable to function in the material world and not yet heedful of their inner spiritual calling. An old soul may try to manage this spiritual crisis with addiction-induced unconsciousness. Most old souls hit bottom trying to live life according to the rulebook they inherited. "Failing" at the game is a good sign that you are awakening.

As old souls learn, they begin to acknowledge there is something greater than this material world, yet they repeatedly get sucked back into the vortex. At some point, the world stops spinning for them. The crisis erupts fully. All systems crash. Old souls experience this as total devastation, the worst possible outcome.

Their life, their reputation, and their identity as they know it are now over.

And yet, in this devastation reside the lessons for spiritual awakening. Old souls can return to those unanswered questions: "What does it all mean?" and "What am I here to do?"

Asking the questions is more important than finding the answers. These questions launch us on our spiritual journey. Over lifetimes, old souls pursue, advance, and then retreat to fear-based thoughts again. Meanwhile, the glowing love of the One pulls them closer. As old souls move toward eleven o'clock, a deep knowing of their spiritual nature arises. They no longer wonder, because they know. Material experience is spiritual transformation.

Old souls may become spiritual leaders or farmers. It does

not matter. Awakening is their full-time occupation. There is no point in attaining desires, and they have nowhere to go, because they are already Home in the One. In other words, an old soul may not achieve much in the material world and may seem unimpressive to younger souls.

At eleven fifty-nine, old souls drop the body one last time, with no sense of loss, and come to rest in their I Am.

In Between

The next step after death, for spirits who are no longer attached to bodies, is to transition to the astral plane. Ram Dass said, "death is absolutely safe" and is like "taking off a tight shoe."[3] Part of what we are here to learn is how to transition in and out of our bodies through death. Some spirits have a difficult time transitioning to the spirit realm after leaving their bodies, as part of their consciousness remains tied to the material world. Some may have difficulty letting go of their physical form and will be fixated on trying to get back in. Perhaps it is like thinking you are stuck in an elevator while ignoring the open door.

In between lifetimes, our consciousness exists on the astral plane. Like sitting in neutral gear waiting for the stoplight to turn green, we wait for the right circumstances for our next birth. Spirits on the astral plane stay connected to events in the material world only if they choose to. Just because someone is dead does not mean their spirit is available to help. For example, a spirit that crossed over due to suicide may be busy healing. Another may have few connections remaining on earth if they were socially isolated or the last of their kin. Some souls have a sense of completion and let go of their attachment to what is happening in the material realm. Many spirits are focused on their own healing or helping others on the astral plane.

Some spirits interact with the material world out of their own self-interest, and so it is important that we pay attention to the energy we attract. Do we invite more light or dark into our lives? Our spirit guides can't protect us from the energy we allow in. Only we can do that through our own conscious choices, learning how to protect ourselves from outside spirits. Imagine a telemarketer is calling to offer their product for sale. Do we pick up the call, or let it go to voicemail? We can have "seniority" over the energy around us by building awareness and running our own energy.

We each have a network of souls whose liberation is tied to our own. Traveling together as a pack across lifetimes, we help each other awaken. Teachers help guide us in the spirit world, just as they do in the material world. Some spirits will allocate part of their consciousness to watching over and caring for their still-living loved ones, desiring to help on their karmic journey of awakening. The fastest superhighway to reach those who have crossed over is through love. Then listen, pay attention to your intuition, and be present to receive any communication.

It took me decades of searching, meditating, praying, and perhaps a head injury to receive my first direct communication from my spirit guide.

My Patient Teacher

In the year after the accident, despite all the cognitive abilities lost, I gained something too: the ability to communicate with Spirit. In the mornings, I eased into a daily meditation practice—make coffee, burn something, pray, and run my energy. Closing my eyes, I would find Teri there waiting for me, right on time. I knew it was her because I felt the indelible sensation of her fingerprints on my heart again. We developed a routine: Teri would offer her hand to me, and I would clasp it, stepping out of my body to explore with her and then back in to write down the experience, like an anthropologist on the astral plane. Teri became my bridge from the material to the spiritual.

One morning, Teri and I flew off together, hand in hand. We flew higher and higher, over treetops that rippled up to a mountainside. At the edge of a forest, we landed in a grassy meadow. The grass poked my bare feet. We wore jewel-encrusted crowns with sparkling white robes that trailed behind us in the sunshine. It was so opulent. I wondered if it was my ego and changed the image. We became humble, dressed in hemp cloth. I changed it again. Now we were merely our naked bodies. But even that was attached to form, so I let our bodies go, and we were just specks of consciousness. Unaffected by my futzing, Teri silently glided upward to a cave entrance. I followed, ducking inward to the darkness.

The cave walls encircled a compacted dirt floor, dimly lit with the golden light of a central fire. The gray silhouettes of beings silently sitting around in a circle were barely visible. I knew this was a council of awakened ones.

From the darkness, a figure stepped forward. Her long gray hair touched the floor, her face was brown and wrinkled, and her black eyes contained galaxies. It was her, the one who had been guiding my river journeys. My spirit guide.

She said, "You have never been alone. Indeed, you are always connected, guided, and sustained by the One's loving presence. Your soul council is with you."

I intuitively knew that my spirit guide and I were not related by blood, and we didn't speak the same language. In fact, she never opened her mouth to utter words, yet, somehow, I knew what she was communicating. Where Teri's communication was fast and high-pitched, hers was slow and methodical.

Over time, I have come to know her as a no-nonsense spirit guide. She is not moved by the drama of the physical plane. She does not mess around. Every word she transmits is crafted for impact. She has seen it all—infant mortality, murder, suicide, death—again and again, and yet she is pure light, drumming with the rhythm of life. I am her student. She is my patient teacher. And I clearly need schooling, consumed with questions related to my attachments, about relationships, work, and what I should do with my life. Meanwhile, she answers different questions, the questions I should be asking, about how to find peace, awaken, and be free. Each morning, she waits for me in her cave of en-lightenment. She is always there, guiding, holding, and loving. She is like a mother who never quits, never dies, never moves on.

Shocked that I finally met my spirit guide after so many years of asking and searching, I couldn't let myself stay with her. I bowed backward out of the cave and returned to the top of my head, easing back into my body. Eyes closed, pen in hand, I lis-tened for any message.

Teri said, "Your number one life lesson is that there is no place where god is not."

My heart immediately responded with a question: "What about loss?"

"What is loss?" Teri asked. "Where could the soul go that love would not find it? Love is a network that connects us across the globe and across planes of existence. In a heartbeat, we can be there, present, one heart, beating together. Feel the richness in your heart, inside your chest, where love resides."

I admitted that I didn't know what to do.

Teri went on. "You worry about what is the next right thought or action. Worries are of the body and small mind. Big Mind, Big Heart knows we are all connected. The web of love is always there, and so it has no worries. Be present in love. Let fear fall away, sliding off your body like armor.

"Your divine nature is being revealed to you. You asked for the school, and now you are taking the curriculum. You have stepped beyond the veil and saw your soul community waiting for you. We are here for you. Our work is not done until yours is done. That is the agreement. My hand will always be there to guide you over. You will know it's my hand because of the fingerprints I left on your heart."

She repeated, "You are guided, loved, and sustained by a power beyond measure."

For the first time, I was not believing. I was not relying on faith. I knew the truth of her words because I experienced it. I met my teacher. I saw my soul council. I felt Teri's touch.

For the first time, I felt specifically loved and cared for—guided by Spirit.

CHAPTER 13

Spirit Communication

When we live a Spirit-guided life, we can own our spiritual abilities. I was not gifted with natural mediumship. I studied and practiced to become an intuitive medium, just as I studied and practiced to become a clinical psychologist. I learned how to ride the bike by getting on it.

I am not special or different. As a child, I did not feel the intrusive presence of departed grandparents. Yet, I was a sensitive kid, Like a piano string, I reverberated with the feelings of others. I parlayed my natural empathy and interest in people's life stories into being a psychologist. I am not special or different, so how is it that I can communicate with spirits that don't have bodies?

I am a good student. I practiced what I was taught.

While raising kids and working full-time, I attended classes to develop mediumship skills. In my morning meditations, I practiced the skills I learned, bringing my consciousness into a higher vibration, stepping out of my body, and using my astral spirit to heal it. I found a mentor who was a locally renowned psychic medium, and she taught me her method for conducting readings. I took notes and practiced daily. But no one could tell me how to be an intuitive medium, just like no one could tell me how to ride a bike. I had to find my own way of communicating with Spirit.

Validation

As I lay on his massage table, a feeling of unease came over me. I had received massages from Graham before and requested him by name at the spa. I never understood what our connection was and wondered if I was attracted to him. He was a fine specimen of a human for sure. His interest in fitness rippled under his t-shirt, and I received the benefit of it in his hands. But curiously, I felt no desire for him, perhaps because I could see the suffering in his eyes.

When I got on the massage table, I began practicing the skills from my mediumship class to heal myself. Without saying a word, I owned the room and removed anyone's leftover energy. I dropped my grounding cord, set my seventh chakra to a clean white, and closed down my lower three chakras. Without effort, I brought my awareness out of my body to the top of my head. Meanwhile, Graham was silently moving through his own routine of loosening my spine with the sheet covering my back, warming up his hands and my skin before we made contact. When his oiled fingers began to find painful nooks in my body, I set about healing it from my spirit, sending my own white healing light where I was storing other people's energy. Pressure, pain, white light, healing. Pressure, pain, white light, healing.

I repeated this practice until anxiety began to build.

I heard the name Mary very clearly and dismissed it. It is my mother's name and my grandmother's name, and so I assumed that I had just found a remnant of their energy in my body during the massage. But that conclusion did nothing to release the grip of unease.

Now I saw the name spelled out for me, slowly, painstakingly, in large red block letters: M A R Y. I tried to send the thought away again.

The big red letters flashed in front of me.

"Okay, okay, I get it," I told Spirit mentally.

Now, I was in a real pickle. Did I want to ask my massage therapist if this information belonged to him, risking total invalidation and judgment for the rest of the massage while I lay there naked, or could I let it go? Ever protective of my ego, I tried to let it be a random thought. But the free-floating anxiety came closer to me when I tried to send the thought away.

I waited as long as I could, until the massage was almost over, before I asked him a question.

"I am wondering if we can play a little game?" I said tentatively. Clearly, this was an awkward invitation for a stranger who was rubbing oil on my body.

"Um. Sure," he replied kindly.

"So, I am studying how to be a psychic medium, and I would like to bring forward information for you and just have you say yes or no to validate it or not. How does that sound?"

"All right . . . " He responded slowly enough that I really didn't know what he thought about this game.

Rather than zeroing in on my target, I started around the edges.

"I'm seeing an 'M' name, a female's name. It sounds like 'Mare.'" Then I offered all kinds of options despite hearing "Mary" yelled at me inside my skull. "It could be Marilyn or Marleen or . . . Mary."

"Well, that's very interesting," he said intellectually. "My grandmother's name is Mary."

At that moment, the anxiety vanished, and I basked in the glory of his validation. Before, all I could see and hear was, "Mary, Mary, Mary." Now, information poured into me.

"I see her as your maternal grandmother, is that so?"

"Yes," he said through a smile. "But, also, my father's mom is a Mary too."

That additional validation hit me like a thunderclap. I saw her on the right side of my screen, where maternal information comes through for me, while paternal is on the left.

"This is on your mother's side," I affirmed, then continued. "I see her holding a little dog with her. And I'm sorry, she is saying it is a yappy dog."

"Oh my god! Oh my god," he exclaimed. I could feel his emotional release as he said, "You have no idea what that means to me." He shared that his Pomeranian had just passed away the week before. While she was the sweetest girl for him, she would have been "yappy" for anyone else.

With those validations, the information continued to flow: his grandfather, who was a carpenter-craftsman, his grandmother's Germanic cooking, his career choices, and his struggles to coparent with his ex-partner. His grandmother closed the reading when he had clearly received enough information to know that he was guided and loved. We both had healthy enough boundaries to end the massage on time, letting the gift from Spirit be what it was and not asking for more.

As I walked out of the room, I floated on pure joy and gratitude that I could be of service in that way.

Spirit Communication

Mediumship, the ability to communicate with Spirit, is not easy. It requires that we decolonize our minds, letting go of what we were taught about the world and our abilities, and heal out of our space all the voices, objections, opinions, and perspectives that we have unwittingly accepted into our psyches over a lifetime. It requires us to stand in our sovereignty and access a deep inner knowing to differentiate between thoughts arising from ego, personal perspective, or small mind from the thoughts, intuitions, and visions coming from Spirit. Directly connected to our ability to meditate, mediumship depends on our capacity to pause, listen deeply, and trust absolutely in our intuition.

Also, mediumship is easy. We communicate with Spirit all the time and just consider it a thought, intuition, or hunch. We get gut feelings, goose bumps, creepy crawlies, or mental images, and we run toward things or away from things without knowing why. We receive these impressions and misattribute the origin to ourselves. I have labeled this "fundamental source misattribution error,"[1] where we mistakenly think our thoughts and feelings are our own, rather than seeing them as energy in our space. Likewise, we receive messages from nature and attribute them to coincidence. We have been socialized to become deaf to this cacophony of communication.

Let's explore the two possibilities—that we are natural mediums, gifted with clairvoyant/audient/sentient abilities, and that, through spiritual practice, we all have the potential for spirit communication.

Natural Mediumship Abilities

Communicating with spirit involves natural ability. Some of us are predisposed, with nervous systems that have heightened sensitivities to the spirit world, just like some people are good with directions and others are perpetually lost. People with natural mediumship abilities often grow up feeling different or "other" and receive messages that they are "too sensitive." Individuals who have inherited psychic and mediumship abilities often appear to be on the spectrum of neurodivergence. Their super-responsive nervous systems leave them on edge as they pick up information around them that others disregard. It is confusing to perceive "extra" sensory information unverified by others. Natural, gifted mediums may turn away from their gift if invalidated, or step into their power if reinforced.

When most people with natural abilities communicate with Spirit, they retain a sense of themselves, their ego and identity. They understand that the voices, imagery, and impressions are coming from outside of them. A smaller portion of people lose their center. Their "center cannot hold," as lawyer and professor Ellen Saks wrote, borrowing a line from poet William Butler Yeats to describe her lived experience with schizophrenia.[2] For this subset of our community, these voices, visions, and spirit communication constitute a confusing array of information originating in here, out there, and everywhere. Western, industrialized culture pathologizes the experience of hearing voices as a "mental illness." Perceptions with no sensory information are labeled hallucinations and delusions, key qualifying symptoms for stigmatized, sticky diagnoses like psychotic disorders. Disconnected from a spiritual context, we simply blame the brain's neurotransmitters. Even the neurotransmitter explanation is not satisfactory, however, and simply demonstrates another correlation.[3]

Actually, it is normal to hear voices. Researchers from Yale University report that "non-clinical hearing voices" occurs on a spectrum that includes "normal," healthy functioning:

> Hallucinations of a loved one are common following bereavement. Non-clinical hallucinations also occur in the general population. Estimates of their prevalence are as high as 28% and only 25% of those . . . meet the diagnostic criteria for a psychotic disorder. Thus, hallucinations may best be described as an extreme of normal functioning rather than a failure of modularity.[4]

Yale created a center to study the experience of hearing voices, the COPE Project, which stands for Control/Influence Over Perceptual Experiences.[5] Pivoting from the customary psychiatric practice of studying suffering people who hear voices and struggle to function, the COPE Project instead focuses on people who hear voices yet function well, without psychiatric support. This group of the "general population" maintains a sense of ego-integrity. The center of their being can hold the experience of hearing voices. One participant described her experience:

> I only experience voices when I want to. I can turn them off and keep them off until and if I decide I want to talk

to them[. . .] It wasn't always that way, though. Once I learned it was even possible to influence my voice-hearing experience, I put effort into developing that skill. It changed my life.[6]

The researchers, still encapsulated within a Western deficit model, hope to learn from this healthy, functioning group of people coping strategies to share with the minority of people who become unbound when hearing voices.

Meanwhile, many Indigenous wisdom traditions celebrate individuals who hear voices and revere their role as shamans.[7] The word shaman represents a person who can interact with the spirit world in altered states of consciousness. Across many wisdom traditions, the unusual experience of hearing voices and seeing visions is understood and valued as a spiritual calling. For instance, the Jivaro of the western Amazon believe that voices are communications from ancestors, plants, animals, or evil spirits. Shamanic initiation entails learning to tell the difference. Among the Yanomami of Brazil, the shaman must undergo a long initiation in which voices and visions are induced to help foster personal and meaningful relationships with spirits, in the hope that the spirits will become allies.[8]

Likewise, in Hindu yogic philosophy, there is an understanding that, along the path of enlightenment, breakthroughs can manifest as breakdowns. Psychiatrist Lee Sanella, co-founder of the Kundalini Clinic in San Francisco, brought to the West the concept of kundalini awakening, states resembling psychosis caused when the chakras fully open and release spiritual energy.[9] Some mental health practitioners are exploring how to integrate a spiritual understanding of kundalini awakening psychosis with mental health treatment.[10] When situated in an understanding cultural context, a community can lovingly hold an individual experiencing kundalini awakening.

In theory, the distinction between a shaman or a medium and someone suffering with mental health challenges is their (a) level of psychological distress, (b) level of functioning in everyday life, and (c) cultural interpretation. In practical application, however, advanced spiritual states can also be distressing at times and make it hard to function in everyday situations, especially when the material world does not mirror your experience.

Am I saying that everyone who hears voices or sees things is having a spiritual experience? Absolutely not. I affirm that our minds can be unhealthy and function poorly. However, I also hold that everyone with lived mental health experience also has a spiritual nature. Therefore, considering the spiritual well-being of people presenting with mental health issues is an important part of the assessment. Similarly, I reject any notion that there is something wrong with me because I hear and perceive things that others do not. In fact, communicating in spirit is one of the most fulfilling parts of my life.

In 1989, psychiatrist Stan Grof and his wife Christina published their book, *Spiritual Emergency: When personal transformation becomes a crisis,* to help Western mental health professionals understand intense, disruptive spiritual experiences.[11] They categorized nine major forms of spiritual emergencies: shamanic crisis, the awakening of kundalini, peak experience episodes, renewal states that involve integrating the light and the dark, psychic openings, past-life experiences, communication with spirit guides, near-death and after-death experiences, experience with non-earthly beings, and possession states. The Grofs described the problem created by the limiting Western mental health perspective for people in spiritual emergency:

The worldview created by traditional Western science and dominating our culture is, in its most rigorous form, incompatible with any notion of spirituality. In a universe where only the tangible, material, and measurable are real, all forms of religious and mystical activities are seen as reflecting ignorance, superstition, and irrationality or emotional immaturity. Direct experiences of spiritual realities are then interpreted as "psychotic"— manifestations of mental disease.[12]

I hear voices not attached to bodies. Am I deranged, or living my best life? Your answer depends on your culture. To be clear, I'm a card-carrying psychologist, and I believe that we can suffer psychologically just as we do physically. Our body can be sick. Our brain can be sick. Classification systems such as the Diagnostic and Statistical Manual (DSM) can be helpful by offering a shared descriptive language system.

Yet, mental health classification systems, including the DSM, can also be extremely harmful, even deadly. All classification systems for psychological suffering arise within a specific cultural milieu, encapsulating the oppressive power dynamics of their time. For example, the current labeling system, the DSM-5, struggles to acknowledge cultural differences, gender on a spectrum, the impact of trauma on our development, the power of social context, and our connection to ourselves, the earth, community, nature, and spirit. Consequently, it invalidates Indigenous knowledge and pathologizes people of color, nonbinary genders and diverse sexualities, people who grow up poor and exposed to trauma, and women. Psychology struggles to appropriately attribute the role of culture, society, socialization, racism, sexism, homophobia, and other pathologies of colonist society in dis-ease. The DSM waves this invalidation away by adding a class of modifiers to diagnoses, so-called V-codes, which are other issues that may be a focus of clinical attention. For example, V-code 62 is a broad catch-all category for social problems, including housing, acculturation, social rejection, and crime, as well as "religious and spiritual problems."[13]

Perhaps one day we will perceive the cultural assumptions in which we swim.[14] For example, instead of diagnosing a person with a body dysmorphic disorder, what if we could label and treat the society that is hyper-fixated on narrow beauty standards? What if we could diagnose systemic racism rather than label the person of color with depressed mood, which could be normalized and expected due to racialized trauma? What if we could acknowledge we are spirits in bodies that can communicate with spirits not in bodies—and see our presentation not as symptoms but as indicators of our spiritual well-being? What if we could transfer power away from the pathologizing, oppressive few who create diagnoses, and instead empower the people? We would diagnose our society as diseased for not acknowledging our spirit. We could guide the person presenting with anxiety to ground, the person with depression to move energy, and the person hearing voices to regulate spirit communication.

I'm a psychologist and also a spirit in a body. I believe that we can have biological, psychological, and spiritual etiologies for our suffering. I strive to integrate my experience of Spirit with the material world. Other cultures include Spirit in their analysis of well-being and treatment of suffering. We can too.

Psychic and mediumship abilities can be a blessing or cause for suffering, depending on an individual's karmic predicament and socio-cultural location. Just as someone with artistic or athletic talent needs to practice their craft or sport, spiritual abilities come with the responsibility for development. Every gifted medium with natural ability must learn how to control when they receive information and when they turn their antennae off. They must learn how to ground and live in the material world ("know your zip code," as Ram Dass said), as well as play on the astral plane.

The first rule of mediumship is that the medium is there to heal themselves. You cannot communicate information from Spirit to others if your own channel is blocked. Similarly, the Big Book of Alcoholics Anonymous says, "The answers will come, if your own house is in order. But obviously you cannot transmit something you haven't got."[15] The same is true for psychic readings. The reader is constantly looking for areas where their own energy is stuck, removing those images in order to read clearly.

My Partnership with A Spirit Guide

I, however, was not gifted with mediumship abilities. I practiced daily to communicate with Spirit. And I wanted more. I always want more.

I wanted to be the next Tyler Henry, Teresa Caputo, John Edward, or James Van Praagh. I wanted to start shaking with anxiety in the grocery store line and feel the pressure to share information with the checkout clerk about her deceased relative. I wanted to break out into a sweat, my body experiencing the cause of death of a client's loved one. I wanted to be an evidential medium, bringing forward the facts—names, dates, places, secret signs—that would utterly convince my client that the spirit world was indeed here. I wanted Hollywood to be my client. I wanted camera crews and film editors who cut out the awkward moments and jumped from validation to validation. I wanted to not have questions anymore, to just know. Everything.

Is that too much to ask?

Laughing at me, with me, in and through me, Meera couldn't care less about the small games my ego plays, my desire to be seen by others. She is not here merely to validate. She is not going to bend over backward to dig up the name of your dog and present it on a platter. Meera is willing to work with my thick head, steeped in skepticism, because we need to awaken now. She is here as a guide, transporting us through suffering to freedom.

Even though I took classes and developed a mentorship with an evidential medium, I had to find my own way. In my morning meditations, my soul council showed me how to conduct mediumship readings. They outlined the structure of the sessions: morning meditation to receive information, opening and closing prayers, orientation for clients, and even when to create a public-facing website.

I have to let go of my own personal concerns—relationship, money, chores, what the heck am I doing with my life—to neutrally receive the information Meera shares. Sitting in front of Meera, I simply bring my client's name forward and see what happens next. Sometimes, when I am trusting and in flow, we start to journey. She brings me into the client's life and shows me their karmic struggles. Other days, I have trouble hearing, and so I give her a blank chalkboard, and she writes her messages down. Sometimes, when I really struggle to get past myself, I give her a question and offer yes/no boxes for her to light up. Pen in hand, I write down whatever comes without judgment. I have a page of notes before I even meet with a client.

The truth is, I don't need Meera, but rather choose to work with her and am grateful for our partnership. Without Meera, I can still achieve states of higher consciousness, step out of my body, and communicate with other spirits. But Meera is special. She is dedicated to the enlightenment of our souls, and so she gets directly to the heart of the issue. Before every session, I am terrified that Meera won't be there, that I will show up to the reading with zero information. But Meera is always there and ready to work. She knows when to start sessions and will end them exactly on time. If I have a 9 a.m. appointment with a client, at 9:55 she will close up shop and stop relaying information, giving me exactly the few minutes I need to end the call. When you make an appointment with a medium, you make an agreement with Spirit, asking them to present at a certain time. They are a punctual bunch. I have never had a session go over the agreed-upon time, even when I'm drifting on the astral plane, listening deeply.

When sitting with a client, I first go through a brief orientation, asking if they have ever had a reading before, and explaining briefly how I work and what our session will look like. I explain that I have already been sitting with them for forty-five minutes and that after we start with a prayer, I will bring that information forward. I offer to record the session so they can relax and just be present. I let them know that we will have time for their questions.

The factual evidence comes into my awareness as whispers. Intellectually, hearing names is the hardest for me because the stigma in my mind doubts that I will get it right. How can you possibly pick a name out of thin air? I will hear an "L" sound, then it builds to "Li." I write that down and let it go. A client's validations help me relax and encourage me to bring the whispers forward.

When I say the "L" name or "Li," and they say that their grandmother was "Ashley Levi, could that be it?"

"Yes!" I want to jump up and shout, "That can definitely be it!" Imagine how hard it is for spirit to break through all the thoughts in my head to give me that sound.

In one reading, I said, "This is kind of funny, but I keep hearing Tom Brokaw."

My client responded, "That is my good friend Tom. He was a real estate broker." Of course he was, why did I ever doubt saying this?

For another client, I saw the number seventeen and bravely said so for no apparent reason.

They replied, "My birthday is on the seventeenth." Yep, thanks again, Meera.

I saw another client's son as a tall sprout with a thin stem. When I presented this seemingly random image, he affirmed that his son had a bone-related growth disorder. Once, I told a client that she regularly went into a womb to light a candle, a healing sacred space, and that she had the wings of Archangel Gabriel wrapped around her, such that she was essentially married to Spirit. Now, it's a little awkward to tell someone she goes into a womb to pray and an angel is her boyfriend, but I have to say what I see. She responded that she prayed to Mary Magdalene and to three angels daily, including Gabriel, and that she may indeed be married to Spirit. Mediumship requires me to trust my guides and my skills more than the voice in my head yelling, "This is utter nonsense!"

As a medium, it is not enough to offer the information. Sometimes the information that we receive is too hot for the client to handle. Meera lets me know when the information is sensitive and to proceed carefully. Occasionally, when I receive information in my morning meditation, I can sense that my client will not be ready to hear it directly. I knew one client would divorce her husband before she even thought about it. When I saw her again six months later, the divorce was unfolding. I rely on my teaching skills to wrap the information in the context of our karmic journey and provide spiritual guidance on how to move through a difficult moment.

One client was slowly lifting the rug to expose her childhood pain. Rather than say it so directly, I said, "I can see your heart chakra pouring out buckets of pain, like buckets of rain. It is a lot of deep healing that you are doing. Other, more mortal souls would crumble under the weight of the pain, so I just want to honor you as a spirit. The fact that you are not a drug addict sitting with a heroin needle in your arm is amazing."

She affirmed that she had heard so many times that people were amazed that she was never on the streets.

I went on, "You are a miracle, but part of that self-sacrifice is shunting off this pain. I see that stuck energy in your fourth chakra and traveling down your arm channels." Here, I switched to teaching mode, explaining, "Your arm channels are your creative channels. So if you are feeling stuck in your creativity, I don't want you to think that is a bad thing or a negative thing. Instead, you can say to yourself that you are doing some deep healing work. That stuck energy may say things to you, like 'I don't know what is true for me,' or 'I don't know what I want to create,' or kind of like a foggy feeling or lack of clarity. I want to speak to you as a spirit and say that means you are moving energy out of your space. Anything you can do to help your energy flow, practice those tools because it will help the indecision clear out of your space."

Good mediumship provides action steps that the person can continue on their own to further their awakening, rather than developing dependency on the medium. Mediumship is not "simply" about receiving information from Spirit and saying what you see. It also involves providing a safe and sacred container for the reading, as well as the interpretative context to help the client understand how stuck energy plays out in our lives.

Validation from clients helps the session to flow, like seeing a signpost on a trailhead. And, I do not need their validation. I've already sat with Meera and seen and written what she wanted me to say. Meera is concerned with the choices my clients make on their path. She reminds them to look past the illusions and remember who they are. She wants us all to know that we are the creators of our path, that we have been given the gift of free will. Meera offers information about where my clients are struggling, where they are allowing other people's energy to drive their own bus. She wants to remind us that we are sovereign. She reminds my hardworking clients that they are worthy of their own time and attention. Meera hopes that we will consider our life lessons and suffering—death, divorce, children, agreements—as stepping stones that deliver us Home. She reminds my clients that standing in their truth will not only set them free, but liberate everyone around them as well.

In one morning meditation, Teri and I bowed to Meera, honoring her power. With a corkscrew in hand, Meera unceremoniously drilled through my skull at my third eye and performed a brain transplant, removing my old way of thinking. This new brain sees Spirit in everything.

Meera is not messing around. She is asking me to wake up now. She is not concerned with perfecting parlor tricks of psychic ability and mediumship. Instead, Meera reveals the raw power of a swirling black hole, where darkness breaks apart light, maintaining the karmic laws of balance, retribution, and equal and opposite reaction. It destroys the material world, chewing up planets and solar systems, the ultimate karmic digestor.

Our Earth is headed toward one. Now.

We need to wake up to our spiritual natures. Now.

CHAPTER 14

Oneness

We live in Oneness. Oneness is who we are, where we are, and how we are. Peace and bliss are our birthright. The suffering caused by separation is the vehicle we use to drive us Home.

Relationships have always been the source of my greatest suffering—and my best teacher.

A Vein of Gold

The predicament of my lifetime came in the form of a man built like a tree. He was me in a man's body, a little weather-beaten with all the childhood trauma, pain, and suffering, all the self-seeking pathways that led us both to god's doorstep. Here we were again in this lifetime, zipped up in new spacesuits, repackaged for one more attempt. He was a special delivery human—a committed bachelor avoiding emotional intimacy and trying to please everyone as if they were his alcoholic father, meanwhile hiding his truth under the rug. And my brave, dumb heart was firmly in the ring, present to do my work. I was fully ready to be at Home in the One as we explored how we ended up as two.

How could I have understood this when I first met him at a sleepover when I was fifteen? My best friend, Phoenix, lived in a remote village surrounded by state and national parks. The land itself had been moving north at glacial speeds over the last 400 million years, starting out in Santa Barbara, breaking off from the North American plate, and crunching its way northward on the Pacific plate, inch by inch, year after year. Her hamlet acted like its own sovereign land, barely associating itself with the affluent county that draped around it like a fur shawl. The families that settled on that land, on top of the Coast Miwok First Peoples, never left once they found it. The homesteaders and the hippies and the wealthy, second-home-owning, old-money San Francisco families and the Chinese who did their laundry all flowed together in one confluence, draining into the bay.

One uneventful day at dusk, as the sun nestled below the hillside next to Phoenix's family's wood cabin, there was a ruckus outside. Truck doors slammed, and a man berated his kids.

"It's my cousins!" Phoenix said with excitement as she raced to open the front door.

He was so beautiful. My cheeks stung, but who had slapped me? Although two years younger than me, pushing through puberty at thirteen, he was already taller and broad in his chest, wearing a red and white baseball uniform. Clark. Pink puffy clouds turned golden and then purple as we chatted on the front porch. And nothing happened. At fifteen, I was going way too fast to slow down for a boy.

Nothing happened except for thirty years of life. His thread wound its way through relationships, travel, art school, addiction, and recovery. Meanwhile, my thread also sewed through addiction and recovery, but followed my family pattern of degrees, academia, marriages, kids, and divorces, weaving in and out of love, in and through spiritual experiences. And then one day, after forty-something circles around the sun, I saw him and swiped right. We made a date to see a movie in the same town where I got sober, on the same block where I had my first psychic reading with Lisa many years prior.

I felt the familiarity of my inner teenager taking hold of the steering wheel. I was so excited to see him as a grown-ass woman, I skipped down the familiar sidewalk as I greeted him.

"Wow," he said, "You are high energy."

"Sorry," I replied as I shrank.

"No," he said with a broad smile, "It's a good thing."

I sat next to him in the movie theater and felt the energy ripple beneath my skin, then rise, arcing between us. It was all I could do to sit in my seat.

When I finally walked into his house, he grabbed my hands and hoisted me up with ease for a kiss, like I was lighter than the logs he slung all day. Feeling his stable foundation, I pushed down into my palms, straightening my arms, locking my elbows, floating my body above his head, improvising our own dirty figure skating routine. My legs pressed out into a straddle V, his face right there where the sun never shines on me, and yet he did. He kissed me there, at the center of my being. It was all so easy and effervescent. Our bodies fit like empty spaces made to be filled up by each other. Like a yoga asana poster, I saw all the positions we could explore over a lifetime.

He stroked my eyebrows, and with my eyes closed, I clearly saw his soul behind his face. I was on both planes simultaneously, making love to his essence while enjoying his beautiful packaging. No attachments, commitments, expectations, limitations, or judgments. Just pure, violent, coursing, pulsating, rolling, shuddering love. I wanted to cry but didn't feel safe. I felt my heart open for him and knew that I would always love him. And I felt my vulnerability, knowing that I was the only one with those feelings. I wrapped his arms around me, soaking in the cuddles I needed. When he drifted off to sleep, I slipped out in the dark, quietly like a fox, creeping back out into the night. On my own, with One who would never leave me.

And after every incredible weekend together, I would see him back online fishing. I didn't understand why he would continue to search after finding god's nectar. Why would he say he missed me, then text instead of call, send emojis instead of words? How can you find a thick vein of gold and not mine it? Worse than that, how could you pick up your axe and labor elsewhere? Confused and mad at god for bringing us together, for making the spark so big, I felt infected. I couldn't get him out of my system. I dragged him everywhere like an army duffel bag that I never got to open—just carried the weight of attachment.

I called up god on the batphone to start hostage negotiations with my sex life: "I know the Bhagavad Gita says I'm supposed to do my duty and devote myself to you and all that, but it feels like you are asking me to be a nun, and I did not sign up for that this lifetime. I want the external validation, please, thank you very much."

Long pause. In the silence, I assumed that, apparently, god was to be my husband.

Trying to find the positive, I offered fake consent: "That's cool, I guess." Being a nun comes with a nice house, a mansion with many rooms. And yet the bottom to my stomach was still missing, and I was breathing my organs out onto the floor.

Finally, I heard, "There is no separation. We are all One."

The solution presented itself. These deep soul connections, these heavenly bodies in my orbit, are all woven into the fabric by the Great Weaver Herself. How could we ever say goodbye? How could we ever be separated? We only have to touch the thread to feel the vibrations ripple through.

The solution to my disconnection tantalized me like a mirage in the desert. I got to decide for myself what love would look like. What if it were unconditional, unattached, devoted, and connected? What if I lived my life as if there was no separation? How would I react when I met another soul? Could I see the One in them? Could I let them be on their journey, capable of free will, and compassionately understand their choices? "Hey, you do you. Go do your dharma. Go to sleep if you need to. Reject me if you must. The One awaits. The journey is timeless, and all is forgiven. There are no mistakes, only lessons in the curriculum of love."

I wanted to take the curriculum. I was so thirsty, I fell down and lapped up the water.

But I was the only one at the watering hole. He was nowhere to be found.

Free will. Ain't that a bitch.

Love Is the Miracle

Let's rewind the clock to before our solar system existed, when our building blocks were just the burp, the excess of a greater explosion that happened long ago, farther away. We cooled, we coalesced, we formed into heavenly bodies that now hold each other in gravitational balance, a solar system with planets and exoplanets. Our planet is the just-right distance from the sun for water to flow as liquid, has enough iron at its core to create a protective magnetic field against solar particles, is wrapped in a warm blanket of atmosphere, and contains the perfect atomic ring of carbon. Abiogenesis, the transition of organic compounds into living matter, occurred somewhere in the dark depths of an ocean, next to a warm hydrothermal vent, when a leaky cell self-replicated for the first time.

Life evolved, and that is a miracle, but in a universe of infinite possibilities, life must also be evolving on other planets. Life diversified and adapted, and whatever promoted survival was carried on. Mass extinctions happened, and some strains of life continued. Mammals evolved and scurried around the feet of towering dinosaurs. They were the underdogs, food for others. In burrows, we tended to our young, groomed their fur, and slept together in a pile. Tending, bonding, and caring were selected for in our genetic code. Specialized pathways evolved in our nervous systems. Dopamine, serotonin, norepinephrine, oxytocin, vasopressin, anandamide, endorphins—different building blocks that trigger our feelings of coziness, relaxation, release, peace, orgasmic flow, bursting joy, and Oneness. We moved from trees to the savanna, and our troops survived with the evolving tools of autobiographical memory, social groups, and communication. We can remember where that tree is located and what time of year it fruits, and we can tell our people about it because our survival depends on their survival. We, the Earth, became capable of loving awareness.

If you are a gambling person, what are the odds that all those photons and quarks would cool, coalesce, change, and evolve into loving conscious awareness?

From a spiritual perspective, how could anything else have evolved? Oneness is expressing Itself all the time in this material universe. This same outcome is happening in other solar systems, too, just via different pathways.

We have a choice. We can attempt to meet our needs through our own self-seeking, or we can open our hearts to compassion for all, including ourselves. Our desires can either be a distraction, or a tool for awakening. What are we going to fill the teacup of our heart with today? Love, or fear?

When we put our spiritual connection above any material attainment, we can meet difficulty with peace. Life cannot harm the soul. We can peacefully float down any river when we allow the One to navigate the rapids. We can face other people's negative judgments without accepting them as our truth. We can surrender our attachment to material gain and instead rest peacefully. Even when it seems like people with power are running the show, we can see and feel the One behind it all, with all the power, playing the game, loving and supporting us in the process. We can live according to my favorite quote from the Big Book of Alcoholics Anonymous:

> Just to the extent that we do as we think God would have us, and humbly rely on God, does God enable us to match calamity with serenity. We never apologize to anyone for depending upon our Creator. We can laugh

at those who think spirituality the way of weakness. Paradoxically, it is the way of strength.[1]

We are all here just playing out our assigned roles, but behind that shtick, we are souls, and behind that, we are One. If we think we are busy helping others, Ram Dass reminds us:

> You start to ask, "Well, whose suffering is it anyway? Whose helping is it anyway?" And the whole idea that "I'll help you" is seen as nonsense. It's like the left hand is caught, and the right hand pulls it out, and the left hand turns to the right and says, "Thank you!" It doesn't work that way, because they're both part of the same body. Who are you thanking? You're thanking yourself, so that on that plane, you realize it's not 'her' suffering, or 'his' suffering, or 'their' suffering. It's one level, you go up, and it's 'OUR' suffering. Then, as it gets depersonalized, it's just 'the' suffering, and out of the identity with the suffering comes the compassion [. . .] There is no longer being compassionate, you are compassion.[2]

When we are One, we easily ask for and receive help. We ask our community to stand with us, not in anger, but in truth. When living Spirit-guided, we use our voice for justice. We say, "Hey, the way you are treating me is not OK," but not for our own validation or empowerment, but so that justice uplifts everyone to a higher state of being. When connected to Oneness, we are both sides of the disagreement—the left hand asking for change, and the right hand asserting sameness.

When we are at Home in the One, we can wield the sword of truth kindly and compassionately comfort those it cuts. We consider:

Do I want to win, or do I want to be free?

Do I want to be right, or do I want to be free?

Do I want justice, or do I want to be free?

We want to be free of all identities so that the One can win, the One can be right, and the One can be just.

When we come Home to Oneness, we honor the Earth for what She has created, for we are Her. We notice that there is no separation between the seasons, the pull of the moon, the flow of water cycles, and us. We exist within these systems. We are these systems. We begin to dig our hands into the earth and grow food. We become oriented to the moons and track the movement of planets, feeling comforted by their rhythmic weaving. We receive messages from Nature and pay attention to Her signs.

We see now that through all the lifetimes, all the love, and all the loss, our rudder has been turned toward the One. We bow down in the sunshine and drink in Source, an ever-present, ever-abundant source of healing. This is ours. We do not need to earn it. Oneness imbues Itself in the love reflected back to us in everyday acts of ordinary kindness. In return, we offer our selfless service to others.[3]

We are on the path of the heart, the road to awakening. It bends before us, and as we round each corner, thinking this time we will see farther ahead, the next curve appears, keeping us in the present moment. We open the doors to our hearts and let everyone in. We love others and ourselves at the same time. There is no separation. There is only love.

The golden light of Source is available all around us. Always. We only have to look within to know that we are specifically guided, loved, and sustained by a power that expresses itself as us in the world.[4] The love and connection that we seek is the healing, radiant light that courses through us, energizes us, and guides us. It is us.

It Was Me All Along

I was brokenhearted about this man who was never in my life, this man who was not capable, not interested, not present, not faithful, not true, not courageous, not mine. My anger turned inward, toward myself, for wanting him, for picking up the rock and letting it go over and over again. I cried great gumball tears. Grief rippled under my skin, pooling and becoming stuck in my joints as the Earth's heavy body pulled it downward. I despaired over what I wanted but could not have. I took his avoidance personally. The pain of loneliness infused its way into my bone marrow, breaking me up from the inside.

The terror of my worst fear visited me daily. Alone. Separate. All I had ever wanted was a steady love. Security. Connection. The kind of companionship where you can just bump elbows with your partner and smile, where you swim in the nurturing goo of the golden yolk. Instead, here I was again, outside the smooth, glossy surface of the eggshell. Vulnerable. Unprotected.

But Oneness would not leave me alone. She would not allow me to sit in my separateness. She showed me that I had been inside Her protective shell all along. Freedom was not on the other side of a door. Enlightenment was not on the other side of a veil. It was all around me. It was me.

Her love for me was carried on hawks' wings. Her eyes watched over me from above. She brought me to him, without protecting me. Over and over, I opened my heart to him only to release him. Oneness brought me an angel, my spirit guide,

Meera. She healed me from the inside out, ministering to my wounds with tender gauze and loving care. And I was willing. Every day, I sat in morning meditation, said a prayer, burned something, and traveled to her for a healing. Meera showed me I had never been alone. I was always connected, guided, and sustained by a loving presence.

What is loss? Where could the soul go that love would not find it? There is no distance that god cannot traverse. Big Mind, Big Heart knows we are all connected. The web of love only stretches, never breaks. The dry, scratchy ropes of fear turned to gelatinous slime and slid off my body; released from the bondage of worry, pain, and separation, I stood radiant, bravely in love, drunk with love, even for those who were unable to love me.

We do not ignore small mind. We are grateful that it has brought us, through its survival skills, to this present moment. Lower chakra energy is useful and contains fun, creative energy. But we are also Big Mind, Big Heart. Living Spirit-guided means moving from this place of evolutionary origin and assuming our place within Oneness.

Source is even bigger than I can conceive. She is fierce and protective and can stretch Her jaws wide and devour whole solar systems in one gulp. She transmutes energy at rest into the raw, awesome building blocks of the universe, digesting and burping out streams of photons and quarks. As a parlor trick, She can blow smoke rings that would burn the crust of the earth off. She is the junk yard that dismantles and tears down any broken jalopies that stand in Her way. She wants me. She claimed me as Hers. She bulldozed my addictions into the ground, even allowed me to build sandcastles of a career before kicking it down, and attached Her strong magnet to the head of any person that blocked Her path. Kali Ma, Alligator Goddess, Pele, the

Destroyer—I am Hers. In Her power, I, Godzilla, cry with laughter as I kick down the skyscrapers of my life.

Every day, I willingly lie down on Her stone altar, offering up my suffering, my heart wide open, pumping blood into the dry grass below. Every day, I traveled to Meera and threw into her central hearth fire all the karmic baggage that stood in the way of my awakening. Attachments, aversions, clinging, desires—I threw my Luis Vuitton treasure trunks into the fire and watched them burn to ash.

Some days, Meera's central fire would overflow with diamonds, crystals, and jewels, thrown away like trash. Who needs them? The soul is not nourished by trinkets. My small mind gets distracted by status and wealth. But love is the soul's medium. Love is what I drink in. Love is what I serve.

Other days, instead of the fire, I'd see a black, swirling orb. With infinite gravitational pull, it wordlessly absorbed all distractions. A kaleidoscope of obsessions rippled on its exterior before being pulled underneath the blackness. Meera's eyes were the same black orbs. She showed me One Heart, One Mind, that is always connected. And then I fell back into this body and this life. Some days, Meera would place a crown on my head, glittering with jewels. I felt unworthy next to the hundreds, thousands of other beings she supports. She reminded me that all life is worthy.

Meera taught me that a true soulmate brings us closer to the One and the truth of who we are. Clark did that just by being himself. Meera showed me that he was a pauper, with empty pockets turned out. He had nothing to offer me. Temporary infatuation could never feed my hungry ghost. Inside my soul was the answer: We are here to heal ourselves.

Meera healed my broken childhood two-heart into One.

Before I was born, I made soul contracts with other precious souls. Sometimes I agreed to heal them, to revisit our past-life relationship. Sometimes I had to choose myself and close those agreements. Often, I could see that the beautiful human before me was not yet on a spiritual path of awakening, not yet ready to let go of material seeking and meet me in Oneness.

Once opened, my heart could not turn off. I went right on loving Clark and was surprised to find him in my chest wherever I went. I bought my groceries while loving him, paid my bills for a house he would never live in, looked up at the stars and thought of him, and went on swiping left while loving him. There was no other choice. I am Love itself. Loving others is what I do. I loved him and accepted that we were not to be in this lifetime. I loved him and healed our past-life agreements in my morning meditations. I loved him and chose myself.

The grace of god brought him to me. A deliciously painful opportunity to burn through so much karmic suffering of desire, longing, and attachment. The Great Weaver binds together opportunities for my heart to open to let more love in. I have repeatedly tried, unsuccessfully, to heal by outsourcing the responsibility to love me. Now, I get to be in love, in full adoration of myself.

I gave my heart to the One and honored the source of love. I found a new Supplier with a super reliable supply chain. Train tracks led to my front door, delivering daily parcels wrapped in brown paper and tied with string: Love. Love universal. My nervous system was rewired. My heart expanded. Healed and connected, I woke up.

A new dilemma emerged: How does one date when awakened?

I trusted in Source. I was already in love. It was just a matter of timing, of the Weaver deciding which threads to bring together, which colors to meld, and when. Opening the dating app, I put up my protection rose and saw drifting before me all the flotsam, the jetsam, the human suffering, the searching, the desperation, the patriarchy, the open lower chakras, the self-abandonment, the judgment, the lies and misrepresentations, the unconscious, the unaware. My own self-loathing was so fully healed that I truly wondered how god was going to manifest a partner in male form.

And so I swiped on and on. I swiped left and left again. Hundreds of times. I saw pictures and read profiles. And even when they looked and sounded good, all I had to do was listen to my intuition for the answer, and she said, "No." I blessed them and prayed for them and swiped them left. Daily, I sat down with my phone and invited god in as I opened the app. And daily, I swiped left, really questioning this practice, wondering how this could possibly be the right method. But my house was a firm train stop on the route of love. She continued to deliver to me every day.

My house was my monastery. I sat in contemplation every day. A pandemic happened, but I was already inside. My daughter and I danced to TikTok. My son and I partnered in taking care of our property. Our dogs and chickens became one pack and walked down the gravel lane together. We were healthy, we were well, and we were in love. I left my job as a dean, stepping out of the tight-fitting heels and into the Crocs of a faculty member. I swiped left and left, and I went on loving Clark, but he had no idea. Rarely, I went on dates.

One night, my fourteen-year-old daughter and I sat down to watch a movie after painting our toes. She moved closer to me, sewing the side of her body to mine, and asked gingerly, "How did your date go?"

I said, "Oh, fine, he is not the one. I love Clark. But he has issues and wants to be alone. That's OK because god is giving me what I need to wake up and be a more spiritually evolved being."

"That is so sad," she said.

"Uggh," I said. "So true."

I became like Rumi's guest house, "every morning a new arrival."[5] I welcomed feelings and loved them all—grief, longing, loneliness, pleasure, connection. Instead of being the wave, I became the ocean, expansive. The world became smaller, like one giant ashram. Where could I go where love was not?

Then one day, as I sat swiping and listening to my intuition, I saw this being's profile picture. Inside of me, my intuition simply said, "Yes."

I stopped in my tracks and listened, shocked that She finally thought some human might possibly be in my life. This one photo held my soul's face with both hands and wouldn't let go. I swiped right and offered my words of introduction. Although it was hard to introduce the magnificence of who I am in just a few sentences, I stammered and tried.

I was about to meet my greatest teacher yet.

Meera's Message: The New Earth

You are filled with Oneness. You are restored to wholeness. You are already free. Go ahead, give yourself permission to move and live from this place. Begin every action from a foundation of self-love. Be rooted in love.

In Oneness, there is no separation, no mine, no yours, no dance of giving and taking away. The resources you worry about are Monopoly money. You cannot take it with you as a spirit, and you didn't actually create it while here. Why grasp onto paper toys? Let it all be a game that you play with kindness. There is so much more waiting for you. The most important resource is the love that you feel in your heart space. The awakened heart loves others no matter their choices.

There is no time, no space, no distance for your prayers to travel. There is only now, the eternal ever-present. Disidentify with your thoughts, your mind, your perspective, wants, and needs, and be with Me, like the drop that joins the ocean.

Your heart knows no darkness. Your mind has no limits. You stand in your freedom of self-expression, simply being the Light you are. Challenges melt away, and you look back amazed. Remember how it was when you had problems? In Oneness, there is no lack, no unmet needs. Desires arise, and they can be fulfilled on earth, or not fulfilled. It doesn't touch you. You are timeless, eternal, ever-present awareness. Your Buddha nature, your Christ consciousness is here. Now.

The old way of being on the earth is ending. The storm is here, and you are living in it: crumbling, dismantling, breaking up of old systems, detritus, wreckage, leakage, cracks, earthquakes. Maya is collecting what is Hers, what karmic debt is due. Stability is transient.

The New Earth is being born. Changes are coming and coming fast. There is some preparing to do, but the more important preparations are in your heart. What you do matters. Your kindness, service, and love are essential. You are being called to radically change your life to live Spirit guided.

In this New Earth, you are fully guided by an inner knowing. Your letting go of old ideas and unlearning of the old ways is complete. All falsehood drops away—all identities, and eventually your body. You are healed and reborn.

You are a beautiful child of god with a magical, loving heart. Rise up and shine. Be of service and receive tenfold in return. Create in the delight of Oneness. Stand in your power, fully unleashed, fully unbound. All of you is connected, available, and engaged. You are cared for, guided, and protected.

Be the Light you are.

Coming Out, Calling In, Coming Home

I am coming out of the psychic closet today. I use that cultural reference with deep respect for my father and millions of others who have been forced to hide an essential organizing truth about themselves. They sought safety in the closet rather than face being diagnosed with a mental "illness" (to use DSM-III era language), forced into treatment, assaulted, jailed, driven to suicide as the only option, or killed. After more than sixty-five years of being locked in a closet, my father is finally living an integrated life, living in love with his husband.

I want to live this integrated life too. I want to own my spiritual beliefs at my workplace. Why is it that it is fine to be a Christian psychologist or a Jewish psychologist, but if you want to identify as a psychic psychologist, you face ridicule? People justify their stigma because science cannot yet explain how non-material forces act in a material world.

Integration is the act of combining parts so that they become whole. Wholeness is one unified state, unbroken, indivisible, complete in itself. Over the last twenty-five years, psychotherapy has taken over the words "integrative" and "integration." Fewer and fewer therapists are aligned with one tradition, cognitive-behavioral or psychodynamic, more and more identifying themselves as integrative therapists who use different modalities depending on the client's presentation.[1] After a psychedelic-assisted therapy session, integration sessions help a client work through, translate, and process the experience with the goal of moving toward greater balance and wholeness.[2] This book has been one long integration session, allowing me to work through internalized stigma, translate my spiritual experiences, and process all the parts of who I am into one Spirit-guided whole.

Why do I need to integrate my psychic abilities at all? Is this even my problem?

No.

It is not just me who needs to combine the parts of myself to become whole again. We all do. Western culture broke itself into parts thousands of years ago, with the deep thinking of Aristotle, Plato, and later, in the 1600s, René Descartes. We are still working on our self-created "mind-body problem." Cultures that honor other ways of knowing remain integrated, although dis-ease spreads as the dominant Western framework inculcates separation. Broadly speaking, Indigenous healing traditions have been recognized as rooted in three core assumptions of holism, interconnectedness, and harmony/balance.[3] In Indigenous wisdom traditions, mind, body, spirit, and nature are one unified whole. Other cultures do not shame people for thinking about their spirit. In fact, those cultures would see the way Western, industrialized cultures have separated their mind from their body from their spirit as deeply problematic and the cause of psychological suffering. Indigenous healing traditions can involve calling a person's spirit back to them.[4] Just as I do every day in morning meditation with big, beautiful, golden suns.

For years, I told my family that my psychic training classes were "meditation classes." Excusing myself from family dinners to attend group trance medium healings, I said, "I have to go meditate." When they asked with interest, "What kind of meditation?" I demurred, saying, "Oh, we just use visualizations." Meanwhile, I had a public-facing website announcing that I was a psychic medium. I was comfortable with strangers knowing this about me. But I shivered inside at the thought that my parents would see it.

I still have healing to do. I still have the roots of colonization in my mind to unlearn. I am still reclaiming my Indigenous Druid ancestors, who tracked the movement of the moon and the stars, celebrated the seasons, brewed healing potions, and danced under the moonlight with mushrooms. The patriarchy baked into my brittle bones still makes me thirsty for validation and drives me to pull my skin taut when alone in front of a mirror. Religious ownership, in my mind, still venerates churches more than my ability to create my own sanctuary, right here, right now, just by sitting down and claiming it so. Technological culture still tells me I need its help to connect with loved ones, when I can travel as a spirit across networks of love to find anyone. I am still reclaiming the pieces of me.

I am not telling anyone what they should believe or how to awaken. This book is an affirmation, a very long one at that, of what I believe, what I know, and what I have experienced. I have directly experienced communicating with spirits that do not have a body. I have healed myself by running my own energy over the past thirty years. I have used protection roses to block others from infiltrating my space. I have received information in mediumship that there is no material explanation for me to know. I have found a source of unlimited love. I am that Love. I am that Light. I am that Peace. I am free.

Spirit Guided and its companion resources leave tools at your feet (linked in the appendix). You have the capacity to sit in the center of your head and see for yourself. You can ground your spirit in your body, increasing your spirit and body's ability to communicate. You can protect yourself from unwanted energy around you. You can clean out your space by running the clean fuel of Earth and cosmic energy. You can restore and heal yourself with golden suns. You can own your energetic space with clarity.

And so, I stand tall here, sovereign. For many others, it is not that difficult to own their psychic abilities and spiritual natures. For me, raised by scientists at the materialistic peak of Western culture, it took me my whole life. I really, really tried to live my life within the bounds of materialism. I tried every concoction of fuel sources—shopping, food, sex, love, exercise, drugs—and still my self-seeking engine tries to convince me, every now and then, that there is a new one we haven't tried. I've almost died three times, due to necrotizing fasciitis as a youngster, my addictions as an adolescent, and my bike accident as an adult.

I am recreating my life, living it the way I want to. I've played the game according to the karma I was born into. I've listened to my parents and been the good girl. I have tried to uphold past-life agreements because others wanted me to. But those train tracks roamed over a wide-open plane until they stopped abruptly, right in the middle of dry brushland, actually taking me nowhere.

When I live my life Spirit-guided, I am limitless. I can solve any problem, restore my insane thinking to sane thinking, create for myself, and live in my truth. I can represent myself with authority and accuracy, not mincing words or making myself smaller for anyone. I can heal the karma of being female, of being white, of being raised by scientists, of wanting so much approval. I can be free, at peace, and in love.

I teach science classes with respect for the discipline and the value of the scientific method as a way of knowing information. I also know that there are other ways of knowing things, that my intuition is valid, and that higher states of consciousness that connect networks of information are possible. I don't need to teach my spiritual beliefs to my students; I can just leave the door open for some of them to walk through if they choose.

I do need to write this book. It is my life's story, the culmination of who I am and all the choices I have made and not made.

We all have our unique paths. This is mine, coming Home to the One. I am here for you on this journey and respect your choices along the way.

I make mistakes every day on my path of awakening. Daily, I forget the super-charged fuel source of Oneness and revert to trying to meet my needs by firing up the self-seeking jalopy. Despite its cockeyed wheels made of wood and a rusting iron frame, I still think it might work this time. I open its gas tank and fuel it up with the seemingly never-ending source of my fears: *Not good enough. This person will leave me. My needs won't be met.* Scarcity. Endings. I have driven down the same streets so many times, I can now watch myself as I do it. *Here I go thinking I need this person to behave differently so I feel safe. Now I'm turning left and pulling out my credit card to buy something I don't need.* On good days, I can watch myself with a Mona Lisa smile, kindly waiting for myself to drive the jalopy until it breaks down—again.

I often find myself caught in a lesson, coveting something I can't afford or wanting someone to respond to me in a particular way. I get impatient with myself, frustrated with my process. *How is it that I am still working on my abandonment issues? When will I ever feel confident in who I am?* Like picking at a scab, now I have two problems—the original issue, and the way my judgments about myself just made it bleed more. In those moments, I can let go of my ego that wants me to be different, to hurry up and awaken already, and accept my human messiness, trusting that this particular difficulty will help me awaken. The first step is always to notice that our attention is caught, mind held captive in the spider's web of desire.

Just yesterday, I made a mistake and missed an opportunity. I showed up for an appointment with a timeshare salesperson with fear and resentment in my heart. I accepted a vacation offer on the terms that I would sit through a two-hour timeshare presentation, firing up the self-seeking jalopy to drive me somewhere—family vacation, fun, pleasure, by any means necessary. I arrived at the appointment already filled with resentment for the number of times the company had called me to confirm my salary income for the year and that I was not married. I felt harassed. I was afraid they would use their powers to convince me to buy something I didn't want. In Twelve-Step terms, I was handing my power over to the sales team. In psychic terms, I had lost my space, given up my seniority.

Worse than that, I was missing out on Oneness all around me.

The young, buff salesman greeted me and instantly asked me personal questions: Why was I here on vacation? What did I want to create for my family? How much money did I want to spend? With firm protection of my space, I answered his questions tersely, not making eye contact, afraid.

But then, Ram Dass tapped me on the shoulder, like the leprechaun he is, and with a twinkly smile said, "Hey! Look at this one here. Look at his incarnation."

The salesman asked me questions about my life, and so I asked him questions about his. He input numbers into a calculator to show me how terrible it was to be a renter and how awesome it would be to be an owner. And I let him do his thing, calmly waiting him out. I was aware of all the managers on the sales floor watching him, judging his performance, and so I played along, going on the tour, watching the video, smiling at him. I felt sorry that I was his one customer that day; there was no way I was going to fuel his self-seeking engine with a commission. Instead, I offered him my validation of who he was: funny, kind, smart, trying to do his best for his girlfriend and his dog.

Had I been Ram Dass, had I been at Home in the One when I arrived, I would have seen who the salesperson really was: Oneness packaged as a little boy who moved from military base to military base. Oneness, whose father remarried four times. Oneness, who got repeated head injuries playing football. Oneness learning how to be in relationship with his girlfriend. Oneness dressed up in drag as a salesperson trying to help me own weeks of time in a hotel. I could have bowed down to him, in deep gratitude and humble awe for all that he had been through in his life to make it to that moment with me. I could have laughed at ourselves playing the game—him in the role of salesperson, me in the role of resistant client—and found that place in my heart where we are One.

Meera says:

> *The divine grace that God has bestowed upon you is this capacity for love. Love is the currency of the new dawn of awakening into which your collective consciousness will rise. Imagine being drunk in love with every person you meet, even your enemies. That is what you call Christ consciousness. That is your magical ability. There is no greater power. Wall Street can tumble, and you will still have the capacity for more love in your life.*

I make mistakes all the time with my family, at work, in everything I do. I forget the truth of who I am and those around me. I care what others think about me. I criticize how I look. I run other people's energy in my space and forget to clean myself out. I pay money to therapists to help straighten me out, even when I have access to my spirit guides and all these psychic tools. And I am OK with my humanness. In fact, I delight in it. When my heart breaks, I can laugh-cry, feeling the suffering and enjoying that I chose this experience. I understand that I am consciousness unfolding. I know I am awakening into my power. For some, it happens instantly. For some, it takes lifetimes.

After thirty years of seeking and practicing on a spiritual path, I have a choice. Do I want to run their information, or do I want to run my own energy? Do I want to be in fear, or do I want to make decisions based on faith—faith that I am specifically guided, loved, and cared for? Do I want to try and get this person to meet my needs, or do I want to first tap into Oneness, the source of everything?

We have a choice today. We have access to all the tools.

Every morning, I sit down, say a prayer, light something, and run my own energy. It is magic to be able to transform myself every day. Teri is there, dressed up as a fairy, waiting for me. With effervescent lightness, she is always ready to giggle at the heaviness of my incarnation. Dick is here, too, in the spirit world, and more and more of my loved ones as they keep crossing over. Ram Dass, cool guy that he is, hangs out with my guides on the causal plane (hey baby, but don't be deceived, he has more lessons to learn too; he'll be back again). Meera is always there when I seek her, patiently guiding. With my friends who are still in a body, sober sisters like Michele and Lisa, this is all that we talk about: what we are letting go of, what we are welcoming in, what the Sunlight of the Spirit is shining on for us. My loved ones continue to love me into wholeness. My family knows I am on a spiritual path, but we don't have to believe the same things to be in love.

In my mediumship readings, I offer validation that my clients are spirits in bodies, that love never dies, and that we all are awakening into Oneness. My clients walk away empowered and sovereign, with practical tools to own their space.

I am here for you on the path of awakening. I don't have your answers. You do. I can help you peek behind the veil to remind you that you are specifically looked after, loved, and sustained.

You are Spirit guided.

I bow down in humble awe to the Light that you are.

Forever Dance

I am happy even before I have a reason.
I am full of Light even before the sky
Can greet the sun or the moon.
Dear companions,
We have been in love with God
For so very, very long.
What can Hafiz now do but Forever
Dance!

—Hafiz

Appendix

The link and coupon code below provides access to a free online companion course for this book. The Essential Grounding Method online course course offers simple, guided meditations for how to own, heal, and run the energy in your body. These skills are the instruction manual we were never given.

As I practiced these life skills for how to be a spirit in a body for more than thirty years, I found them to be life-changing. They are the most important spiritual practice I do. Can you imagine not brushing your teeth for a day, for a week, for a year? That is how I feel about energy hygiene practices. I don't want to run someone else's life force energy in my body. *Yuck.* I want to be sovereign, with access to my full spiritual abilities of clairvoyance, clairaudience, clairsentience, and so on.

By practicing these spiritual skills, you will be able to:

- Process feelings and heal with lightning speed,

- Remove from your body/mind other people's energy, and

- Have full access to your information, power, and sover-eignty as a spirit.

I have brought the best of my college teaching experience to this online offering. It is clear, simple, and concise. I use these tools daily, and my freedom continues to grow exponentially. I hope that, through them, you find your freedom too.

ESSENTIAL GROUNDING METHOD COURSE

catherineannewilliams/grounding

At checkout enter coupon code: **spiritguided**

BOOK STUDY QUESTIONS AND GUIDELINES

catherineannewilliams.com/book-study

Endnotes

Introduction

1   Jeffery Jones, "In U.S., 47% Identify as Religious, 33% as Spiritual," Gallup Poll, effective September 22, 2023, https://news.gallup.com/poll/511133/identify-religious-spiritual.aspx.

2   Jill Bolte Taylor, *My Stroke of Insight: A Brain Scientist's Personal Journey* (Viking, 2008).

3   Laura Lynn Jackson, *The Light Between Us* (Random House, 2015).

4   Gabriel Popkin, "World Wide Web Underground Network Microbes Connects Trees Mapped for the First Time," *Science*, effective May 15, 2019, https://www.science.org/content/article/wood-wide-web-underground-network-microbes-connects-trees-mapped-first-time.

5   Alcoholics Anonymous, *Alcoholics Anonymous*, 4th ed. (Alcoholics Anonymous World Services, 2002), 84.

Part 1: The Problem is the Solution

Chapter 1: Crashing

1   David Robson, "There Really Are 50 Eskimo Words for Snow," *Washington Post*, effective January 13, 2013, https://www.washingtonpost.com/national/health-science/there-really-are-50-eskimo-words-for-snow/2013/01/14/e0e3f4e0-59a0-11e2-beee-6e38f5215402_story.html.

2   Vinod Menon, "20 Years of the Default Mode Network: A Review and Synthesis," *Neuron* 111, no. 16 (2023): 2469-87.

3   Peter Gay, *Freud: A Life for Our Time* (W. W. Norton, 2006).

4   Anton Loonen and Svetlana Ivanova, "Circuits Regulating Pleasure and Happiness: The Evolution of Reward-Seeking and Misery-Fleeing Behavioral Mechanisms in Vertebrates," *Frontiers in Neuroscience* 9 (2015): 394.

5   Daniel Lieberman and Michael Long, *The Molecule of More: How a Single Chemical in Your Brain Drives Love, Sex, and Creativity—and Will Determine the Fate of the Human Race* (BenBella Books, 2018).

6   Lisa Miller, *The Awakened Brain: The Psychology of Spirituality* (Penguin Books, 2021), 25.

7   Miller, *The Awakened Brain*, 164.

Chapter 2: Admitting Bottom is the Price of Admission

1   Maja Marstrand-Joergensen, Martin Madsen, Dea Stenbæk et al. "Default Mode Network Functional Connectivity Negatively Associated with Trait Openness to Experience," *Social Cognition Affective Neuroscience* 16, no. 9 (2021): 950-9.

2   Sok-in Ho, I-Mei Lin, Jen-Chuen Hsieh, and Cheng-Fang Yen, "EEG Coherences of the Default Mode Network Among Patients Comorbid with Major Depressive Disorder and Anxiety Symptoms," *Journal of Affective Disorders* 361 (2024): 728-738.

3   As cited by Lisa Miller, *The Awakened Brain: The Psychology of Spirituality* (Penguin Books, 2021), 119.

4   "List of animals that have passed the mirror test," Cognition Animal, effective April 15, 2015, https://www.animalcognition.org/2015/04/15/list-of-animals-that-have-passed-the-mirror-test/; Carrie Arnold, "Monkey in the Mirror," *Scientific American*, effective March 1, 2011, https://www.scientificamerican.com/article/monkey-in-the-mirror/.

5   Istvan Molnar-Szakacs and Lucina Uddin, "Self-Processing and the Default Mode Network: Interactions with the Mirror Neuron System." *Frontiers of Human Neuroscience* 7 (2013): 571.

Chapter 3: The Magic is in the Group

1   Umberto Castiello, Cristina Becchio, Stefania Zoia et al. "Wired to be Social: the Ontogeny of Human Interaction," *PLoS One* 5, no. 10 (2010): e13199.

2   Elliot Aronson, *The Social Animal*, 9th ed. (Worth Publishers, 2004).

3   Giacomo Rizzolatti and Laila Craighero, "The Mirror-Neuron System," *Annual Review of Neuroscience* 27 (2004): 169-92.

4   Katja Guenther, "'It's All Done With Mirrors': V.S. Ramachandran and the Material Culture of Phantom Limb Research," *Medical History* 60, no. 3 (2016): 342-58.

5   Lea Winerman, "The Mind's Mirror," *Monitor on Psychology* 36, no. 9 (2005): 48.

6   Francesca Ferri, Francesca Frassinetti, Francesca Mastrangelo, Anatolia Salone, Filippo Ferro, Vittorio Gallese, "Bodily Self and Schizophrenia: The Loss of Implicit Self-body Knowledge," *Conscious Cognition* 21, no. 3 (2012): 1365-74; Peter Enticott, Haley Kennedy, Nicole Rinehart et al. "Mirror Neuron Activity Associated with Social Impairments but not Age in Autism Spectrum Disorder," *Biological Psychiatry* 71, no. 5 (2012): 427-33.

7   Richard Katz, *Indigenous Healing Psychology: Honoring the Wisdom of the First Peoples* (Healing Arts Press, 2017).

8   Katz, *Indigenous Healing Psychology*, 96.

9   Katz, *Indigenous Healing Psychology*, 100.

Chapter 4: Barriers to Oneness

1   Michaeleen Doucleff, "Can Dogs Smell Time? Just Ask Donut the Dog," *NPR*, effective December 22, 2022, https://www.npr.org/sections/goatsandsoda/2022/12/22/1139781319/can-dogs-smell-time-just-ask-donut-the-dog.

2   "Can Animals Predict Earthquakes?" United States Geological Survey, accessed June 1, 2023, https://www.usgs.gov/faqs/can-animals-predict-earthquakes.

3   Deborah Byrd, "How Do Flocking Birds Move in Unison?" *EarthSky*, effective April 30, 2023, https://earthsky.org/earth/how-do-flocking-birds-move-in-unison/.

4   Yangfan Zhang and George Lauder, "Energy Conservation by Collective Movement in Schooling Fish," *eLife*, effective February 20, 2024, https://elifesciences.org/articles/90352.

5   Gabriel Popkin, "'Wood Wide Web'—The Underground Network of Microbes that Connects Trees—Mapped for First Time," *Science*, effective May 15, 2019, https://www.science.org/content/article/wood-wide-web-underground-network-microbes-connects-trees-mapped-first-time.

6   Richard Schwartz, *No Bad Parts: Healing Trauma and Restoring Wholeness with the Internal Family Systems Model* (Sounds True, 2021), 65.

Chapter 5: This Is Your Brain on Oneness

1   Definitions matter in the drug industry. A drug is defined as any substance (other than food) that is used to prevent, diagnose, treat, or relieve symptoms of a disease or abnormal condition, see https://www.fda.gov/drugs/drug-approvals-and-databases/drugsfda-glossary-terms#D.

2   Kimon de Greef, "The Pied Piper of Psychedelic Toads," *New Yorker*, effective March 21, 2022, https://www.newyorker.com/magazine/2022/03/28/the-pied-piper-of-psychedelic-toads.

3   Margaret Osborne, "Don't Lick This Toad National Park Service Says," *Smithsonian Magazine*, effective November 7, 2022, https://www.smithsonianmag.com/smart-news/dont-lick-this-toad-national-park-service-says-180981092/.

4   The Multidisciplinary Association for Psychedelic Studies (MAPS) has a robust archive of resources on psychedelic studies, see https://maps.org/take-action/resources/.

5   "Wikipedia: Tassili Mushroom Figure," Wikimedia Foundation, last modified May 1, 2025, https://en.wikipedia.org/w/index.php?title=Tassili_Mushroom_Figure&oldid=1219659697; Bernard Lowry, "New Records of Mushroom Stones from Guatemala," *Mycologia* 63, no. 5 (1971): 983-993; Hesham El-Seedi, Peter De Smet, Olof Beck, Goran Possnert, and Jan Bruhn, "Prehistoric Peyote Use: Alkaloid Analysis and Radiocarbon Dating of Archaeological Specimens of Lophophora from Texas," *Journal of Ethnopharmacology* 101, no. 1-3 (2005): 238-242.

6   With humility, I acknowledge that I cannot possibly summarize and unitize Indigenous wisdom. As Katz says, "There is no unitary Indigenous perspective or set of agreed-upon perspectives." Richard Katz, *Indigenous Healing Psychology: Honoring the Wisdom of the First Peoples* (Healing Arts Press, 2017), 80. Some of what I present here is based on teachings I received from Indigenous wisdom keepers during my graduate certificate studies in Psychedelic Assisted Therapy and Research at the California Institute of Integral Studies in 2023.

7   Jerry Brown, "The Immortality Key: The Secret History of the Religion with No Name," *Journal of Psychedelic Studies* 5, no.1 (2021): 5-8.

8   Brian Muraresku, *The Immortality Key: The Secret History of the Religion with No Name* (St. Martin's Press, 2020).

9   Jerry Brown and Julie Brown, "Entheogens in Christian Art: Wasson, Allegro, and the Psychedelic Gospels," *Journal of Psychedelic Studies* 3, no. 3 (2019): 142-63.

10   Tom Schroder, "'Apparently Useless': The Accidental Discovery of LSD," *The Atlantic*, effective September, 2014, https://www.theatlantic.com/health/archive/2014/09/the-accidental-discovery-of-lsd/379564/; Alfred Hoffman, *LSD My Problem Child* (McGraw-Hill Publishing Company, 1980), https://maps.org/images/pdf/books/lsdmyproblemchild.pdf.

11   Richard Doblin, Merete Christiansen, Lisa Jerome, and Brad Burge, "The Past and Future of Psychedelic Science: An Introduction to This Issue," *Jouranal of Psychoactive Drugs* 51, no. 2 (2019): 93-7.

12   Robert McDonnell, John Moriarty, Ian Cabe, and Emily Higgins, "AA, Bill Wilson, Carl Jung and LSD," *Journal of Analytical Psychology* 69, no. 4 (2024): 550-80.

13   Robin Carhart-Harris and Guy Goodwin, "The Therapeutic Potential of Psychedelic Drugs: Past, Present, and Future," *Neuropsychopharmacology* 42, no. 11 (2017): 2105-13.

14   Walter Pahnke, *Drugs and Mysticism* (Harvard University, 1963).

15   Rick Doblin, "Pahnke's 'Good Friday Experiment': A Long-term Follow-up and Methodological Critique," *Journal of Transpersonal Psychology* 23, no. 1 (1991): 1-25.

16   Katherine Maclean, Jeannie-Marie Leoutsakos, Matthew Johnson, and Roland Griffiths, "Factor Analysis of the Mystical Experience Questionnaire: A Study of Experiences Occasioned by the Hallucinogen Psilocybin," *Journal of Scientific Study of Religion* 51, no. 4 (2012): 721-37; "Pahnke-Richards Mystical Experience Questionnaire", Open Computing Facility University of California at Berkely, accessed November 10, 2024, https://www.ocf.berkeley.edu/~jfkihlstrom/ConsciousnessWeb/Psychedelics/Pahnke-Richards_Mystical_Experiences_Questionnaire.pdf.; Walter Pahnke and William Richards, "Implications of LSD and Experimental Mysticism," *Journal of Religion and Health* 5, no. 3 (1966): 175-208.

17   Jasmine Virdi, "Psychedelics and the Default Mode Network," *Psychedelics Today*, effective 2020, https://psychedelicstoday.com/2020/02/04/psyche-

delics-and-the-default-mode-network/; Rebecca Smausz, Joanna Neill, and John Gigg, "Neural Mechanisms Underlying Psilocybin's Therapeutic Potential - The Need for Preclinical in Vivo Electrophysiology," *Journal of Psychopharmacology* 36, no. 7 (2022):781-93; Frederick Barrett and Roland Griffiths, "Classic Hallucinogens and Mystical Experiences: Phenomenology and Neural Correlates," *Current Topics in Behavioral Neurosciences 36 (2018)*: 393–430.

18   Calvin Ly, Alexandra Greb, Lindsay Cameron et al. "Psychedelics Promote Structural and Functional Neural Plasticity," *Cell Reports* 23, no. 11 (2018): 3170-82.

19   Jerry Brown, "The Immortality Key: The Secret History of the Religion with No Name," *Journal of Psychedelic Studies* 5, no.1 (2021): 5-8.

20   Barbara Tomasino, Sara Fregona, Miran Skrap and Franco Fabbro, "Meditation-related Activations are Modulated by the Practices Needed to Obtain it and by the Expertise: An ALE Meta-analysis Study," *Frontiers in Human Neuroscience*, 6 (2013): 346.

21   Tomasino et al. *Frontiers in Human Neuroscience*, 6.

22   Lisa Miller, *The Awakened Brain: The Psychology of Spirituality* (Penguin Books, 2021).

23   Miller, *The Awakened Brain*, 158.

24   Miller, *The Awakened Brain*, 157.

25   Walter Pahnke and William Richards, "Implications of LSD and Experimental Mysticism," *Journal of Religion and Health* 5 (1966): 175-208.

26   Julia Sullivan and IFS Institute, "The 8 C's of Self-leadership Wheel," IFS Foundation, effective 2020, https://foundationifs.org/images/banners/pdf/The_8_Cs_of_Self_Leadership_Wheel.pdf.

27   Lisa Miller, *The Awakened Brain: The Psychology of Spirituality* (Penguin Books, 2021), 162.

28   Simon Vossel, Joy Geng, and Gereon Fink, "Dorsal and Ventral Attention Systems: Distinct Neural Circuits but Collaborative Roles," *Neuroscientist* 20, no. 2 (2014): 150-9.

29   Try activating your dorsal attention network with this fun test: https://www.youtube.com/watch?v=vJG698U2Mvo.

30   Kathryn Devaney, Emily Levin, Viabhav Tripathi et al. "Attention and Default Mode Network Assessments of Meditation Experience during Active Cognition and Rest," *Brain Science* 11, no. 5 (2021): 566.

31   Antonietta Manna, Antonino Raffone, Mauro Perrucci et al. "Neural Correlates of Focused Attention and Cognitive Monitoring in Meditation," *Brain Research Bulletin* 82 (2010): 46-56.

32   Lisa Miller, *The Awakened Brain: The Psychology of Spirituality* (Penguin Books, 2021), 7.

33   Ralph Metzner, *Allies for Awakening: Guidelines for Productive and Safe Experiences with Entheogens* (Green Earth Foundation & Regent Press, 2015), 9.

Part 2: How to Get Home

Chapter 6: How the Spiritual and Material Interact

1   Judea Christine, *OmniChakra: Psychic Intuitive Development Through the Chakras* (Author, 2024).

2   Gabe Hiemstra, "Yuj: 10 Definitions," Wisdom Library, accessed October 29, 2024, https://www.wisdomlib.org/definition/yuj.

3   Tyson Yunkaporta, *Sand Talk: How Indigenous Thinking Can Save the World* (HarperOne, 2020), 39.

4   Ram Dass, "Ram Dass Quotes," accessed November 1, 2024, https://www.ramdass.org/ram-dass-quotes/.

5   "This Month in Physics History: May 1801: Thomas Young and the Nature of Light," American Physical Society, effective May 2024, https://www.aps.org/archives/publications/apsnews/200805/physicshistory.cfm.

6   Monica Grady, "Can Physics Prove if God Exists?" BBC, effective March 1, 2021, https://www.bbc.com/future/article/20210301-how-physics-could-prove-god-exists.

7   Etzel Cardeña, "The Experimental Evidence for Parapsychological Phenomena: A Review," *American Psychologist* 73, no. 5 (2018): 663-77, 665.

8   "Spooky Action at a Distance," Wiktionary, accessed November 1, 2024, https://en.wiktionary.org/wiki/spooky_action_at_a_distance#:~:text=-

Calque%20of%20German%20spukhafte%20Fernwirkung,interact%20instantaneously%20over%20a%20distance.

9   These quantum mechanics concepts are mathematical concepts; therefore, any attempt to wrap language around them is not fully accurate.

10   Rafi Letzter, "Giant Molecules Exist in Two Places at Once in Unprecedented Quantum Experiment," *Scientific American*, effective 2019, https://www.scientificamerican.com/article/giant-molecules-exist-in-two-places-at-once-in-unprecedented-quantum-experiment/.

11   E. Buks, R. Schuster, M. Heiblum, D. Mahalu, and V. Umansky, "Dephasing in Electron Interference by a 'Which-path' Detector," *Nature* 391, no. 6670 (1998): 871-4.

12   Bernard d'Espagnat, "The Quantum Theory and Reality," *Scientific American* 241, no. 5 (1979): 158–81.

13   Lisa Miller, *The Awakened Brain: The Psychology of Spirituality* (Penguin Books, 2021), 99.

14   Etzel Cardeña, "The Experimental Evidence for Parapsychological Phenomena: A Review," *American Psychologist* 73, no. 5 (2018): 663-77.

15   Dark matter is the gravitational effects that pull galaxies together. The concept of dark energy is a placeholder term for the expansion of the universe. "According to the most recent studies, the universe is 5% baryonic matter, 27% dark matter, and 68% dark energy. Baryonic matter consists of the atoms of which you and everything you interact with is made. This includes stars, galaxies, planets, and just about everything else astronomers can visually observe." Brown Particle Astrophysics Group, "Dark Matter," Accessed October 10, 2025, https://particleastro.brown.edu/dark-matter/#:~:text=According%20to%20the%20most%20recent%20studies%2C%20the,about%20everything%20else%20astronomers%20can%20visually%20observe, para. 5.

16   Confirmation bias is a common cognitive error where we prefer information that confirms previously learned beliefs/knowledge because we like to be consistent with ourselves; see Carol Tavris and Elliot Aronson, *Mistakes Were Made (But Not by Me): Why We Justify Foolish Beliefs, Bad Decisions, and Hurtful Acts* (Harvest Books, 2008).

17   Tyson Yunkaporta, *Sand Talk: How Indigenous Thinking Can Save the World* (HarperOne, 2020), 32.

18   Neil Douglas-Klotz, *The Hidden Gospel: Decoding the Spiritual Message of the Aramaic Jesus* (Quest Books, 1999).

19   Douglas-Klotz, *The Hidden Gospel.*

20   Neil Douglas-Klotz, *Prayers of the Cosmos. Reflections on the Original Meaning of Jesus's Words* (Harper One, 1990).

21   Neil Douglas-Klotz, *The Hidden Gospel: Decoding the Spiritual Message of the Aramaic Jesus* (Quest Books, 1999), 1.

22   Rupert Spira, *"Awareness is Known by Itself,"* Youtube, effective *August* 14, 2020, https://www.youtube.com/watch?v=eXviDUwjqQM#:~:text=its%20 own%20limitations%20on%20everything%20that%20it,we%20truly%20 are%20is%20simply%20pure%20awareness.

23   Unfortunately, with the rise of intravenous drug use there is an increase in the cases of necrotizing fasciitis. The cure remains the same: early diagnosis, antibiotics, and removal of tissue; Jordan Carter, Michael Polmear, Rami Khalfia, and Giberto Gonzales, "Incidence and Treatment of Necrotizing Fasciitis of the Upper Extremity in IV Drug Users Admitted to a Level 1 Center," *Journal of the American College of Surgeons* 231, no. 4 (2020): e171.

24   T. Rouse, M. Malangoni, and W. Schulte, "Necrotizing Fasciitis: A Preventable Disaster," *Surgery* 92, no. 4 (1982): 765-70.

Chapter 7: Our Spiritual Nature

1   David Chalmer, "Facing Up to the Problem of Consciousness," *Journal of Consciousness Studies* 2, no: 3 (1995): 200-19.

2   "Lewis S. Bostwick," Mystic Explorers, accessed November 1, 2024, https://www.mysticexplorers.com/lewis-bostwick?rq=bostwick.

3   "About Church of Divine Man," Berkely BPI, Accessed November 1, 2024, https://www.berkeleybpi.com/about-church-of-divine-man.

4   Marco Masi, "An Evidence-based Critical Review of the Mind-brain Identity Theory," *Frontiers of Psychology* 14 (2023): 1150605.

5   René Descartes, "Meditations on First Philosophy in which are Demonstrated the Existence of God and the Distinction between the Human Soul and the Body (1639)," Marxists Internet Archive, accessed September 20,

2025, https://www.marxists.org/reference/archive/descartes/1639/medita-tions.htm, para 25.

6   "How Is This Possible?" Windbridge Research Center, accessed November 1, 2024, https://www.windbridge.org/how-is-this-possible/.

7   Marco Masi, "An Evidence-based Critical Review of the Mind-brain Identity Theory," *Frontiers of Psychology* 14 (2023): 1150605.

8   Robert Sapolsky, *Monkeyluv: And Other Essays on Our Lives as Animals* (Scribner, 2005), 70.

9   Antonio Demascio, *Descartes Error: Emotion, Reason, and the Human Brain* (Penguin Books, 2005), 252.

10   Paul Bloom, *Descartes' Baby: How Child Development Explains What Makes Us Human* (William Heinemann, 2004), 227.

11   "How Is This Possible?" Windbridge Research Center, accessed November 1, 2024, https://www.windbridge.org/how-is-this-possible/.

12   Christopher Koch, "What is Consciousness?" Scientific American, effective June 1, 2018, https://www.scientificamerican.com/article/what-is-con-sciousness/.

13   Marco Masi, "An Evidence-based Critical Review of the Mind-brain Identity Theory," *Frontiers of Psychology* 14 (2023): 1150605.

14   David Chalmer, "Facing Up to the Problem of Consciousness," *Journal of Consciousness Studies* 2, no: 3 (1995): 200-19.

15   Phillip Goff, *Galileo's Error: Foundations for a New Science of Consciousness* (Pantheon, 2019), 3.

16   Thomas Nagel, "What Is It Like to Be a Bat?" *The Philosophical Review* 83, no. 4 (1974): 435–50.

17   Thomas Nagel, *Mind and Cosmos: Why the Materialist Neo-Darwinian Conception of Nature is Almost Certainly False* (Oxford University Press, 2012).

18   "Support for the Survival of Consciousness Explanation," Windbridge Research Center, effective 2019, https://windbridge.org/factsheets/WRC_sur-vival.pdf.

19   Bruce Greyson, "Near-death Experiences and Spirituality," *Zygon* 41, no. 2 (2006): 393-414.

20   Pim van Lommel, Ruud van Wees, Vincent Meyers, and Ingrid Elfferich, "Near-death Experience in Survivors of Cardiac Arrest: A Prospective Study in the Netherlands," *Lancet* 358, no. 9298 (2001): 2039-45.

21   Bruce Greyson, "Near-death Experiences and Spirituality," *Zygon* 41, no. 2 (2006): 393-414, 398.

22   Christopher Kerr, James Donnelly, Scott Wright et al. "End-of-life Dreams and Visions: A Longitudinal Study of Hospice Patients' Experiences," *Journal of Palliative Medicine* 17, no. 3 (2014): 296-303; Peter Fenwick, Hilary Lovelace, and Sue Brayne, "Comfort for the Dying: Five Year Retrospective and One Year Prospective Studies of End of Life Experiences," *Archives of Gerontology and Geriatrics* 51, no. 2 (2010): 173-9.

23   Jim Tucker and F. Don Nidiffer, "Psychological Evaluation of American Children Who Report Memories of Previous Lives," *Journal of Scientific Exploration* 28, no. 4 (2014): 585-96.

24   Matthew Sarraf, Michael Woodley, and Patrizio Tressoldi, "Anomalous Information Reception by Mediums: A Meta-analysis of the Scientific Evidence," *Explore* 17, no. 5 (2021): 396-402.

25   Jurgen Kremer, *Psychology in Diversity in Psychology: Introduction to Psychology for the 21st Century* (Kendall Hunt, 2017).

26   Ram Dass, *The Only Dance There Is: Talks at the Menninger Foundation, 1970, and Spring Grove Hospital, 1972* (Anchor, 1974), 50-1.

27   Helen Santoro, "The Push for More Equitable Research is Changing the Field," *Monitor on Psychology* 54, no. 1 (2023): 49.

28   Marco Masi, "An Evidence-based Critical Review of the Mind-brain Identity Theory," *Frontiers of Psychology* 14 (2023): 1150605, 2.

29   Helané Wahbeh, Dean Radin, Julia Mossbridge, Cassandra Vieten, and Arnaud Delorme, "Exceptional Experiences Reported by Scientists and Engineers," *Explore* 14, no. 5 (2018): 329-341; to learn more about telepathy, I recommend this podcast: Ky Dickens, *The Telepathy Tapes*, Apple Podcasts (2025): https://thetelepathytapes.com/.

30   Lisa Miller, *The Awakened Brain: The Psychology of Spirituality* (Penguin Books, 2021), 102.

31   Miller, *The Awakened Brain,* 102.

32   Marco Masi, "An Evidence-based Critical Review of the Mind-brain Identity Theory," *Frontiers of Psychology* 14 (2023): 1150605.

33   Masi, *Frontiers of Psychology* 14, 3.

34   "How Is This Possible?" Windbridge Research Center, accessed November 1, 2024, https://www.windbridge.org/how-is-this-possible/, para. 2.

35   Steve Taylor, "Do Psi Phenomena Exist? A Debate (Part One)," Psychology Today, effective May 29. 2020, https://www.psychologytoday.com/us/blog/out-the-darkness/202005/do-psi-phenomena-exist-debate-part-one, para 4.

36   Ram Dass, "Relative Realities," accessed November 1, 2024, https://www.ramdass.org/relative-realities/, para. 6.

37   Ralph Adolphs, "The Unsolved Problems of Neuroscience," *Trends in Cognitive Sciences* 19, no. 4 (2015): 173-5.

38   Imants Barušs and Julia Mossbridge, *Transcendent Mind Rethinking the Science of Consciousness* (American Psychological Association, 2016).

39   See Phillip Goff, "Why the Mystery of Consciousness Is Deeper Than We Thought," *Scientific American*, effective July 3, 2024, https://www.scientificamerican.com/article/the-mystery-of-consciousness-is-deeper-than-we-thought/; Annika Harris, *Conscious: A Brief Guide to the Fundamental Mystery of the Mind* (Harper, 2019).

40   Frederico Faggin, *Irreducible: Consciousness, Life, Computers, and Human Nature* (Essentia Books, 2024); Tom Campbell, "Overview of My Big TOE", accessed September 18, 2025, https://www.my-big-toe.com/theory/overview-of-my-big-toe/.

41   David Loy, *Nonduality: A Study in Comparative Philosophy* (Humanity Press, 1988).

42   See Robert Pepperell, "Consciousness as a Physical Process Caused by the Organization of Energy in the Brain." *Frontiers of Psychology* 9 (2018): 2091.

43   Marc Russo, Danielle Santarelli, and Dean O'Rourke, "The Physiological Effects of Slow Breathing in the Healthy Human," *Breathe 13*, no. 4 (2017):

298-309; Nestor, James, *Breath: The New Science of a Lost Art* (Riverhead Books, 2020).

44   Jason Hao and Michele Mittelman, "Acupuncture: Past, Present, and Future," *Global Advances on Health and Medicine 3*, no. 4 (2014): 6-8.

45   H. MacPherson, E.A. Vertosick, N.E. Foster et al. "The Persistence of the Effects of Acupuncture After a Course of Treatment: A Meta-analysis of Patients with Chronic Pain," *Pain 158, no. 5 (2017): 784-93.*

46   Madhav Goyal, Sonal Singh, Erica Sibinga et al. "Meditation Programs for Psychological Stress and Well-being: A Systematic Review and Meta-analysis." *JAMA Internal Medicine 174*, no. 3 (2014): 357-68.

47   I support an inclusive view on treatment: We can heal our bodies, minds, and spirits through physical medicine, psychological, and spiritual healing modalities. I approach my own health issues from a "both/and" perspective: I want to know what Western medicine and integrative health systems recommend, and I run my own healing energy.

Chapter 8: Learning Through Relationship

1   Anthony DeCasper, Jean-Pierre Lecanuet, Marie-Claire Busnel, Carolyn Granier-Deferre, and Roselyne Maugeais, "Fetal Reactions to Recurrent Maternal Speech," Infant Behavior and Development 17, no. 2 (1994): 159-64; Viola Marx, Emese Nagy, "Fetal Behavioural Responses to Maternal Voice and Touch," *PLoS One* 10, no. 6: (2015): e0129118; Erica Neri, Leonardo De Pascalis, Francesca Agostini et al. "Parental Book-reading to Preterm Born Infants in NICU: The Effects on Language Development in the First Two Years," *International Journal Environmental Research and Public Health* 18, no: 21 (2021):11361.

2   Ian Bushnel, "Mother's Face Recognition in Newborn Infants: Learning and Memory," *Infant and Child Development* 10, no. 1-2 (2001): 67-74; Sarah Jessen, "Maternal Odor Reduces the Neural Response to Fearful Faces in Human Infants," *Developmental Cognitive Neuroscience* 45 (2020): 100858.

3   Ellen Boundy, Roya Dastjerdi, Donna Spiegelman et al. "Kangaroo Mother Care and Neonatal Outcomes: A Meta-analysis," *Pediatrics* 137, no. 1 (2016): e20152238.

4   Evan Ardiel and Catherine Rankin, "The Importance of Touch in Development," *Pediatrics and Child Health 15*, no. 3 (2010): 153-6.

5   Beatrice Beebe, Daniel Messinger, Lorraine Bahrick et al. "A Systems View of Mother-infant Face-to-face Communication," *Developmental Psychology* 52, no. 4 (2016): 556-71.

6   Naomi Scatliffe, Sharon Casavant, Dorothy Vittner, and Xiaomei Cong, "Oxytocin and Early Parent-infant Interactions: A Systematic Review," *International Journal of Nursing Science* 6, no. 4 (2019): 445-53; Gabriela Markova, "The Games Infants Play: Social Games During Early Mother–Infant Interactions and Their Relationship With Oxytocin," *Frontiers in Psychology* 9 (2018).

7   Donald Winnicott, "Transitional Objects and Transitional Phenomena; A Study of the First Not-me Possession," *International Journal of Psychoanalysis* 34, no. 2 (1953): 89-97.

8   Jude Cassidy, Jason Jones, and Phillip Shaver, "Contributions of Attachment Theory and Research: A Framework for Future Research, Translation, and Policy," *Developmental Psychopathology* 25, no. 4 (2013): 1415-34.

9   My insecure attachment style keeps me preoccupied with the amount of love and connection I am receiving in relationships. I highly recommend attachment theory for understanding relationship patterns; see Amir Levine and Rachel Heller, *Attached: The New Science of Adult Attachment and How It Can Help You Find – and Keep – Love* (Tarcher, 2012).

10   Melissa Nachmias, Megan Gunnar, Sarah Mangelsdorf, Hornik Parritz, and Kristen Buss, "Behavioral Inhibition and Stress Reactivity: The Moderating Role of Attachment Security," *Child Development* 67, no. 2 (1996): 508-22.

11   Jude Cassidy, Katherine Ehrlich, and Laura Sherman, "Child-parent Attachment and Response to Threat: A Move from the Level of Representation," in *Nature and Development of Social Connections: From Brain to Group, ed.* Mario Mikulincer and Phillip Shaver (American Psychological Association, 2013).

12   Stan Tatkin, *Wired for Love: How Understanding Your Partner's Brain and Attachment Style Can Help You Defuse Conflict and Build a Secure Relationship* (New Harbinger, 2012).

13   Tatkin, *Wired for Love.*

14   Daniel Sznycer, John Tooby, Leda Cosmides et al. "Shame Closely Tracks the Threat of Devaluation by Others, Even Across Cultures," *Proceedings of the National Academy of Sciences* 113, no. 10 (2016): 2625-30, https://doi.org/10.1073/pnas.1514699113.

Chapter 9: Psychic Abilities

1   Connie Wang, Issac Hilburn, Daw-An Wu et al. "Transduction of the Geomagnetic Field as Evidenced from alpha-Band Activity in the Human Brain," *eNeuro* 6, no: 2 (2019): 0483-18.

2   "Paranormal Encounters," Yougov, effective Oct 20, 2022, https://today.yougov.com/society/articles/44141-paranormal-encounters-yougov-poll-october-12-2022.

3   Layne Redmond, *When the Drummers Were Women: A Spiritual History of Rhythm* (Three Rivers Press, 1997).

4   Brian Muraresku, *The Immortality Key: The Secret History of the Religion with No Name* (St. Martin's Press, 2020).

5   Muraresku, *The Immortality Key*.

6   Phillip Goff, *Galileo's Error: Foundations for a New Science of Consciousness* (Pantheon, 2019), 14.

7   "Report on an Offer of Apology, on Behalf of the American Psychological Association, to First Peoples in the United States," American Psychological Association, effective February, 2023, https://www.apa.org/pubs/reports/indigenous-apology.pdf; for a reimagined introduction to the field of psychology that honors Indigenous wisdom, I recommend Jurgen Kremer, *Psychology in Diversity in Psychology: Introduction to Psychology for the 21st Century* (Kendall Hunt, 2017).

8   500 Women Scientists Leadership, "Silence Is Never Neutral; Neither Is Science," *Scientific American*, effective June 6, 2020, https://www.scientificamerican.com/blog/voices/silence-is-never-neutral-neither-is-science/.

9   Cat Bohannon, *Eve: How the Female Body Drove 200 Million Years of Evolution* (Knopf, 2023).

10   Melissa de Witte, "Is Psychological Research Racially Biased?" Greater Good Magazine, effective 2020, https://greatergood.berkeley.edu/article/item/is_psychological_research_racially_biased.

11   As cited by Jennifer Reiling, "Psychic Research," *JAMA* 295, no. 20 (2006): 2422.

12   Etzel Cardeña, "The Experimental Evidence for Parapsychological Phenomena: A Review." *American Psychologist* 73, no. 5 (2018): 663-677, 665.

13   Cardeña, *American Psychologist* 73, no. 5.

14   William James, *Varieties of Religious Experience: A Study in Human Nature* (Oxford University Press, 2012).

15   William James, "*1896 Societal for Psychical Research President's Address,*" Public Knowledge Project, https://journals.sfu.ca/seemj/index.php/seemj/article/download/211/174.

16   Michael Mumford, Andrew Rose, and David Goslin, "An Evaluation of Remote Viewing: Research and Applications," American Institute for Research, effective, 1995, https://www.cia.gov/readingroom/docs/CIA-RDP96-00791R000200180006-4.pdf.

17   Caroline Watt and Marleen Nagtegaal, "Reporting of Blind Methods: An Interdisciplinary Survey," *Journal of the Society for Psychical Research* 68, no. 875[2] (2004): 105–14.

18   Leslie John, George Loewenstein, and Drazen Prelec, "Measuring the Prevalence of Questionable Research Practices with Incentives for Truth Telling," *Psychological Science* 23, no. 5 (2012): 524–532; Steven Roberts, Carmelle Bareket-Shavit, Forrest Dollins, Peter Goldie, and Elizabeth Mortenson, "Racial Inequality in Psychological Research: Trends of the Past and Recommendations for the Future," *Perspectives on Psychological Science* 15, no. 6 (2020): 1295–1309.

19   Samah Khaled Zahran "What is PSI? From anti-parapsychology to PSI as a Next Scientific Revolution: Theoretical Rreviews and Hypothesized Vision," *American Journal of Applied Psycholoy* 5, no. 2 (2017): 33-44.

20   Larry Dossey, "Spirituality and Nonlocal Mind: A Necessary Dyad," *Spirituality in Clinical Practice* 1, no. 1 (2014): 29–42.

21   Etzel Cardeña, "The Experimental Evidence for Parapsychological Phenomena: A Review." *American Psychologist* 73, no. 5 (2018): 663-677, 665.

22   Cardeña, *American Psychologist* 73, no. 5, 665.

23   Cardeña, *American Psychologist* 73, no. 5., 663

24   Stephan Schmidt, "Can We Help Just by Good Intentions? A Meta-analysis of Experiments on Distant Intention Effects," *The Journal of Alternative and Complementary Medicine* 18, no. 6 (2012): 529-33.

25   Schmidt, *The Journal of Alternative and Complementary Medicine* 18, no. 6, 69

26   Chris Roe, Charmaine Sonnex, and Elizabeth Roxburgh, "Two Meta-analyses of Noncontact Healing Studies," *Explore* 11, no. 1 (2014): 11-23.

27   Thomas Rabeyron, "Why Most Research Findings About Psi Are False: The Replicability Crisis, the Psi Paradox and the Myth of Sisyphus," *Frontiers in Psychology* 11 (2020): para. 5.

28   Dean Radin, Marilyn Schlitz, and Christopher Baur, "Distant Healing Intention Therapies: An Overview of the Scientific Evidence," *Global Advances in Health and Medicine* 4 (1_Suppl) (2015): 67–71.

29   Bethany Butzer, "Bias in the Evaluation of Psychology Studies: A Comparison of Parapsychology Versus Neuroscience," *Explore* 16, no. 6 (2020): 382-391.

30   Jill Bolte Taylor, *My Stroke of Insight: A Brain Scientist's Personal Journey* (Viking, 2008).

31   Dean Radin, *Entangle Minds: Extrasensory Experiences in a Quantum Reality* (Simon & Schuster, 2006).

Chapter 10: Our Body, Our Greatest Teacher

1   "Spiritual bypass" was coined by John Welwood in 1984 when he "noticed a widespread tendency to use spiritual ideas and practices to sidestep or avoid facing unresolved emotional issues, psychological wounds, and unfinished developmental tasks" Tina Fossella and John Welwood, "Human Nature, Buddha Nature: An Interview with John Welwood," *Tricycle: The Buddhist Review* 20, no: 3 (2011): 1-18, 1.

2   Molly Sargen, *"Biological Roles of Water: Why is Water Necessary for Life?"* Harvard University Science in the News, effective September 26, 2019, https://www.scribd.com/document/519419174/Biological-Roles-of-Water-Why-is-water-necessary-for-life-Science-in-the-News.

3   Emeran Meyer, Rob Knight, Sarkis Mazmanian, John Cryan, and Kirsten Tillisch, "Gut Microbes and the Brain: Paradigm Shift in Neuroscience," *Journal of Neuroscience 34*, no. 46 (2014): 15490–96.

4   Jeremy Appleton, "The Gut-Brain Axis: Influence of Microbiota on Mood and Mental Health." *Integrative Medicine* 17, no. 4 (2018): 28-32.

5   Appleton, *Integrative Medicine* 17, no. 4.

6   Caitlin Cowan, Alan Hoban, Ana Ventura-Silva et al. "Gutsy Moves: The Amygdala as a Critical Node in Microbiota to Brain Signaling," *BioEssays* 40, no. 1: 1700172.

7   Albert Bandura, Dorothea Ross, and Sheila Ross, "Transmission of Aggression through Imitation of Aggressive Models," *Journal of Abnormal and Social Psychology* 63, no. 3 (1961): 575-82.

8   "TV and Smart Phones May Hamper a Good Night's Sleep," NPR: Talk of the Nation, effective March 11, 2011, https://www.npr.org/2011/03/11/134459354/TV-And-Smart-Phones-May-Hamper-A-Good-Nights-Sleep.

9   Juliet Diaz, *The Altar Within: A Radical Devotional Guide to Liberate the Divine Self* (Row House, 2022), xvi.

10   Ester Meerwijk, Judith Ford, and Sandra Weiss, "Brain Regions Associated with Psychological Pain: Implications for a Neural Network and its Relationship to Physical Pain," *Brain Imaging and Behavior* 7, no. 1 (2013): 1-14.

11   For suicide prevention and support resources, visit https://www.nimh.nih.gov/health/topics/suicide-prevention.

12   To learn more about this "smush" caused by cultural gender programming, see Kasia Urbaniak, *Unbound: A Woman's Guide to Power* (Tarcher, 2020).

Part 3: Arriving

Chapter 11: Uncovering the Soul From the Layers of Identities

1   Ram Dass, "An Evening with Ram Dass NYC, 1985 – Part 3," YouTube, effective June 1, 2008, 8 min., 52 sec., https://www.youtube.com/watch?v=n-VrFp_5FfNk&list=PL1D9B4E2F9092826B&index=10.

2   Ram Dass, "An Evening with Ram Dass NYC, 1985 – Part 3," YouTube.

3   Ram Dass, "An Evening with Ram Dass NYC, 1985 – Part 3," YouTube.

4   Ram Dass, "An Evening with Ram Dass NYC, 1985 – Part 3," YouTube.

5   Ram Dass, "An Evening with Ram Dass NYC, 1985 – Part 3," YouTube.

6   Ram Dass, "An Evening with Ram Dass NYC, 1985 – Part 3," YouTube.

Chapter 12: Learning from Experience

1   Ram Dass used the clock as a metaphor for the soul's journey: Ram Dass, "Who Are You?" Podcast, Here and Now, Ep. 106, Audio: 53:36, 1976). For a more detailed description of soul ages, I recommend the 1-10 scale in Ainslie MacLeod, *The Instruction: Living the Life Your Soul Intended* (Sounds True, 2009).

2   Ram Dass, *Ram Dass Quotes*, accessed November 1, 2024. https://www.ramdass.org/ram-dass-quotes/.

3   Ram Dass, "Dying is Absolutely Safe," accessed November 1, 2024, https://www.ramdass.org/dying-is-absolutely-safe/.

Chapter 13: Spirit Communication

1   With a nod to the helpful psychological concept of Fundamental Attribution Error, a cognitive error we make when we have a discrepancy between how we explain our own problematic behavior (by blaming external factors) and how we explain other people's behavior (by blaming their personality).

2   Elyn Saks, *The Center Cannot Hold: My Journey Through Madness* (Grand Central Publishing, 2008); William Butler Yeats, "The Second Coming," Poetry Foundation, accessed September 24, 2025, https://www.poetryfoundation.org/poems/43290/the-second-coming.

3   I am not describing a purely causal relationship where hearing voices is always spirit communication; rather, I am suggesting it can be that so-called "psychotic disorders" can have a body, mind, and/or spirit etiology.

4   Albert Powers, Megan Kelley, and Phillip Corlett, "Hallucinations as Top-down Effects on Perception," *Biological Psychiatry: Cognitive Neuroscience Neuroimaging* 1, no. 5 (2016): 393-400.

5   Yale COPE Project. 2023. "The Yale COPE Project." Effective December 2, 2025. https://www.powerslab.net/.

6   "Yale COPE Project to Study How People Control Their Voices," *Mad in America*, September 2019, accessed December 2, 2025.

7   An excellent book on the treatment of health issues, cultural humility is by Anne Fadiman, *The Spirit Catches You and You Fall Down* (Farrar, Straus and Giroux, 1997).

8   "Shamanism," Understanding Voices, accessed November 1, 2024, https://understandingvoices.com/exploring-voices/voices-and-spirituality/case-studies/shamanism/.

9   Lee Sanella, *The Kundalini Experience: Psychosis or Transcendence* (Integral Publishing, 1987).

10   Mini Sharma, Mondeep Dhankar, and Deepak Kumar, "Awakening of Kundalini Chakras Presenting as Psychosis-A Case Report," *Indian Journal of Psychological Medicine* 44, no. 5 (2022): 526-8.

11   Stanislav Grof and Christina Grof, *Spiritual Emergency: When Personal Transformation Becomes a Crisis* (G. P. Putnam's Sons, 1989), 3.

12   Grof and Grof, *Spiritual Emergency.*

13   Jacek Prusak, "Differential Diagnosis of 'Religious or Spiritual Problem'—Possibilities and Limitations Implied by the V-code 62.89 in DSM-5," *Psychiatria Polska 50, no. 1 (2016): 175-86.*

14   To learn more about efforts to destigmatize, normalize, and integrate the experience of hearing voices and seeing visions, visit https://www.hearing-voices.org/#content and https://understandingvoices.com/.

15   Alcoholics Anonymous, *Alcoholics Anonymous, 4th ed.* (Alcoholics Anonymous World Services, 2002), 164.

Chapter 14: Oneness

1   Alcoholics Anonymous, *Alcoholics Anonymous, 4th ed.* (Alcoholics Anonymous World Services, 2002), 68; edited for gender neutrality.

2   Ram Dass, "If You Think You are Free You Can't Escape," Love Serve Remember Foundation, accessed November 1, 2024, https://www.ramdass.org/think-free-cant-escape/.

3   For the most accessible text on selfless service and the Bhagavad Gita see Edward Viljoen, *The Bhagavad Gita: The Song of God Retold in Simplified English* (St. Martin's Essentials, 2019).

4   This affirmative prayer adapted from Dr. Edward Viljoen, the Center for Spiritual Living Santa Rosa, see www.cslsr.org.

5   Jalal Al-Din Rumi *The Essential Rumi*, Translated by Coleman Barks, Reynold Nicolson, A.J. Arberry, and John Moyne (HaperCollins, 2004).

Conclusion

1   Cristina Zarbo, Giorgio Tasca, Francesco Cattafi, and Angelo Compare "Integrative Psychotherapy Works." *Frontiers in Psychology* 6 (2016).

2   Geoff Bathje, Eric Majeski, and Mephina Kudowor, "Psychedelic Integration: An Analysis of the Concept and its Practice," *Frontiers in Psychology* 13 (2022): 824077.

3   Bathje, Majeski, and Kudowor, "Psychedelic Integration".

4   Jurgen Kremer, *Psychology in Diversity in Psychology: Introduction to Psychology for the 21st Century* (Kendall Hunt, 2017).